THE GUARDIAN/QUARTET ELECTION GUIDE

Q————————————————————

DAVID McKIE, CHRIS COOK AND MELANIE PHILLIPS

QUARTET BOOKS
LONDON   MELBOURNE   NEW YORK

First published by Quartet Books Limited 1978
A member of the Namara Group
27 Goodge Street, London W1P 1FD

Copyright © 1978 by David McKie, Chris Cook
and Melanie Phillips

ISBN 0 7043 3231 0

Typeset by Bedford Typesetters Limited

Printed in Great Britain by
Hazell Watson & Viney Limited, Aylesbury, Bucks

Introduction

This Guide is the third in a series which began with the 1970 General Election. We have altered the format a little this time, introducing in the Issues section a more comprehensive account than before of who did what, and when, during the period since the last election. As before, we have supplemented the text with a great many tables, most of them drawn from the increasingly comprehensive and ingenious pages of government statistical publications (one of the few areas of government which can unquestionably be said to have gone from strength to strength over the past 10 years).

The fact that the book is so peppered with statistics does not in any way imply that elections could or should, in our view, be settled on figures alone. Many of these figures, for a start, are rough guides rather than totally precise indicators, and many are subject to revision: the famous £800 million balance of trade deficit which Labour inherited in 1964 turned out, after many cross checks and recalculations, to be only around half that figure. Nor can one mechanically ascribe everything which happened between 18 June 1970 and the last day of February 1974 to the activities of Mr Heath's government, and everything that has happened thereafter to Labour. Faith in the omnicompetence of government, indeed, has taken some heavy knocks in the period covered by this book, and one of the themes of the Conservative campaign this time may be the contention that successive governments have attempted to invade too many areas of the nation's economic and social life, to the ultimate detriment – despite their good intentions – of all concerned.

We don't, in other words, assume that the performance of British government over the past 10 years could ever be judged solely by the figures we have assembled here. What we do try to do in this book is to provide a consumer guide to British politics, compiled on as neutral a basis as we can contrive, which will at least arm the voter with the material he needs to ask necessary (and troublesome) questions of politicians – and to challenge some of the carefully tailored accounts of recent events which will be put out by the parties during the campaign. And since MPs in these days of narrow majorities or none at all have been showing a refreshing tendency to think for themselves rather than simply do as the Whips tell them, we have provided rather more voting tables than in previous Guides, especially on those issues, like Europe, devolution, and the reform of the law on abortion, which cut clean across party lines.

We have also, in the best traditions of recent government, vastly expanded our work force since the 1974 Guide: a third contributor, Melanie Phillips, has joined Chris Cook and David McKie. This represents a 50% increase, substantial even by Whitehall standards, though not, we would respectfully point out, much above some of the recent increases in Health Service administrative staff which we record on p. 107. Since we hope to make these Guides a regular feature of British elections, we would welcome suggestions for additions to (or even subtractions from) the material we have included this time.

1 July 78   David McKie

Part I
The Record

Part I
The Record

Prologue

The coming General Election, the eleventh time the nation has gone to the polls since 1945, will take its place in history – whatever its outcome. Will Labour, for the first time ever, win a third successive General Election? Or will Margaret Thatcher become the first woman Prime Minister in British history? It is not only the fate of the two largest parties that is at stake. Will the Liberals be able to reverse the tide that has flowed against them throughout this Parliament? Or will the Scottish Nationalists emerge as the third largest party at Westminster, maybe even holding the balance of power if the election sees a close-run race?

For the impending General Election, Labour will go to the country defending its solid list of achievements in office. But the nation will cast its verdict, not just on that record but on the dramatic circumstances in which Harold Wilson returned to power after the election of February 1974 – an election which marked a decisive turning point in post-war British politics.

The Coming of the General Election of February 1974

The General Election of February 1974 was one of the most extraordinary in British history. It was held against a background of a state of emergency and a three-day week. These, in turn, were the twin products of the oil embargo, imposed by the Arab countries after the Arab-Israeli war, and the government's confrontation with the miners (the latest and most fateful in a

11

series of battles between the Heath government and the unions). The miners' dispute originated in the overtime ban which began in November 1973, a month after 11 Arab countries had announced a 5% drop in oil production. At the same time, the electrical engineers banned out-of-hours work. The Heath government met the challenge head on: a state of emergency was proclaimed and the Bank Rate hoisted to 13%. In December, the crisis measures intensified: a 63°F limit on office heating and a 50 mph speed limit were imposed. The three-day week was announced and television hours curtailed. Meanwhile, the industrial scene worsened further when the railwaymen's union, ASLEF, banned overtime and began a policy of non-cooperation. The nation was well and truly at a crisis point.

There were three possible outcomes: the unions could back down; the government could back down; or a compromise could be hammered out. With the failure of the TUC initiative of 9 January (when the TUC pledged that if the miners were treated as a special case, this would not be cited as a precedent by other unions) the chances of compromise faded. The government steadfastly stood firm – and, in mid-January, ministers predicted a four-day week might soon be possible. The miners responded swiftly and devastatingly: they proposed to stage an all-out strike rather than a ban. The battle lines were now drawn. Heath at last decided to appeal to the country (a course of action the hawks in the party had been advocating throughout January). On Thursday 7 February at 12.45 pm in a statement from Downing Street it was announced that the nation would go to the polls on 28 February. Nearly 50 years after the miners had endured defeat in the 1926 General Strike, they had now embarked on a battle in which their strength was very different.

The Election Campaign

For the campaign, Heath was determined to keep the issue straightforward and uncomplicated. His strategy throughout remained exactly as he had outlined it in his opening broadcast. He had defined the issue: the need for a strong government to overcome inflation, one which was able to succeed against any group of workers, however powerful. It was on that issue that the British people must decide their votes. He summarised it most succinctly on 12 February. The issue before the nation was:

whether this country is now going to return a strong government with a firm mandate for the next five years to deal with the counter-inflation policy . . . a firm incomes policy, which Parliament will approve. The challenge is to the will of Parliament and a democratically elected government.

The same theme was vigorously pursued in the party manifesto, *Firm Action for a Fair Britain*. 'The choice before the nation today, as never before,' it proclaimed 'is a choice between moderation and extremism.' They would amend the social security system to see that the tax-payer no longer had to subsidise strikers and their families while union funds were left undisturbed. But the Conservatives offered fairness too: they would introduce reviews of pensions twice yearly, instead of once; they would introduce changes in the Industrial Relations Act to see there was conciliation before legal action; they would enhance the powers of the Price Commission. During the campaign, indeed, Heath represented the Conservative government as the union of all those groups who had no union to protect them, but who suffered the results of the demands made by the unions on behalf of those who had. The Conservative campaign thus showed a peculiar blend of aggression and moderation.

The Labour strategy was to prevent Heath at all costs from choosing the ground for the fight. But the party had a difficult defensive action to fight. They needed to show the electorate that they were moderate and responsible people who could get the country out of the mess into which the Conservative administration and the harsh facts of world politics had jointly dumped it. Gradually, they developed a persuasive theme: Labour had got the country out of its mess in 1964–70 and left it financially strong. Now Labour was ready to take on that thankless job again.

Just as, in the run-up to the 1970 election, Wilson had been faced during the campaign with unexpected blows, so now was Heath. On top of the index of retail prices announced on 15 February (which showed a 12-month rise of 20p in the £) came the disastrous trade figures of 25 February – the final Monday of the campaign. The figures revealed the biggest deficit in the country's history. Added to these problems was the bombshell announcement of Enoch Powell who, having denounced the election as immoral in a manner befitting a prophet from Wolverhampton, went on to say he would not be fighting the election and, in a theatrical coup which even an Old Testament prophet would have admired, announced he had already cast a postal vote for Labour.

If Powell's antics seemed like predictable treason, there then came the startling statement by the CBI director-general,

Campbell Adamson, that the Industrial Relations Act introduced by the Conservatives had 'sullied every relationship at every level between unions and employers and ought to be repealed rather than amended'. Even more damaging was his remark that a Conservative victory would not solve the country's problems.

All this coincided with the production of new figures by the Pay Board (which was examining the miners' pay claim) which seemed to demonstrate that the miners had a very good case. Heath's strategy of keeping the issue to the one theme of who governed had been knocked off course. At the same time, there were reports from worried Conservatives of the threat from the Liberals in many constituencies.

While Conservative and Labour politicians were embroiled in the election, the February contest offered a unique opportunity for the Liberal and Nationalist parties. Never before had the Liberals faced an election while riding so high in the opinion polls. Never had the opportunity to transform a by-election revival into a General Election breakthrough seemed so possible. An immediate consequence of this Liberal and Nationalist optimism was seen in the nominations. Of the 2135 candidates nominated, no less than 517 were Liberals, the highest total the party had ever fielded (exceeding the 513 brought forward in 1929 and the 475 who contested the 1950 election). All 36 seats in Wales were contested by Plaid Cymru, while the SNP fought all but one of the seats in Scotland.

The main lines of the Liberal manifesto followed the resolutions adopted at the 1973 Annual Conference. The party laid much emphasis on a permanent prices and incomes policy backed by penalties for those whose actions caused inflation. Among other proposals put forward by the party were a statutory minimum earnings level; profit sharing in industry; a credit income tax to replace the means test and existing allowances; pensions of two-thirds the average industrial earnings for married couples; a Bill of Rights; the replacement of the Housing Finance Act and a permanent Royal Commission to advise Parliament on energy policy.

The Result

The election campaign fought in February 1974 was bitter. The stakes could not have been higher. And in the event, the electors produced a result that had never before taken place in post-war politics. For the first time since 1929, the election gave no party an over-all majority. The Labour Party won 301 seats (287 in 1970), the Conservative Party 296 (330 in 1970), and the

14

Liberal Party 14 (6 in 1970). Other parties, with a total of 23 seats, held the balance of power. The Ulster Loyalists won 11 seats, the Scottish National Party 7 seats, Plaid Cymru two seats. In Ireland, the SDLP won one seat. And two Independent Labour MPs were elected – Dick Taverne at Lincoln and Eddie Milne at Blyth.

Some 78·7% of the electorate voted – the highest poll since 1959. During the 1960s the proportion of the electorate voting had fallen at each election, but even the 1974 result was still below the record polls of 84·5% in 1950 and 82·6% in 1951.

The results were a disaster for the Tory Party which lost 1·2 million votes in spite of the higher poll and only won the support of 38·1% of the voters (11·9 million votes). The Labour Party polled 11·7 million votes, 500,000 less than in 1970, and won the support of 37·2% of the voters. Labour lost less votes to the Liberals and Nationalists than did the Tories and so regained some of the seats lost in 1970. Although the Labour share of the vote fell 5·8% the Tory share fell 8·3%.

The most striking feature of the election was the drop in support for both Labour and Tory parties. The Labour Party received its lowest share of votes since 1931 and the Tories received less support in 1974 than they had done for over 50 years.

Perhaps the nearest parallel to the 1974 result was that of 1929. Then, Conservative and Labour between them polled 75·2% of all votes cast and the outcome was also a minority Labour government.

By far the chief beneficiaries of the decline in Conservative and Labour support were the Liberals and Nationalists. The performance of the Liberals was perhaps the single most outstanding feature of the February election. Having entered the contest with their hopes the highest for a generation, they came out of the battle with a staggering 6 million votes, but a mere 14 seats. The only Liberal gains were Cardiganshire and Colne Valley (from Labour), Bodmin and the Isle of Wight from the Conservatives and the new seat of Hazel Grove, won by the former Liberal MP for Cheadle, Michael Winstanley.

However, the greatest Liberal achievement in February 1974 was not in seats won, or even in the remarkable personal triumphs of leading Liberals, but in votes polled. But in only a few of these seats was the Liberal total good enough to run the winners close – mostly in Conservative-held seats. In only 14 Conservative-held seats were Liberals within 4000 votes of victory, while the Labour citadels had hardly suffered at all from the Liberal advance.

After the 6 million votes polled by the Liberal Party, the greatest success in the election for the smaller parties was undoubtedly that won by the Nationalists in Scotland. Unlike the Liberals, the SNP came out with a dramatic increase in its parliamentary representation. The party had entered the election defending two seats (Western Isles and Glasgow Govan). Although Govan was lost to Labour, the SNP returned 7 members to Parliament, a major success for a party that had never won a single seat in a General Election until 1970.

These SNP gains were mainly at the expense of the Tories, who went down to defeat in Argyll, Moray and Nairn, Banff, and Aberdeenshire East, while Labour lost Stirlingshire East and Clackmannan and also Dundee East. Several of the SNP victories were little short of spectacular, although the SNP failed to make any real impression in Glasgow or Edinburgh. Apart from these relative setbacks, however, the SNP had every reason for satisfaction. Compared to 11·4% of the Scottish vote in 1970, they obtained 21·9% on this occasion. Only 6 deposits were lost (compared with 43 in 1970) and with its best results in exactly those areas most affected by the impact of the North Sea oil boom, the February 1974 election provided the SNP with a potential springboard for a further major parliamentary advance.

The stalemate results of the election provided Heath with an acute problem. Although the Conservatives had fared badly, no other party had an over-all majority. In this situation, Heath did not offer his resignation immediately, but entered into discussions with Jeremy Thorpe, the Liberal leader, to see if the basis existed for a working arrangement. During the weekend of 1–4 March, the nation awaited the outcome of these talks. After internal soundings in the party, Thorpe declined any arrangement. This was a very significant moment – for the failure of these talks weakened the Conservatives throughout 1974. For when Wilson came to form his administration he knew that a majority for an anti-Labour government was unlikely in the Commons.

Hence, after one of the most dramatic confrontations in British politics, and an election result unheard of since 1929, Labour returned to power. For Heath, the politics of confrontation had ended in failure.

The Return of Harold Wilson

Wilson became Prime Minister again on 4 March, at the head of the first minority Labour government since 1931. As in 1964, when he had first become Prime Minister, the new Premier acted swiftly and determinedly.

Wilson decided that, although Labour had taken office as a minority government, it would govern as if it had a majority. There would be no retreat from the election manifesto and no alliances with other groups. There was no point in compromise, since any rebuff in the House of Commons could be met with an appeal to the country – and he knew that the other parties would be reluctant to force another election immediately.

The New Government

The new Cabinet showed a mixture of old and new faces: Callaghan went to the Foreign Office; Jenkins was at the Home Office and Denis Healey was given the crucial job of Chancellor. Among the more surprise appointments, Michael Foot became Secretary of State for Employment and Wedgwood Benn became Secretary for Industry. For the first time in British history, the Cabinet contained two women members – Barbara Castle at Social Services, and Shirley Williams in the new post of Secretary of State for Prices and Consumer Protection. The Cabinet was again a balanced mix of left-wingers and the right.

The whole of the 1974 Parliament was dominated by the prospect of another General Election. Once Wilson had ruled out a coalition with any other group it was indeed inevitable that another election would have to follow shortly. Wilson himself appears to have decided at a very early stage that it should be in the autumn. And so it was. The 1974 Parliament lasted six months – the shortest Parliament in British history since 1681.

As in 1964, Wilson sought from the start to create an immediate impression of decision and firmness. Thus, within a few days of the first Cabinet of 5 March, the miners' strike was settled and the three-day week and the state of emergency came to an end. The Pay Board was abolished, and the policy of compulsory wage restraint finally ended in July 1974. The Price Code and the Price Commission were, however, retained. An immediate freeze was imposed on all rents, while a Queen's Speech was drafted promising pension increases, stricter price controls, and food subsidies. Among other decisions were the ending of the much criticised entry charges for museums (which the Conservatives had imposed), and the speedy abandonment of controversial plans for a third London airport at Maplin. Initial moves were also put in progress to end the Channel Tunnel project, but Concorde was allowed to go ahead. In other areas, also, the Government seemed to be acting with purpose and determination. In deference to left-wing antagonism to the ruling military juntas in Greece and Chile, naval visits to these two countries were cancelled in March. In April Reg Prentice (the Secretary for Education) acted to speed the shift towards comprehensive education and Anthony Crosland as Secretary for the Environment took measures to discourage the sale of council houses. Labour had less success in its attempts to restore the £10 million in taxation and in pension funds to those unions who had refused to acknowledge the Industrial Relations Act – and in the end the government suffered a parliamentary defeat.

The Social Contract

This activity, though important, masked the crucial issue before the country: the state of the economy and in particular the crucial problem of inflation. The indices for 1974 told their own story: during the 6 months of the 1974 Parliament, prices rose by 8% and wages by 16%. The *Financial Times* Share Index, which had stood at 313 on 1 March fell to 202 by 20 September – a larger decline in the real value of shares since 1972 than had happened after the Great Crash of 1929. Nor were these phenomena confined to Britain. Throughout the world, stock markets were collapsing and prices soaring. It was this crisis, or rather Heath's handling of it, that had brought Wilson back to power. It would be Wilson's handling of it which determined whether Labour itself stayed in power. Wilson and the government put their faith in the Social Contract.

During the election campaign an agreement between the Labour Party and the TUC had been announced (the Social Contract) (see pp. 44–5).

The government's faith in the Social Contract underlay the Budget tactics planned by Healey at the Exchequer. During this short Parliament, the Chancellor introduced two Budgets, on 26 March and 22 July. The first Budget, presented three weeks after returning to power, was only mildly deflationary in its intended effect on demand (see p. 53).

One unforseen effect of Healey's 26 March Budget was to add to the liquidity problems facing many companies. This, plus warnings from such key economic advisers as Harold Lever that the danger of a serious recession was increasing, led to Healey's second Budget, on 22 July. This second Budget – with an election on the way – was mildly expansionary (see p. 53).

Given the political situation at the time, these Budgets were tactical rather than strategic measures. After October 1974, the weaknesses of both the Social Contract and Healey's Budgets became more obvious as the economic indices worsened. But

18

in 1974, it must be admitted, Healey had little enough room for manoeuvre. On the industrial front, there was mounting anxiety at the prospect of serious union rebellion against the government's economic policies.

For despite the Social Contract and the prospect that the new government would enjoy a period of industrial peace, there was a series of unofficial strikes. Although in April, the engineering union, led by Hugh Scanlon, refrained from pressing a £10 a week pay claim, there was almost constant trouble in the motor industry. In May, widespread disruption occurred on the railways as a result of action by the locomen, led by Ray Buckton. In July there was a prolonged strike by hospital workers. Like the government, the unions also had their eyes on an autumn election and to some extent militancy was restricted by this consideration. But these industrial troubles were portents of coming strains in the Social Contract.

The Conservative Opposition

Heath's defeat in the February election had meant a profound shift of power not only between the parties but within them. Heath's defeat had led to considerable dismay at his leadership. His critics increased. But they too were unwilling to lock the party in a leadership struggle while an election loomed. With Heath's second defeat in October, the floodgates were opened for his departure as leader (see p. 27). Meanwhile Labour as well as Conservatives were keeping an anxious eye on the Liberals and Nationalists whose performance in February had been at the expense of both major parties.

The Scottish Nationalists

With the advent of a minority Labour government, and with it the probability of an early second General Election, it was imperative for the Liberals and Nationalists to maintain their momentum. For the Scottish Nationalists, this was a considerably easier task than for the Liberals. Oil and devolution continued to occupy much political attention. Both issues clearly aided the SNP. The party received a further boost when, after its success in February, it was joined by its most famous recruit so far, Sir Hugh Fraser, the Scottish millionaire.

Further evidence of increased support for the SNP came in the May local elections. Although Labour easily dominated the cities, and did especially well in Strathclyde, the SNP achieved some successes. At Cumbernauld the SNP secured an over-all majority. In East Kilbride they finished as the largest single party, while they took second place in many Glasgow seats. These were significant results, for they showed the party's growing appeal in the new towns and in areas such as the Clyde which had been Labour for a generation. Meanwhile the SNP probably benefited from the increasing discussion in the Tory ranks over devolution. At the Conservative Party Conference in Ayr during May, Edward Heath launched a major five-point plan for Scotland which he pledged a future Conservative government to introduce. Its proposals included the creation of a Scottish Development Fund, to deal with the new environmental problems brought by oil, and the establishment of a Scottish Assembly.

Heath's proposals were immediately attacked by SNP chairman William Wolfe as 'half-baked' and, he added, 'The people of Scotland are in no mood to be bought off by the broken leader of a discredited party.'

These were confident words; but the SNP had every reason for confidence, for the Nationalist tide was clearly flowing strongly in Scotland.

The Liberals in the Short Parliament

In England the Liberals were not finding the political course so easy. The invitation from Heath for Thorpe to support a Conservative administration had only served to emphasise that the party could easily indulge in fratricidal warfare if talk of coalition was not handled very carefully. Although Liberal support in the opinion polls held relatively steady during 1974, the absence of by-election contests prevented the Liberals from achieving renewed momentum.

The two most significant happenings for the Liberals during this short parliament were the launching of a 'coalition campaign' and the defection of Christopher Mayhew from Labour.

The Liberal 'coalition campaign' was launched in a party political broadcast on 25 June by David Steel, the party's Chief Whip. The broadcast, with its appeal for a 'Government of National Unity', stated that Liberals would be 'ready and willing to participate in such a government if at the next election you give us the power to do so'. In an ITV interview the same evening Thorpe stated that such a government of National Unity 'reflects the views of millions of people'.

In July Liberal attempts to foster a realignment in politics seemed to achieve a marked step forward with the defection of Christopher Mayhew, a former Labour minister and MP for Woolwich East, to the Liberal ranks. His defection increased the number of Liberal MPs to 15 and was accompanied by very wide press coverage. But those who expected further defections from sitting Labour members were to be disappointed. Meanwhile, the Liberals began frenetic activity to revitalise derelict constituency associations so that the party could fight virtually every constituency in the coming election. By the late summer of 1974, both Liberals and Nationalists were prepared for the largest-ever assault on the two-party system, whenever the election might be called.

The October 1974 Election

Despite the government's success in exploiting its weak parliamentary position, it had become clear during the summer that it would seek a new mandate from the electorate at the earliest opportunity. The summer was noteworthy for the large number of policy statements to emanate from the government. Meanwhile, the Labour Party remained ahead in the opinion polls. The signs were right for Wilson. In September 1974 he took the plunge.

The Dissolution of Parliament announced on 20 September 1974 ended the shortest parliament of the present century. It had been opened by the Queen on 11 March and had lasted a mere 184 days. For only the second time this century, two General Elections had occurred within the same year, the first such occasion being 1910.

A record number of candidates (2252 compared to 2135 in February) was nominated for the 10 October election. This highest-ever figure was partly explained by the 619 Liberals fielded in October – a rise of 102 on the February total, and an all-time record for the party. Every seat in England and Wales (except for Lincoln) was contested by a Liberal. Only Argyll, Glasgow Provan and Fife Central were not fought by Liberals in Scotland. Another party to greatly increase its tally of candidates was the National Front, who nominated 90 candidates compared to 54 in February, partly emboldened by municipal election successes in areas of high immigrant concentrations.

There was little new or unexpected in the campaign. Labour urged the electorate to give it a majority to finish the job on which it had embarked; the Conservatives were still partly on the defensive after February.

The Outcome

Despite widespread predictions that Labour would win with a comfortable majority, the result proved to be yet another cliff-hanger. As more and more Conservative-held marginal seats stubbornly defied the swing to Labour, computer forecasts of

Labour's eventual over-all majority became lower and lower. In the event, Labour won 319 seats, the Conservatives 277, Liberals 13, the Scottish Nationalists 11 and Plaid Cymru three. The Conservatives had polled 10,462,583 votes (35·8%), Labour 11,457,079 (39·2%), the Liberals slipped to 5,346,754 (18·3%) while the combined Nationalist vote in Wales and Scotland passed the one million mark for the first time.

Labour's majority, though even smaller than the photo-finish result of 1964, was in fact, in terms of practical politics, considerably more comfortable than it appeared. Labour's majority over the Conservatives was a healthy 43, while Labour's majority over Conservatives and Liberals combined was still 30.

In all, Labour gained 19 seats, for the loss of only one constituency (Carmarthen) to Plaid Cymru. The Conservatives suffered 22 losses with only two gains – Hazel Grove and Bodmin, both taken from the Liberals. The Scottish Nationalists gained 4 seats (all from the Conservatives) to take their total to 11.

Over the whole country, Labour achieved a swing of 2·2% from Conservative. If this swing had occurred uniformly in each constituency, Labour would have achieved an over-all majority of 25. Labour, in fact, could only achieve a small swing of 1·2% in the key Conservative-held marginals that they needed to win.

Particular interest in the results of October 1974 centred round the Liberal and Nationalist challenge. As we have seen, for the October election, the third parties entered the contest in a mood of optimism and at times euphoria. The Liberals, fortified by 6 million votes in February, and with a massive field of 619 candidates, were in buoyant mood.

When, however, the results were announced, it was the Scottish Nationalists who had achieved the most substantial advance. Thus SNP representation increased from 7 to 11 and Plaid Cymru went up from 2 to 3, but the Liberals fell back from 15 (if Christopher Mayhew is included) to 13. Even so, Liberal and Nationalist representation combined was higher than at any previous occasion since the 1930s.

Meanwhile, the total Liberal vote had fallen from the 6,063,470 (19·3%) cast in February to 5,346,754 (18·3%) in October. This decrease tended to disguise the fact that, with 102 more candidates than in February, their vote in most constituencies had fallen quite considerably. In 93% of constituencies contested by Liberals on both occasions, the Liberal share of the vote declined. The party had lost its momentum and faced the prospect of a difficult period under a Labour government.

Tackling Inflation

The extremely close victory was not at all what Labour had wanted – for it was likely to mean that, in the near future, by-election losses, to say nothing of defections, would produce a minority government. Wilson, however, went on as if all was well and the government's legislative programme was outlined in the Queen's Speech on 19 November. Most of the proposals were expected. They included legislation for a development land tax, the phasing-out of private practice from the National Health Service, the extension of the dock labour scheme to inland depots and the abolition of selection in secondary education. Many of these proposals – particularly on 'pay beds' and comprehensive education – were bitterly attacked by the Conservative opposition. But the most far-reaching proposal in the Queen's Speech was the promise of legislation – albeit by a very protracted time-table – to establish Scottish and Welsh assemblies.

All these proposals, however, presupposed that the government could win the battle of the economy where inflation was the key factor (see pp. 45ff).

Wilson faced a most difficult situation. The year had seen a simultaneous failure to meet all four main policy targets – adequate economic growth, full employment, a stable balance of payments, and stable prices. The volume of consumer spending fell for the first time in 20 years, and by January 1975 over 700,000 people were unemployed, over 140,000 more than at the beginning of the previous year. Despite this, the balance of payments deficit on current account was the largest ever recorded and retail prices in January 1975 were over 19% higher than in January 1974. Moreover, the wages policy within the 'Social Contract' was increasingly seen not to be working.

By early 1975 it was evident that this policy had not succeeded. Some wage settlements were of the order of 30%.

The 1975 Budget and the £6 a Week Pay Policy

The Budget introduced by Denis Healey on 15 April 1975 was, in his own words, 'rough and tough'. It was certainly stringent (see p. 54).

It was followed by what was effectively a compulsory wages policy. In July 1975 the government announced that there would be a limit of £6 per week on pay increases, £6 representing 10% of average earnings. There were to be no exceptions to this, and those earning more than £8500 a year were to get nothing at all. The government had the prior agreement of the TUC to such a policy, and the TUC agreed to try to persuade its members to comply. The policy was voluntary to the extent

23

that there were no legal sanctions against individual unions, but in a different sense there were very powerful sanctions operating through the Price Code. No firms could pass on in price rises any part of a pay settlement above the limit: this applied not only to the excess but to the whole of the increase. Up until April 1976 the limit apparently was not breached, and this was possibly due as much to these sanctions and to the recession in the economy as to the voluntary cooperation of trade unions. Apart from avoiding the threat of penalties on trade unionists, this form of sanctions had the advantage of covering all payments made at the plant level. The government's twin measures – Budget and wages policy – to reduce the rate of inflation, implemented during a serious world-wide recession, led to a sharp rise in unemployment.

The 1976 Sterling Crisis

As 1976 continued, the most alarming feature, however, was the behaviour of sterling. Once again, the Labour government faced a crisis of confidence in the pound. On 1 January 1976, the £ had stood at $2·024. By 28 September it had collapsed to $1·637. This was a frightening debilitation. It could neither be blamed (or explained) merely on Britain's balance of payments deficit nor on the high internal rate of inflation. The real fear lay in the future course of the economy, the failure of business confidence to revive and, perhaps more than anything else, the inability of the government to contain public expenditure – fears of this PSBR (Public Sector Borrowing Requirement) had been heightened on 19 February by the publication of the White Paper *Public Expenditure 1979–80*. Although, as the oil factor aided Britain's recovery, the sterling crisis subsided, it had made 1976 very reminiscent of the unhappy days of 1966–8.

The National Enterprise Board

The problems on the economic front, and the narrowness of Labour's electoral victory did not deter the party from beginning to implement significant changes in industry. Back in 1974, Labour had published its White Paper, entitled *The Regeneration of British Industry*. Its main proposal, the creation of a new National Enterprise Board, was included in the Industry Bill, introduced into Parliament in January 1975 and finally enacted in November (see p. 82ff).

Even before the National Enterprise Board was in operation, state acquisitions in the private sector had rapidly mounted. By early 1976, the companies which were wholly or partly owned by the State included Ferranti, Alfred Herbert, British

Leyland, Rolls-Royce, Dunford and Elliot, Triang and Harland and Wolff. A further major extension of state ownership came about as a result of the Aircraft and Shipbuilding Bill (see p. 85).

Of very great importance were the government's moves to control the exploitation of North Sea oil. Labour was determined that the State should secure a substantial share of the returns of North Sea oil extraction and it was also particularly worried at the large number of foreign-owned oil companies involved in these operations. Hence, in February 1975, a bill was put forward proposing a Petroleum Revenue Tax (see p. 79).

The Common Market Referendum

The Labour Party's manifesto for the October election had promised that within a year the people would decide 'through the ballot box' whether Britain should stay in the European Common Market on the terms to be renegotiated by the Labour government, or reject them and leave the Community. This formula left the option open between a referendum and yet another election in 1975. On 22 January the Government announced that they would bring in a Referendum Bill. The White Paper published on 26 February established that there would be a national count. The decision was to be by simple majority on the question 'Do you think the UK should stay in the European Community?' In the debate on the White Paper, the principle of this direct consultation of the electors, a hitherto unknown British constitutional practice, was approved in the House of Commons by 312 votes to 262, 5 Conservatives voting with the government and one Labour MP with the Opposition. The government's original intention for a single national declaration was lost during the debate. On a free vote on 23 April it was decided by 270 votes to 153, against strong government advice, that the result should be declared regionally: a Liberal motion for declaration by constituencies was lost by 264 votes to 131.

On 18 March Wilson informed the Commons that the Government had decided to recommend a Yes vote. The Cabinet, however, was split 16 to 7. The No faction numbered Michael Foot (Secretary of State for Employment), Tony Benn (Industry), Peter Shore (Trade), Barbara Castle (Social Services), Eric Varley (Energy), Ross (Scotland) and Silkin (Planning and Local Government). It was an extraordinary state of affairs. Should the rebel ministers resign? Wilson neatly resolved the problem by stating that, while dissident ministers would otherwise be free to express themselves as they wished, all ministers speaking from the despatch box would reflect government policy. Apart from the dismissal of Eric Heffer, the Minister of State for Industry, this extraordinary Cabinet agreement to differ on a vital issue operated without resignations right through the referendum.

Though the Cabinet remained intact, the divisions within the Labour ranks remained as wide as ever. On 19 March, a resolution signed by 18 out of 29 members of its National Executive recommended to a special party conference, successfully demanded by the left wing, that the party should campaign for withdrawal from the EEC. Later, in the Commons vote on the government's pro-market White Paper, 145 Labour MPs went into the No lobby, against 137 Ayes and 33 abstentions. The special conference on 26 April voted two to one for withdrawal.

Following the EEC summit meeting in Dublin on 10 and 11 March, when the assembled heads of government ratified certain decisions favourable to Britain which were regarded as part of the renegotiation, the government's White Paper, *Membership of the EEC: Report on Renegotiation* was published on 27 March. After describing the better terms which the government claimed it had won, it concluded: 'Continued membership of the Community is in Britain's interest . . . In the government's view the consequences of withdrawal would be adverse.'

The White Paper went on to consider general questions like sovereignty, the European Parliament, Community legislation, the value of membership for Britain's world role, and the effects of withdrawal, which, it said, would threaten the political stability of Western Europe.

In the House of Commons on 9 April the White Paper was endorsed by a margin of 226 votes (393 to 170), more than double the majority of 112 recorded in October 1971 for the principle of entering the EEC. In many respects, the claims and counter-claims of the debate had all been heard before. The Yes side had a clear propaganda advantage in the support of most business firms, who did not hesitate to use their money, their advertising power and their communications with their workers, and of the great majority of the national and regional press. The contest cut right across party lines. Politicians as far apart as Enoch Powell and Michael Foot united in the No lobby.

The Yes lobby included such unusual allies as the Labour Cabinet majority, the bulk of the Tory and Liberal parties, the Confederation of British Industry, the National Farmers Union and the City of London. Three pamphlets were duly delivered to every household in the kingdom. One was the government's 'popular version of the White Paper'. The others, each half the size, were produced by the umbrella organisations 'Britain in Europe' and 'The National Referendum Campaign', and were straightforward exercises in public relations. The outcome fulfilled the best hopes of the pro-marketeers. Turnout was high and the majority for Yes was over two to one (see p. 142).

The outcome, though a triumph for the ardent champions of Britain in Europe – most particularly Edward Heath – was also a triumph for the astute political tactics of Harold Wilson. The left of his party had been appeased by the fact of the referendum, the right by its result, and the Wilson–Callaghan combination, having at last come down on the Yes side, backed by the electorate, gained prestige as a national leadership. Other consequences also followed the Yes vote. Labour belatedly sent a team to the European Parliament, and British trade unionists joined the appropriate bodies. Labour had survived the Common Market issue. With almost as many divisions, the first steps were taken to put the Devolution Bill on to the Statute Book (see Part II ch. 15) and Labour pursued the search for a solution to the continuing troubles in Ulster (see Part II ch. 19).

Margaret Thatcher at the Helm

If Wilson faced a plethora of difficulties, the going was no more easy for the leaders of the two main opposition parties. Although many Conservatives had been deeply critical of Heath's leadership in the wake of the February election defeat, the proximity of another election kept this discontent in check. The October election defeat opened the flood-gates to an attack on his position. Long before October many Conservatives had disliked his personal style. Now they possessed two further grounds of attack. A commander who has lost two campaigns in quick succession, having himself chosen the battle-ground, the timing and tactics for a decisive conflict, is implicitly marked out for replacement. With the Conservative Party now in the wilderness, it seemed the right moment to rediscover a basic philosophy around which it could unite in regaining power. This task clearly needed a new leader. Despite the clamour for his replacement, Heath defiantly held his ground, waiting for the report of the Home Committee which had been set up to consider the future method of choosing the party leader. The Home Committee duly recommended that when the party was in opposition, there should be an annual election by all MPs. Heath accepted these proposals on 23 January 1975; it was then announced the date when the first round of the ballot

27

would take place would be 4 February.

In addition to Heath, two other candidates came forward: Margaret Thatcher, Heath's Secretary of State for Education, and Hugh Fraser, the MP for Stafford and Stone. This first ballot was clearly a vote of confidence, or no-confidence, in Heath. In this respect it was decisive. Margaret Thatcher received 130 votes, Edward Heath 119, Hugh Fraser 16, and there were 11 abstentions. Heath instantly stood down from the contest. Four more former Ministers, William Whitelaw, James Prior, John Peyton and Sir Geoffrey Howe, declared themselves candidates for the second ballot whilst Hugh Fraser withdrew. Whitelaw was widely tipped to emerge as the heir of the Heath vote. The outcome, however, was somewhat unexpected. The result of the second ballot on 10 February made a third unnecessary. With 146 votes out of 271 cast, Margaret Thatcher had a clear over-all majority. William Whitelaw received 76 votes, Sir Geoffrey Howe and James Prior 19 each, and John Peyton 11. For the first time, a major British party had chosen for its leader a woman who might one day become Prime Minister.

Margaret Thatcher's victory was widely interpreted as a swing to the right by the Conservatives. For the leadership vote had led not merely to defeat for Heath but also for such centre-moderates as Whitelaw and Howe. Margaret Thatcher's new team, however, was in most respects made up of a fair cross-section of the party, although the dropping of such 'liberals' as Robert Carr, Peter Walker and Nicholas Scott and the appointment of Sir Keith Joseph to take charge of policy and research rather disguised the fact.

The key shadow cabinet appointments were announced on 18 February. William Whitelaw remained deputy leader, with special charge of devolution policy. Among the most important changes Reginald Maudling took over Foreign and Commonwealth affairs from Geoffrey Rippon. Sir Geoffrey Howe replaced Robert Carr as shadow Chancellor. An important change was also announced in the party organisation with the appointment of Lord Thorneycroft, a former Chancellor of the Exchequer, to be Chairman.

The series of Conservative by-election victories under Margaret Thatcher rather disguised the fact that Conservative policy on industrial and economic matters was somewhat sketchy. With the Conservatives seemingly taking almost every Labour stronghold that came vacant (including the Stechford division of Birmingham, which became vacant when Roy Jenkins took up his post as President of the Commission) such policy gaps seemed immaterial. Margaret Thatcher was already, or so it seemed, set fair for No. 10 Downing Street. But as the General Election drew nearer, some of the doubts about both her policies and personal style began to be heard.

The Thorpe Affair

The October 1974 election had seen a distinct loss of momentum by the Liberals from their position in February. Historically, under every previous Labour administration, Liberals had always suffered a loss of support, partly as disaffected Tories who had voted Liberal went back to their old allegiance. After October 1974, this was repeated. In the by-elections up to the Lib-Lab 'pact' of March 1977, the Liberal vote showed a persistent decline (see p. 216).

This decline in the Liberal vote was partly cause and partly consequence of the most unedifying circumstances which eventually led to the resignation of Jeremy Thorpe from the Liberal leadership. By 1976, Thorpe had been party leader for 9 years. Some of his critics were suggesting the time was ripe for a change, to give a successor time to prepare for an election. Thorpe's luckless association with a collapsed secondary bank did nothing to mute this criticism. It was the affair of Norman Scott, however, which finally unseated him. Scott, a former male model, alleged that he had had a homosexual relationship with Thorpe. Despite Thorpe's denials, the affair refused to die down. On 10 May, against a background of bad by-election results, Thorpe resigned.

His resignation as leader of the party, against this background of accusation and innuendo left the Liberals in a dilemma. The party had not yet finalised its new method of electing a party leader. As a stop-gap measure, on 12 May Jo Grimond agreed to resume the leadership on a temporary basis. Once the Liberals had agreed their new plan to elect a leader (a highly complex system involving the setting up of an electoral college based on constituency associations) Steel and Pardoe fought for the leadership. In the most democratic election for the leadership of a British political party, Steel won a comfortable victory.

The Resignation of Harold Wilson

Unlike the sad departure of Jeremy Thorpe, and unlike the ousting of Heath, which had been widely forecast, the resignation of Harold Wilson was as dramatic as it was totally unexpected. Wilson's resignation was announced on 16 March 1976, but it was revealed that he had informed the Queen of his decision the previous December – a decision Wilson insisted he had secretly formed in March 1974. He declared he had three main reasons for resigning: his long career in Parliament (on the Front Bench for 30 years and in the Cabinet for over 11), including a period as Prime Minister spanning 8 years; secondly, he argued that he should not remain so long that younger men were denied the chance to take his place (although, at 60, Wilson seemed in his political prime and his eventual successor, Jim Callaghan, was older); thirdly, and perhaps the most important factor, Wilson argued that his successor would need time to impose his style and strategy for the rest of the Parliament.

These were sound reasons, although far from sufficient to prevent continued speculation on any secret reasons Wilson might have withheld. Certainly, his critics were ready to argue that the Prime Minister had quit with three major crises looming on the horizon – the economic crisis, including the steady slide of sterling on the foreign exchanges, a deep left–right split in the party and an ever-decreasing parliamentary majority which might force an election on the country.

Wilson did not accept a peerage, but on 22 April it was announced that he had received the Order of the Garter. Wilson's own Resignation Honours list (a 'leak' of its contents was carried in the *Sunday Times* on 2 May) produced a furore, most particularly from the left of the Labour Party. Many of the names involved financiers or entertainment tycoons whose contributions to national politics were not always immediately apparent.

The Fight for the Labour Leadership

Wilson's shock resignation opened the way for a highly significant contest for the Labour leadership. Six candidates stood in the first ballot – the left-wingers represented by Michael Foot and Tony Benn. Callaghan was widely regarded as the front-runner of the moderate camp, although Roy Jenkins's supporters were more optimistic than events were to justify. On the first ballot, Michael Foot polled 90 votes, Callaghan 84, Jenkins an unexpectedly low 56, Benn a creditably high 37, Healey a poor 30 and Crosland 17.

Soon after the result was announced Roy Jenkins, who came third, stated that he was standing down from the contest. A similar announcement had come from Tony Benn, who said he would support Michael Foot. Crosland, who drew only 17 of the 314 votes cast, was automatically eliminated. In the ballot on the second round, both Callaghan and Foot consolidated their positions as the leading contenders. Callaghan topped the poll with 141, Foot polled 133 and Healey 38. In the third and final ballot, most of Healey's supporters duly switched to Callaghan, who won by 176 votes to Foot's 137.

Although Callaghan had eventually triumphed, the result was a striking demonstration of support for Michael Foot, who had not merely inherited the votes of Benn's supporters but had clearly picked up some support from the three losing right-wing candidates. No doubt Foot's style and personal charisma accounted for some of this appeal, but the result was confirmation that a substantial leftward move had taken place in the Labour Party over the past decade.

Callaghan Takes Over

Callaghan became Prime Minister on 5 April 1976. Few contrasts could have been more marked than that between the new Premier and his predecessor. Callaghan, a chapel-goer, teetotaller and non-smoker, was 64 when he became Premier. In contrast to Wilson's brilliant academic career at Oxford, Callaghan had had only an elementary and secondary school education. He had made his career as a civil service tax officer, but growing involvement in trade union affairs had seen him rise to become assistant secretary of the Inland Revenue Staff Federation in 1936. Elected MP for Cardiff South in 1945, he held junior office under Attlee. Under Wilson he had been successively (even if not always successfully) Chancellor of the Exchequer, Home Secretary and Foreign and Commonwealth Secretary.

Although the leadership election had confirmed the growing power of the left in the Labour Party, Callaghan from the first adopted the tough 'above faction' line that was to dominate his premiership. Thus he told the Parliamentary Party, he would not tolerate 'minority groups' trying to 'foist their views' on the party.

In his first television broadcast as Prime Minister, Callaghan reiterated that the most important task would be to drive on with the vital job of bringing down the rate of inflation. Callaghan's Cabinet team, though relying on many of the stalwarts of the Wilson era, showed some important changes. Healey (whose Budget was due the day after Callaghan became Prime Minister) was confirmed as Chancellor. Foot became Lord President and Leader of the House, replacing Edward Short and reflecting his strength in the party. Crosland became Foreign Secretary, Shore replaced Crosland as Environment Secretary, Dell became Secretary of State for Trade and Albert Booth took over from Foot at Employment. Among other significant changes, Shirley Williams became Paymaster General as well as Secretary for Prices and Consumer Affairs, while Barbara

31

Castle left as Social Services Secretary, being replaced by David Ennals. Barbara Castle, a veteran left-wing campaigner, (and, declared Crossman in his *Diaries*, of Prime Ministerial calibre but for the fact that she was a woman) had not enjoyed an easy time with the medical profession. Although Roy Jenkins remained as Home Secretary, he was to resign within a short while to become President of the European Commission. The untimely death of Anthony Crosland in February 1977 led to the promotion of David Owen to be Foreign Secretary, the youngest person to hold the post since Eden.

The Lib-Lab Pact

That the Callaghan administration lasted so long before an election was called was due to the working arrangement it came to with the Liberals. Within a short time of taking office, the growing unpopularity of the government had been witnessed in a series of humiliating by-election losses. By the end of 1976, Labour had lost such strongholds as Walsall North and Workington to the Conservatives (see p. 216ff).

Excluding the Speaker and his three Deputies, the government's over-all majority had fallen to one by January 1977. Even this majority was dependent upon the two members of the break-away Scottish Labour Party and the two non-Unionists from Northern Ireland, all of whom usually supported the government.

Weakened by by-election losses, the Labour government was faced in March 1977 with almost certain defeat on a Conservative vote of 'no confidence', since the Nationalists had stated that they would vote against Labour.

By the time of the weekend prior to the Conservative vote of censure, Callaghan's only hope of surviving as Prime Minister and avoiding an immediate General Election lay in a deal with the Liberals. The pressures on Callaghan mounted when David Steel, the Liberal leader, and Reg Prentice, the rebel Labour MP for Newham, stated that their conditions were an agreed policy 'in the national interest' for the next two years. So identical was Prentice's tone that it seemed clear he had been colluding with the Liberals. At the same time, the votes of a majority of the Ulster Unionists seemed certain to be cast against the government.

When the terms of the deal were made public, Liberal scepticism that Callaghan had got by far the better of the deal mounted (and insult was added to injury by press reports that an unnamed Cabinet minister was declaring that the Liberals had been bought 'for nothing').

On the Labour side, four Cabinet ministers were reported to be against the deal – led by Environment Secretary Peter Shore with Energy Secretary Tony Benn equally opposed, if perhaps preoccupied with taking notes of the Cabinet for his memoirs. On the Liberal side, Cyril Smith proved the most voluble sceptic in the parliamentary party. In the country at large, most Liberals were prepared to 'wait and see', and there were only a few outraged Liberals who resigned rather than see their party supporting Labour in office. At the opposite extreme, the Lib-Lab pact had a hard ride at the Young Liberals' April Conference at Weston-super-Mare. Young Liberal Chairman Steve Atack argued that Liberals should attack Labour from the left, not from the centre.

In many ways, however, the pact represented a sensible assessment of the practical political situation. Neither Labour nor the Liberals wanted an election. For Steel, the pact represented a move towards possible future deals in a hung Parliament – and hence electoral reform. But if this deal gave Liberals more influence than for many years at Westminster, in the country it did nothing to restore a disastrous slump in Liberal fortunes. In the first nation-wide test of Liberal support (the May 1977 local elections) the Liberals fared disastrously and in by-elections their vote plummeted. Against this electoral background, and amid increasing growls of discontent from the Liberal ranks, the Lib-Lab pact seemed as if it might crumble over the question of direct elections to the European Parliament.

On 26 November 1977, the Liberal Party Council passed a resolution calling for a special Liberal Assembly to be held if the House of Commons failed to pass the regional list system for direct elections to the European Parliament because of the opposition of a substantial number of Labour back-benchers. Although the resolution supported continuing the Lib-Lab pact, thus confirming the decision of the September 1977 Liberal Assembly, it was clear that trouble was likely over European elections.

The Blackpool Liberal Assembly

On 13 December, the Liberals were faced with exactly what they had feared. Some 114 Labour MPs, including four members of the Cabinet, voted for an amendment supporting the 'first-past-the-post' system rather than the Liberal-backed regional list. The result was the calling of a special Liberal Party Assembly to meet in Blackpool on 21 January 1978.

The Blackpool Assembly focused the internal wranglings in

the party. The 'Liberals Against the Pact' had the persuasive support of such figures as Cyril Smith and Andrew Ellis, the Liberal candidate in Newcastle Central. Steel, in a powerful speech, catalogued what he saw as the achievements of the pact. Steel's arguments won the day. At the end of the debate, 520 delegates voted for the immediate ending of the agreement, 1727 voted to continue the pact until at least after the 1978 Finance Act and to let its termination be decided by Steel in consultation with the party's senior officers and the parliamentary party.

Among all the vicissitudes of the Lib-Lab pact, it was Callaghan who certainly gained most from it. It had bought him time – time for the economy to improve and time also to attempt to put the lengthy and controversial Devolution Bill on to the Statute Book.

Labour and the Economy

Of the difficulties inherited by James Callaghan, the crucial problem still remained the management of the economy, now deep into recession (see p. 48). It was against a difficult economic background, and with the £6 limit due to end in July 1976, that Healey introduced his Budget.

The Budget of April 1976 was broadly neutral in its intent (see p. 54). Its most important and novel aspect was the offer of tax cuts conditional on the unions agreeing to a limit of around 3% on pay increases from July. If the government secured such agreement, the single person's allowance would be increased by £60 to £735 and the married person's allowance by £130 to £1085.

Such an agreement was made in May 1976 with a new limit aimed to hold average wage increases to 4·5% in the year starting in August 1976. Price controls were also maintained, but there was some relaxation to encourage industrial investment. As important as restrictions on pay increases was a reduction in the soaring amount of government expenditure. Hence, during 1976, a vigorous campaign was mounted in favour of cuts in public expenditure. Concern that the government was borrowing excessively to finance this spending also led to weakness of sterling on the foreign exchange markets. In July, to avert a further fall in the value of sterling, substantial cuts were announced in the government's spending plans for 1977–8 and interest rates were raised to record levels (see p. 65). These measures were not sufficient, however, to prevent a dramatic slide in the £ during the autumn which forced the government to seek a $3900 million loan from the International Monetary

Fund. To obtain this assistance, further cuts in public expenditure, amounting to £3000 million over the next two years, and increases in taxation, were imposed in December.

The sterling crisis of 1976 marked the low point of the government's struggle with the economy. During 1977 and 1978, definite signs of recovery began. Though the economy was still in recession – in February 1977 an enormous total of 1,420,000 people were unemployed and output was hardly rising – the benefits of North Sea oil were beginning to transform the balance of payments. For 1977 as a whole the balance of payments showed an actual surplus. The pound was riding higher, helped partly by the continuing weakness of the dollar. Even the rate of inflation – though uncomfortably high in comparison with Britain's major competitors – was at last reduced to single figures. The signs of economic recovery were reflected in the April 1978 Budget (see p. 56), although a reminder of the varying fluctuations of economic life came with the renewal of a 'credit squeeze' in early June (see p. 51).

Labour and Devolution

The most difficult – as well as the most significant – legislation which Callaghan inherited was the Devolution Bill. It provided another delicate issue which had already deeply divided the Labour Party.

The need for some degree of devolution had been given added urgency by the dramatic gains of the Scottish National Party in the October 1974 election. Equally worrying to Labour as a longer-term threat were not the 11 SNP gains but the 42 seats in which the SNP was now the challenger. No fewer than 35 of these were Labour-held.

Devolution had thus become urgent politics for Labour. For if Labour lost its Scottish electoral base, its chances of once again forming a majority government at Westminster would be minimal. But what form should devolution take?

As early as April 1969, the Labour government had appointed a Royal Commission on the Constitution under the chairmanship of Lord Crowther. Following the latter's death in February 1972, Lord Kilbrandon, a Lord of Appeal in Ordinary and a member of the Commission since its inception, was appointed chairman. The Commission's findings were published in October 1973.

All the members of the Commission accepted that there was some dissatisfaction with the present system of government and that some change was desirable. They also unanimously rejected extreme solutions, such as the division of Great Britain into three sovereign states or the creation of a federation. Beyond this, however, they failed to reach agreement. Two of the Commission's members disagreed sufficiently fundamentally to produce a lengthy memorandum of dissent. The remaining 11 who signed the majority report in fact produced five different schemes, although some of these had elements in common. The most popular scheme, which was advocated by 8 members when applied to Scotland and by 6 when applied to Wales, proposed the creation of regional assemblies for Scotland and Wales elected on the basis of proportional representation.

Initially the Kilbrandon Report was not received very favourably. However, with the continuing successes of the Nationalist parties, Labour gradually came over (despite the opposition of the Scottish Executive of the Labour Party) to supporting devolution with elected assemblies for Scotland and Wales. In June 1974 the Labour government published a consultative document which set out 7 possible schemes for greater devolution. In September 1974 a White Paper was published, *Democracy and Devolution: Proposals for Scotland and Wales*, and following further discussions, a second White Paper, *Our Changing Democracy: Devolution to Scotland and Wales* was produced in November 1975 (see Part II ch. 15).

They contained far-reaching proposals with very great constitutional significance. Within the Labour Party in Parliament there was likely to be strong opposition – not only from anti-devolutionists in Scotland such as Tam Dalyell, the Labour MP for West Lothian, but also from an English 'backlash' opposed to special treatment for Scotland. At the same time that opposition in Labour's own ranks was growing, the Conservatives were also hardening their position. Although the Opposition had in principle supported the creation of a Scottish Assembly since the late 1960s, in 1976 the party decided officially to oppose the government's legislation – although a number of senior Conservatives opposed the change of attitude by the party.

These political difficulties were reflected in the fate of the Scotland and Wales Bill, and the subsequent difficult passage through Parliament (see p. 131ff).

At long last, devolution, provided that Scotland and Wales gave the necessary assent in the referendums, was, by mid-1978, near to becoming a reality, but whether this move would satisfy the Nationalists – and whether indeed they would secure Labour's electoral flank in Scotland – remained to be seen, although Labour's comfortable victory in the Garscadden and Hamilton by-elections and the SNP set-backs in the local elections were extremely encouraging signs.

Labour and Ulster

In addition to the Common Market and devolution, Labour also inherited the intractable question of the Ulster troubles. In the closing months of the Heath administration, direct rule in the province had been ended on 1 January 1974 with the coming into operation of the main provisions of the Northern Ireland Constitution Act.

Labour, however, inherited a near hopeless legacy. Right from the start, the political position of the new Executive was weak. Its position was worsened by the result of the February general election in Northern Ireland in which 11 out of the 12 seats were won by Loyalist candidates opposed to the Executive. None of the Unionist candidates supporting the Sunningdale agreement was elected and 11 of the 12 seats were won by anti-Sunningdale Unionists who achieved a total of 367,000 votes (51·1% of the Northern Ireland poll). The election had thus sent back to Westminster a collection of MPs all but one of whom were opposed to the power-sharing settlement.

The Chief Executive, Brian Faulkner, and his deputy, the SDLP leader, Gerry Fitt, soldiered on bravely until its collapse occurred in May 1974. Following the ratification of the Sunningdale Agreement in the Assembly, the Ulster Workers' Council initiated strike action, at first interfering with the supply of electricity and later extending this to a large part of the economy. The UK government's refusal to negotiate with the Council led to the resignation of the Chief Executive, Brian Faulkner, and his Unionist colleagues. As a result the Assembly was prorogued and direct rule resumed.

In an attempt to get a new political initiative going in Ulster, it was announced in July 1974 that a constitutional convention was to be elected so as to give the people of Northern Ireland, through elected representatives called together for this purpose, an opportunity to put forward recommendations as to how the province should be governed. Elections were held in May 1975. The result was a massive loyalist landslide, with the United Ulster Unionist Council taking 46 seats, the SDLP 17, the Alliance Party 8 and the Unionist Party of Northern Ireland a mere 5. From the start of the Convention's deliberations, the UUUC made it clear that it would not agree to the inclusion of opposition members in a future cabinet. Thus the Convention failed to produce a unanimous report. However, its recommendations, which were submitted to the government in November 1975, revealed that there was all-party agreement that direct rule should be ended and a Northern Ireland assembly

37

and executive re-established, and the UUUC did propose that powerful all-party committees should be created in the assembly. The Convention was re-convened for one month at the beginning of February 1976 but was dissolved finally on 5 March and direct rule from Westminster continued.

Terrorism from both Protestants and Republicans continued throughout 1976. The collapse of a general strike call by Ian Paisley early in 1977 reinforced Mason's prestige as Northern Ireland Secretary, but any solution of the problems of the province seemed as remote as ever (see also Part II ch. 19).

Labour's Domestic Legislation

Although devolution had occupied a great deal of parliamentary time (though far less than the Conservatives thought desirable), by 1978 Labour could point to a substantial legislative achievement. Callaghan had inherited from Wilson a large number of controversial bills. Although there were some that were to be severely mauled, some important legislation had gone through – despite strong opposition – in the House of Commons, where the government's small majority was frequently threatened, and in the House of Lords. The Lords attempted to make major changes in 6 bills, but the conflicts eventually centred around two measures – the Dock Work Regulation Bill and the Aircraft and Shipbuilding Industries Bill. The former was returned to the Commons with its main provision transformed by the Lords, but the defection of two of its own back-benchers prevented the government restoring its original proposal. Continuing difficulties over the Aircraft and Shipbuilding Industries Bill forced its re-introduction at the beginning of the 1976–7 session. It eventually became law in March 1977 but only after the Government had made important concessions, notably dropping the nationalisation of the ship-repairers (see p. 85).

Among the main legislative measures, Callaghan could point to the Police Act, establishing a Police Complaints Board to take part with the police in investigating complaints against the police by the public. There was also the Health Services Act, providing for the progressive withdrawal of private medicine from National Health Service hospitals; the Education Act, requiring local education authorities to submit proposals to abolish selection in secondary education; and the Race Relations Act, which created a new Commission for Racial Equality.

With devolution out of the way, with the legislative decks virtually cleared and with the worst of the economic recession behind it, the way was clear for Callaghan to time his appeal to the country.

Part II
The Issues

Part II
The Issues

1 The Management of the Economy

All political parties, at all times, want power – however unappetising the prospect of having to exercise that power, and to take the awkward and painful decisions which go with it, may look to the outside world. Yet only a masochist of a particularly devout order could have positively gloried in the prospect which faced the new Labour government when Harold Wilson moved into Downing Street on 4 March 1974.

The brave bid by Edward Heath and his Chancellor Anthony Barber to burst their way out of Britain's long period of economic stagnation by a sustained and unflinching commitment to economic growth had, by the end of 1973, begun to come badly unstuck. There were the consequences of the Heath government's terminal encounter with the miners – leading to the imposition of the three-day week, extensive industrial disruption and a costly loss of production – waiting to be cleared up. But most of all, the new government had to come to terms with the belated assertion of economic power mounted after the Middle East war by the Arab oil states, which had led first to shortages of essential supplies and then to a quadrupling of the price of oil – a sharp enough shift to throw the whole economy of the western industrial world into confusion, and to threaten people in Britain with an abrupt reduction in the steadily advancing standards of life to which (though only, for the most part, by living beyond their means) they had become accustomed.

'It is not often,' the quarterly report of the National Institute of Economic and Social Research observed in February 1974,

41

'that a government finds itself faced with the possibility of a simultaneous failure to achieve all four main policy objectives – of adequate economic growth, full employment, a satisfactory balance of payments and reasonably stable prices.' But all that, and more, now faced the incoming Chancellor, Denis Healey.

The Heath break for growth had indeed brought results. Between 1972 and 1973 – after the Heath government, faced with unemployment at the million mark and the need to save great companies like Rolls-Royce and the Clyde shipyards from swelling those totals still further, reversed its previous policies to go unconditionally for growth – the Gross Domestic Product grew by about 6%, against an annual average of less than 3% for the 10 years before.

The Barber Boom Bursts

But like every previous attempt in this series, the Heath–Barber dash for growth brought problems in its train. 'The problems of success' Heath had called them in the summer; but it was very soon clear that there was more to them than that. As usual, greater domestic spending power quickly produced a richer market for imported goods. The import bill for the first quarter of 1974 proved to be almost half as much again as the bill for the same quarter a year earlier. Fatally for the Heath government, which along with many others had not fully foreseen it, commodity prices were growing at a record rate – faster even than in the Korean war (see table 1·11). The volume of exports declined. The deficit on visible trade in the third quarter of 1973 was £606 million; in the fourth it was £1019 million – greater than the *annual* deficit which had created a crisis for the British economy as Labour came into office in 1964. There was an adverse trade balance at the end of the year of £2375 million – offset by a surplus on invisible trade of £1165 million, but still leaving Britain over £1200 million in the red on current account.

The money supply, an index less venerated in the Conservative Party then than it is today, showed, on the M 3 basis (see table 1·16) a 28% expansion on the year. Inflation, too, was reaching new heights. The retail price index climbed 12 percentage points in the year from January 1973 to January 1974. Industry, as in every previous expansion, complained that it was starved for materials, components and skilled men, and was buying in imports, and bidding up wages, accordingly. Already, Chancellor Barber had made modest attempts at damping down the economy, with public spending cuts in May and a boost for interest rates to a record 11·5% in July – followed by a further rise to 13% in November.

On 17 December, the Chancellor came forward with a package which seemed to throw the previous policy into reverse. With the oil crisis upon us, and the dispute with the miners coming to a head, he announced a programme of cuts in public spending amounting to £1200 million – much the biggest programme of cuts which any Chancellor had ever brought forward. Details of this package, and of the many subsequent budgets, mini-budgets, mere statements and other announcements of financial chop and change, can be found in table 1·1.

The domestic elements in this crisis would have been bad enough, but the multiplication of oil prices gave it a new dimension outside the experience of Chancellors, in Britain or elsewhere. Heath and Barber insisted in the last days of government that savage deflation, designed to see that other countries took a heavier share of the coming oil deficit than we did, would be the wrong route out of trouble. 'There is an acute danger,' Heath said on 13 December, 'that if we all independently resort to deflationary measures for the sake of our individual balances of payments, we shall set off a disastrous slump in the level of world trade. It will require all the effort and all the farsightedness of which the international community is capable to escape this consequence.'

Healey took the same line. The answer was for the western industrial nations to keep cool, collaborate, avoid competitive deflation which would only make the coming recession worse, and reach civilised agreements for recycling the Arab oil surpluses. Such sentiments were echoed by many but observed by few. Western countries, led by France but with Britain not so very far behind, were soon busy (to the anger of the Americans) constructing their own bilateral deals with oil producers to offset the bills they were destined to have to pay. And while Healey's anti-deflationist declarations were applauded in principle, great economies like the United States and Japan were quickly set on the road to deflation, unemployment and deepening recession.

The Labour government in Britain, however, stood by what it said. It had several reasons for doing so. For one thing, it genuinely believed what it was preaching (and knew the outgoing government had preached it too). It was anxious to bring peace where there had, until recently, been confrontation, and throwing many thousands out of work was unlikely to contribute to that. And it also knew that it might before long have another election to fight. Others, therefore, might opt for instant suffering, but Britain would not.

Labour 1974: a Contract for Inflation?

The main plank of Labour's policy – sketched out in opposition, developed through the short Parliament of 1974 – was the relationship with the trade unions which came to be known as the Social Contract. The machinery of wage restraint – though not of price restraint – was to go. (The same Bill which abolished the Pay Board strengthened the powers of the Price Commission.) Like the incoming Conservative government of four years before, the Labour government of February 1974 tore down the institutions of wage control it had inherited. The Conservatives' Phase Three could continue until it ran out naturally in July. (Labour anyway lacked the Commons majority to terminate it.) But even that was set aside for those groups judged to be especially deserving. The miners took 22%, and soon the barriers were lifted again for the teachers and for the nurses and paramedicals (some of whom had rises of 50% or more) to be signalled through.

The spirit of the Social Contract was clear enough. The Labour government would pursue a series of policies – the abolition of hated Conservative legislation, increases in subsidies and social benefits, the extension of public ownership – which they and the unions alike believed to be in the national interest. In return for that, the unions would moderate their bargaining power in wage negotiations. But the formula on which the Social Contract, in its role as arbiter of wage settlements, was based turned out to be ambiguous. The unions were entitled to such settlements as would enable them to keep pace with the rising cost of living. But was that supposed to compensate for the rise which had already taken place – or to shore them up against the rises which might take place in the future? 'If settlements can be confined to what is needed to cover the increase in the cost of living,' said Healey in his supplementary budget of 12 November 1974, 'we can reasonably expect to see a decrease in the rate of inflation in the coming year.' But the accumulation of settlements well above what was needed to compensate for past price rises quickly demonstrated that the Chancellor's was a minority interpretation of the deal.

At first, this was barely reflected in prices. And, on 22 July 1974, the Chancellor brought in a package of measures designed to keep prices down – including a cut in the rate of Value Added Tax (VAT), an extension of food subsidies, new aid for ratepayers and a mitigation of increases in council house rents. During the campaign for the October election, by restricting his statistical base to a three-month period which embraced the immediate consequences of these measures, Healey was able to argue that the rate of inflation had been brought down to a mere 8·4%. But the respite, such as it was, did not last long. By January 1975, the retail price index was showing an increase of 20% on the previous year; by June inflation was running at a rate of 26%.

The conventional analysis of this inflation attributed most of it to the breakdown of control over wages. The great boom in commodity prices was over. As the Chancellor said himself in his first budget of 1975, wages were now the main fuel of inflation. If we persisted, almost alone among the industrialised countries, with our current rates of inflation, there would clearly be very serious consequences for our trade and our balance of payments. The government, the Chancellor said, had honoured its side of the Social Contract: the Trades Union Congress (TUC) had stood by its guidelines; but these guidelines had not been universally observed. Pay was running 8% to 9% ahead of prices: unless there was restraint, the consequence 'could only be rising unemployment, cuts in public spending, lower living standards for the country as a whole, and a growing tension throughout society'.

But while to many on the government side this looked like a signal for a renewed experiment with incomes policy (though there was a certain reluctance to say so, especially before the referendum on British membership of the EEC was safely out of the way), opinions on the Conservative side were sharply divided. Since the February 1974 defeat, there had been growing attention for the monetarist explanation for our economic ills, an explanation which – to summarise it somewhat brutally – made incomes policy look largely irrelevant; if too much money was circulating, the theory said, then inflation would result as inevitably as night followed day. This did not mean that if you got the money supply right, all other problems would disappear: what it said was that while you had got the money supply wrong you had no real prospect of salvation. Even before the October election, in a speech at Preston on 5 September, Sir Keith Joseph, who had been Heath's Secretary of State for Health and Social Services, began to reinterpret recent economic history in these terms. The election of Margaret Thatcher, on 11 February 1975, both because it represented a repudiation of the Heath leadership and because she was known to be much influenced by Joseph, put monetarist theory closer to the heart of Conservative policy-making than Heath would ever have permitted.

Strictly applied, it diminished the blame to be attached to the government for what was now happening, tracing much of

45

it back to the headlong expansion of the money supply under Heath and Barber. (Healey, indeed, had been thought something of a monetarist himself for the assaults he had launched on Barber on this score.) But it also furnished a base from which the Conservatives now launched a prolonged campaign against the Labour government's failure to reduce the Public Sector Borrowing Requirement (PSBR) because of its cowardly refusal, as they saw it, to make stringent cuts in public spending.

May 1975: Mr Jones Intervenes

A month after Healey in his budget speech warned of the grim alternatives to self-restraint, a programme for wage control emerged from the trade union movement. The Transport and General Workers' (TGWU) leader, Jack Jones, proposed that there should be a flat rate wage award, universally applied. On 25 June the General Council of the TUC approved a 6-point set of guidelines built on this principle, and on 11 July the government published a White Paper making it the centrepiece of its new wages policy. It allowed a maximum increase of £6, with no increase at all for those earning more than £8500 (the TUC had wanted a ceiling of £7000). There would be sanctions on employers who did not comply: grants and contracts would be put at risk. The government could not give the TUC the price freeze it wanted – that would jeopardise investment and so threaten employment – but controls would be tightened. 'A plan to save our country,' the White Paper called it: if we did not succeed in drastically reducing our present disastrous inflation, then the people of Britain would be engulfed 'in a general economic catastrophe of incalculable proportions'. (For details of this and subsequent stages of the Labour policy, and comparisons with the Conservative policy of 1972–4, see table 1·6.)

The Commons approved the strategy on 22 July by 262 votes to 54 on a vote forced by Labour left-wingers (see table 20·2) after the defeat of a Conservative amendment welcoming the assault on inflation but condemning the government for failing to act on public spending. The Liberals commended the measures, though with reservations. The Labour MPs opposing the policy called it a capitulation to pressure from enemies of the British Labour movement.

But again there was an ambiguity. The Chancellor regarded the £6 as an upper limit, not as a universal entitlement. The TUC saw it as a standard increase. The TUC view prevailed. But the new policy made impressive progress. Settlements fell dutifully into line. The inflation rate was gradually checked – though by international standards (see table 1·4) it remained exceptionally high. And the wave of industrial disputes which had often attended incomes policies failed to materialise. On a monetarist analysis, the Chancellor's success, such as it was, lay mainly in his recapture of control of the money supply; but elsewhere, as the opinion polls showed, it was the Jones initiative which took the credit.

But other key indicators gave little comfort. Much of the world, after a year of brutal recession, was now on the way to recovery. The United States economy, through a fiscal policy which sought expansion at the cost of a doubled budget deficit, was by 1976 taking off again. Japan was emerging, though cautiously, from a year which had brought it its first drop in output since the war. In Britain, too, production was depressed, down to the level of the three-day week. But unemployment, which had been held while rates in other countries climbed, was only now beginning to climb, while rates in other countries stabilised. The huge payments deficit of 1974 was halved in 1975, but only at the cost of recession. The living standards of the British people, as measured by their real personal disposable income (RPDI) advanced only by a fraction in 1975, and fell back in 1976 to the levels of 1974. (For Britain's performance in these years of recession, and comparisons with other countries, see tables 1·4 and 1·8.)

Despite many dire predictions, the incomes policy moved safely into a second phase in the summer of 1976. In his budget speech on 6 April 1976, Healey offered one set of tax concessions while holding another in reserve. Tax cuts worth £930 million were guaranteed; but on top of that there would be a further £370 million package if the unions would accept a new pay ceiling equivalent to about 3% on wage increases. The agreement which was subsequently reached with the unions did not in fact fall quite within these guidelines; the out-turn was expected to be nearer 4·5%. But the additional tax concessions were made anyway.

The over-all effects of the Chancellor's measures at this stage remained severely deflationary. He had several times renounced the use of unemployment as an economic regulator. 'Deliberately to adopt a strategy which requires mass unemployment would be no less an economic than a moral crime,' he had said in his budget of November 1974. And there had been a succession of government announcements (see table 6·5) designed to preserve or create jobs. But their main effect was to prevent unemployment becoming even worse: they could not by their nature be sufficient to get it moving substantially down (see also Part II ch. 6).

1976: Recession and a Vanishing Pound

No country had emerged unscathed from the crisis which followed the rise in oil prices. But on all tests the United Kingdom, in 1975 and 1976, seemed to be doing conspicuously worse than average. The charts on pages 58–9 tell the story. Our GDP and industrial output remained stagnant while those of competitor countries recovered. Our unemployment had grown higher just when other countries were bringing theirs down. Our price inflation was the most severe in Europe and our wage inflation was surpassed only by Italy's. And 1976 saw a new threat developing. The exchange rate which had been declining slowly since the end of 1973 began to slip faster until it precipitated, in the autumn, a sterling crisis far greater than that which had swamped the new Prime Minister, James Callaghan, when he was Chancellor in 1967.

There had been heavy inflows into Britain's reserves immediately after the oil crisis developed. Though they were greeted at the time as a heartening sign of Britain's continued standing in the world, they came in time to be an element of additional insecurity. For a while, they cushioned the British against the consequences of what was happening elsewhere in the economy – and particularly, an increase in the rate of inflation way above what other countries were experiencing. The inevitable reckoning seems to have begun with an attempt by the Treasury at the beginning of March to engineer a fall in the rate to make our goods more competitive in export markets. Unhappily, once the selling started, others joined in, and the Treasury was unable to call a halt.

On 5 March, the value of the £ fell for the first time below $2 (until 1967 it had been worth $2·80; the post-devaluation rate was $2·40). Despite a $806 billion drawing on the International Monetary Fund (IMF) in May and a further $5300 million standby arrangement with 8 western central banks, confidence in the £ continued to collapse. The Conservatives demanded instant and severe cuts in public spending; it was the Chancellor's reckless failure to curb public expenditure, they said, which had caused our creditors to despair of us. Almost any piece of bad news – and there were plenty – was now enough to set off a further slide.

A package of public expenditure cuts of around £1000 million, produced by the Chancellor on 22 July (see table 2·4) did little to check the decline. The culmination came in September, during a Labour Party conference which seemed to suggest to the outside world that Labour's 'moderates' had finally lost control. Extensive nationalisation plans were approved; it was agreed to launch a public campaign against the Labour government's spending cuts. The Chancellor, on his way to an IMF conference in Manila, telephoned the Treasury from Heathrow to check on the latest state of the £ and was so overcome by what he heard that he cancelled his trip and went straight back to Whitehall, announcing that he was working on an application for a further standby arrangement with the IMF. That he had missed the IMF's own conference, and had taken the unseemly course of speaking about his application in public before he had communicated his intentions in private, were enough on their own to guarantee him somewhat frosty treatment from the IMF; and the continuing reluctance within the British government to swallow the medicine which the IMF found appropriate made the subsequent negotiations all the tougher. And at Blackpool, where he delivered a robust defence of the policies the government had been pursuing to a conference which thirsted for full-blooded socialist solutions, there was much enthusiastic booing among the cheers which greeted him.

The sealing of the IMF deal finally stopped the flow – but only at the price of a further round of public spending cuts, this time on something like the scale which the Conservatives had been demanding. After a long, anguished and well-publicised argument in Cabinet, during which the strategy of the Labour left for an abandonment of orthodox remedies in favour of a more socialist programme of recovery was examined and rejected, the Chancellor came to the Commons on 15 December to announce cuts of £1000 million in the programme for 1977–8 and £1500 million in that for the year beyond – savings which along with other measures, including the sale of a £500 million block of oil shares recently acquired by the government, were expected to reduce the PSBR by nearly £2000 million in the first year and £3000 million in the second. The Public Expenditure White Paper of January 1977 produced a further scaling down of plans.

The Conservatives regarded this as a vindication of the advice they had been giving all along; the Labour left saw it as the eradication of socialism from the government's programme. Already, on 10 March 1976, they had defeated the government by refusing to endorse the projected spending cuts in the 1976 Public Expenditure White Paper. Now they threatened they would do the same again. The result was the deal with the Liberals which produced the Lib-Lab pact and saved the government from defeat on a confidence motion – and the beginning of a new chapter in Labour's management of the economy.

1977: A Little Moment of Euphoria

The transformation was startling. From the time of the IMF deal, the £ had begun to strengthen, the reserves to accumulate once more. But the return of confidence came faster than anyone had expected. The Chancellor was able to come forward with another tax-cutting budget in 1977 and to sustain its proposals despite his failure to negotiate a third round of wage restraint with the unions; he was back in October with more and the promise of more again in the spring of 1978 – though the tax cuts he made now still did not restore anything like the depredations of the past four years. The Conservatives attributed the change in climate to the belated arrival of sound financial managers in the shape of the men from the IMF. The Liberals put it down to the greater stability which the Lib-Lab pact had brought to the government and the country. The Chancellor regarded it as the outcome of his long struggle with adversity.

Hardly had we ceased worrying about the weakness of the £ than we began to fret over its strength. On 31 October 1977, unable to hold the rate down except by measures such as a wider relaxation of exchange controls, which the government was unable to contemplate – mainly for fear of lost investment and lost jobs at home – the Treasury announced that the £ was to be freed to float upwards; which it promptly did, until at one point it was nestling only a few cents short of the $2 parity which few had expected to see again.

It was unreal – boosted by the expectation of oil revenues which would not last for ever, and would leave us all the more vulnerable when they had gone. It was damaging the competitiveness of our exports. (The City favoured a high exchange rate, industry a low one.) An agitated debate began about how the revenues could best be used. The Labour left favoured a programme of industrial reconstruction predominantly through government intervention and state investment. The Conservatives thought the main use should be to produce personal and corporate incentives for private industry. The government, which published a Green Paper on this theme in March 1977, favoured a blend of public and private investment but gave special weight to the need to develop alternative sources of energy which could serve after the North Sea oil ran dry.

By the spring of 1978, however, the euphoria was fast abating. You could hardly talk of recovery: production remained depressed – in 1977 it was still not yet back to the level of five years before – though investment seemed at last to be growing; unemployment, despite every ingenious scheme which the government could contrive, remained for some time becalmed around the 1·5 million mark. The Chancellor had held out hope through the winter of a major tax-cutting budget, but when the time arrived he found his room for manoeuvre desperately constrained. The expected boom on the balance of payments seemed to be vanishing already, with the trade figures showing the familiar signs of greater spending power sucking in more and more imported goods. Inflation was at last down into single figures, and Phase Three of the incomes policy, built on a minimum of TUC agreement (table 1·6) but backed by a government determination to exploit all available sanctions to the full was faring better than expected, with the hope that the target figure of 10% would be overshot by perhaps no more than a further 4%. But there remained abundant signs that it might before long turn up again rather than go further down.

Indeed, the Chancellor was forced into yet another bout of emergency action on 8 June 1978 after the £ had once again fallen into decline following his Spring Budget. The City was worried enough by the original Budget arithmetic, fearing that the projected size of the Borrowing Requirement had dangerous implications for the money supply and so for inflation. But the Chancellor's predicament was made even worse when the Opposition parties combined on 8 and 10 May to carry amendments to the Finance Bill cutting the standard rate of income tax by an additional 1p and introducing further alleviations for the better-off. Before that vote, some measure of further restriction had begun to look distinctly likely: after it, it became inevitable. On 8 June, Healey announced tough new restrictions on bank credit, a further 1% rise in Minimum Lending Rate to 10%, and a 2·5% addition to employers' national insurance contributions. Just as some of the indicators – especially consumer spending – were beginning to show a bit of buoyancy, the prospect appeared that the top would be knocked off the expansion. Still more revisions were necessary when the Liberals refused to back the 2·5% surcharge.

The apocalyptic quartet whose presence the NIESR had noted as Labour came back to power still threatened as the election approached: inadequate growth, high unemployment, a queasy balance of payments, and a destabilising level of inflation.

Labour's left condemned the failure to break out of the old, tried, and in their view discredited, system of orthodox deflationary policies, rather than their own 'alternative strategy' of industrial reconstruction through extensive state intervention behind protectionist walls. The Liberals put special weight on the instability of British government, the chop and change for largely party purposes which had robbed industry of what it had always needed most of all to encourage investment and enhance productivity: a climate of continuity. The Conservatives said that Britain's troubles in these years had been substantially of the government's manufacturing, chiefly because of the Chancellor's failure to read the writing on the wall, his reluctance to cut public spending, his inconsistent governing of the money supply.

The Conservatives put their hope in an 'enterprise package' of major cuts in direct taxation, balanced by increases in indirect taxation where necessary, and most of all by an attack on public spending. Only three areas – defence, law and order, and people identified as genuinely in need – were regarded as deserving candidates for more public money. They did not entirely repudiate the concept of incomes policy, though Mrs Thatcher sometimes came near to it, with her enthusiastic endorsement of the system of free collective bargaining to which so much of the trade union movement now thirsted to return. But it was clear that a Conservative policy would maintain a tight hold on wages in the public sector, which it could directly control. And there was also a developing interest in moving towards a system of incomes policy built on German lines: employers and unions would come together annually with the government, in some forum comparable to the National Economic Development Council (NEDC), to assess the size of the income 'cake' available for the coming year and discuss how the money should be distributed.

The Liberals had made a tighter grip on inflation, one of the conditions of their pact with Labour. They were the one party to advocate in the elections of 1974 a statutory control of incomes, arguing that wage increases over the prescribed norm should be removed through the tax system. They continued to make this case in Parliament, though at the Liberal Assembly of 1977 it was unexpectedly rejected by the grass-roots party.

Certainly it could be said, as the election approached, that the worst should now be over, and the decline in living standards arrested. But Britain was emerging out of a grim past into a deeply uncertain future. It had always been inevitable, once the oil states had spoken, that there would be grievous setbacks, and a curbing of ambitions, for Britain as for other States in the industrial west. The question which the Opposition parties asked and the government was required to answer was whether Labour's management of the economy had exacerbated the inevitable problems – rather than saving us, as the government claimed, from still worse.

Table 1·1: PRINCIPAL GOVERNMENT ECONOMIC MEASURES 1973–8

(For further details of tax policy see Part II ch. 3; for incomes policy see table 1·6; for public spending cuts see table 2·4)

CON

1973

6 March **BUDGET.** VAT to be fixed at 10% with car tax also set at 10%. Allowances raised, especially for elderly. Action to close tax loopholes on North Sea oil. Pensions to rise.

21 May Public expenditure cuts: £500 m taken from 1974–5 programme.

17 December £1200 m cuts in public spending, including defence £178 m; capital expenditure on nationalised industries £264 m; roads and transport £212 m; education, libraries, arts £182 m; health and social services £111 m. Surtax surcharge, credit and HP controls.

LAB

1974

26 March **BUDGET.** Taxes up £1387 m in full year. Basic and higher rates of tax up 3% (top rate by 8%). Allowances up (single £595 to £625; married £775 to £865). Corporation tax up 2% to 52% (small companies 48%). VAT extended to cover confectionery, soft drinks, ice-cream, etc, petrol and other fuels. Reductions on interest relief – withdrawn on second home mortgages, mortgage ceiling fixed at £25,000, all other relief on private loans removed. Tightening of exchange controls on direct and portfolio investment. All social security rates to be increased, with contributions up for employers (at cost of £500 m) and down for employees. Nationalised industry charges (coal, electricity, steel, post and telecommunication, rail passenger and freight) all to rise. Additional £500 m to be set aside for food subsidies, and £70 m for housing subsidies to cover rent freeze. Public expenditure cuts: a further £50 m off defence, Concorde programme cut, Maplin plan frozen (scrapped in July). Cigarettes, wine, beer, spirits, off-course betting all up.

22 July VAT down to 8%. Rate relief for ratepayers facing increases of more than 20%. Help for tenants through increase in needs allowance on rents. Food subsidies: £50 m extra to be allocated from Budget £500 m. Regional Employment Premium (REP) doubled to £3 (men). Dividend controls eased.

12 November Income tax – new age allowance introduced. VAT on petrol up from 8% to 25%. Social security payments to be increased in April 1975 and again in December. Family allowances up to 60p for second child, 50p third and subsequent. Nationalised industry subsidies to be phased out. Companies: relief on stock appreciation (temporary measure until report of official committee examining inflation accounting). Initial investment allowance for industrial buildings increased and bigger tax allowances for insulation. Relaxations on price code (Healey says inflation has made it 'more rigid than intended'). Sterling guarantees to be dropped at end of year. Oil taxation bill promised; Capital Transfer Tax to be implemented.

1975

30 January Public Expenditure White Paper. Added £4650 m to 1975–6 programme; £4400 m to 1976–7; £3800 m to 1977–8; and £3650 m to 1978–9 (as against December 1973 White Paper).

12 February £215 m package designed to save or create 70,000 jobs. £55 m for industrial investment; £50 m for construction industry; £16 m for Temporary Employment Subsidy (TES) to avoid lay-offs where there is prospect of jobs reappearing; £30 m for job creation schemes; £55 m for training programmes.

15 April **BUDGET.** Taxes up £1250 m in full year. Income tax: basic and higher rates up further 2 percentage points except for top (98%) rate. Allowances up (single £625 to £675, married £865 to £955). VAT 25% rate for certain 'luxury' goods. Beer, wine, spirits, cigarettes all up; road tax up 60%. Stock appreciation relief continued; further relief on price code to encourage investment for exporting. Additional £20 m in 1975–6 and £30 m 1976–7 for training. Nationalised industry subsidies reduced to £70 m in 1975–6 against £550 m in 1974–5 and will phase out altogether by April 1976. Nationalised industry investment programmes cut by £100 m. Public expenditure cuts of £901 m in 1976–7; food subsidies to be cut by £150 m and housing £65 m. Start of child benefit scheme fixed for April 1977.

11 July Linked with Phase One of incomes policy. Price restrictions (if possible, on voluntary basis) on selected commodities judged to be of particular significance in family budgets. Food subsidies up £70 m in 1976–7. Increase in council rents pegged to 60p per week. Introduction of temporary employment subsidy to be speeded up. Introduction of cash limits announced for 1976–7.

17 December HP down payments reduced and maximum repayment time extended. Additional funds for Manpower Services Commission and TES. Government to finance counter-cyclical steel stock piling scheme for BSC at cost of £70 m in current year.

1976

19 February Public Expenditure White Paper. Public expenditure to grow a further 2·6% in 1976–7 but cuts of £1621 m in 1977–8 programme and £2974 m in 1978–9.

6 April **BUDGET.** Linked to Phase Two of incomes policy. Mix of conditional and unconditional tax cuts. Pensions, age allowances and child allowances to be raised unconditionally; increases in personal allowances from £675 to £735 single and £955 to £1085 married, conditional on settlement of Phase Two. VAT 25% rate cut to 12·5%. Similar cut affects petrol, but hydrocarbon fuel duty is raised. Beer, wine, spirits, cigarettes up. More measures to help employment including extension of TES scheme to end of 1976. Curb on fringe benefits promised.

54

30 June Government White Paper, *The Attack on Inflation*, sets out details of Phase Two. Price code changes estimated to put 10% on corporate profitability; no change in dividend control.

22 July £952 m cuts in public spending programmes; 2% increase in employers' national insurance contributions from April 1977.

15 December Further public spending cuts in line with undertakings given to IMF. £1016 m cut from 1977–8 programme and £1513 m from 1978–9. Sale of £500 m Burmah Oil shares acquired by BP during Bank of England rescue of Burmah. Alcohol and tobacco up; phase-out of food subsidies to be accelerated and REP to be scrapped.

1977

27 January and *25 February*. Public Expenditure White Paper. Cuts of £1624 m in 1977–8 programme and £649 m in 1978–9.

29 March **BUDGET.** Income tax reductions totalling £2·25 billion in a full year; £960 m contingent on satisfactory arrangements for next phase of pay policy. Personal allowances up by £70 to £805 (single) and £140 to £1225 (married). Level of entry to higher tax brackets raised £1000 to £6000. Threshold for surcharge on investment income raised £500 to £1500. Foreign earnings: tax relief on 25% of earnings of people working overseas for 30 days or more in a year. (*Conditional:* cut in basic rate of income tax from 35% to 33%.) Petrol up, tobacco up, vehicle excise duty up (cars up 25% to £50). Temporary employment subsidy extended for a further 12 months; £100 m extra for construction in inner cities. Employment subsidies for small companies and for jobs for the disabled. Stock relief continued for industry; relief on corporation tax for small companies (effective rate 42%). Exchange controls: stronger powers to be sought on sterling borrowing by foreign-owned UK companies.

15 July Amendment of Budget in light of subsequent incomes policy developments. Income tax basic rate cut one point to 34% instead of two points as intended in Budget. Personal allowances up by a further £40 to £845 (single) and £70 to £1295 (married) as a result of government defeats in committee (the 'Rooker-Wise amendments'). Child benefit to go up in April 1978 to £2·30 for all children. Milk subsidy up to prevent threatened 1·5p per pint increase. Eligibility for free school meals widened. Increase in petrol duty of 5·5p per gallon, announced in Budget, rescinded (despite the Lib-Lab pact, the Liberals refused to vote for it). Electricity: aid for poor households to be given next winter. £70 m additional aid for key sectors of industry and £100 m extra for construction. Dividend controls: 10% limit maintained.

26 October Further increases in tax allowances, backdated to April – single allowance up £100 to £945 and married up £160 to £1455 with all others increased accordingly. £10 tax-free bonus for pensioners at Christmas. Public spending to go up £1 billion next year including £400 m on construction, £20 m on overseas aid, £9 m on law and order. Mobility allowance to increase. Capital transfer tax – threshold for personal liability raised, business relief against CTT raised. Exchange controls eased.

1978

12 January Public Expenditure White Paper. A plan for 'resumed and continuing expansion'. Adds £1614 m to programme for 1978–9, £1090 m to programme for 1979–80, and £1830 m to programme for 1980–81 (compared to 1977 plans).

11 April **BUDGET.** Allowances up (single by £40 to £985, married by £80 to £1535). Lower tax band introduced at 25%; threshold for 40% rate raised. Help for small companies, including raising of Corporation Tax profits limit. Wider exemptions from VAT. High tar cigarettes up; all other cigarettes and alcohol spared. Price of school meals pegged; free milk for 7-to-11-year-olds with help of EEC subsidy. Child benefit up to £4 in April next year but interim £3 rate in November. £50 m to bring new hospitals into use, provide extra kidney machines etc. £40 m for school and college building and retraining teachers. More money for prisons, police, magistrates' courts, probation services. Corporation tax level held, stock relief continues until permanent scheme devised. Farmers to be allowed to average returns from two years for income tax purposes. Pensions to rise in November. Profit sharing incentive scheme to be introduced.

Table 1·2: BRITAIN'S GROWTH RATE 1964–76

Annual average increases in gross domestic product, at constant factor cost, as measured by the average of three methods of estimating GDP

Annual average percentage increases:

From ▼ \ To ▶	1965	1966	1967	1968	1969	1970	1971	1972	1973	1974	1975	1976	
1964	2·9	2·2	2·2	2·6	2·6	2·5	2·4	2·4	2·8	2·4	2·0	2·1	1964
1965		1·6	1·8	2·6	2·5	2·4	2·3	2·8	2·4	2·0	2·0		1965
1966			2·1	3·1	2·8	2·6	2·4	2·4	2·9	2·5	2·0	2·0	1966
1967				4·0	3·2	2·8	2·5	2·5	3·1	2·5	2·0	2·0	1967
1968					2·4	2·2	2·0	2·1	2·9	2·3	1·7	1·8	1968
1969						1·9	1·9	2·0	3·0	2·2	1·6	1·7	1969
1970							1·8	2·1	3·4	2·3	1·5	1·6	1970
1971								2·4	4·1	2·5	1·4	1·6	1971
1972									6·0	2·5	1·1	1·4	1972
1973										−0·8	−1·2	−0·1	1973
1974											−1·6	0·3	1974
1975												2·1	1975

To get the growth figure for a single year, simply read down the column for that year till you reach the final figure: e.g. during the year 1970 GDP grew 1·9% on 1969; in 1973 GDP grew 6% on 1972. For longer periods, find your start year in the left-hand column, and then read across to the appropriate column for your terminal year. Thus, from the end of 1964 to the end of 1970, GDP grew at an annual rate of 2·5%. From the end of 1970 to the end of 1973, GDP grew by 3·4% annually. From the end of 1973 to the end of 1976 GDP fell at an annual rate of 0·1%.

SOURCE: *Economic Trends*, October 1977

Table 1·3: THE INTERNATIONAL GROWTH LEAGUE

Gross domestic product per head of the population in OECD countries at current prices, and exchange rates in US dollars

	1961			1966	
1	United States	2851	1	United States	3827
2	Canada	2167	2	Iceland	3045
3	Sweden	2021	3	Sweden	3043
4	Switzerland	1773	4	Canada	2898
5	New Zealand	1591	5	Switzerland	2522
6	Luxembourg	1585	6	Denmark	2309
7	Australia	1544	7	France	2148
8	W Germany	1477	8	Luxembourg	2103
9	*United Kingdom*	*1439*	9	New Zealand	2083
10	France	1435	10	W Germany	2081
11	Denmark	1421	11	Australia	2049
12	Norway	1363	12	Norway	2036
13	Iceland	1353	*13*	*United Kingdom*	*1931*
14	Belgium	1310	14	Belgium	1910
15	Finland	1235	15	Finland	1883
16	Netherlands	1045	16	Netherlands	1638
17	Austria	983	17	Austria	1420
18	Italy	769	18	Italy	1209
19	Ireland	679	19	Japan	1030
20	Japan	564	20	Ireland	948
21	Greece	471	21	Spain	868
22	Spain	435	22	Greece	774
23	Portugal	300	23	Portugal	456
24	Yugoslavia	276	24	Yugoslavia	456
25	Turkey	196	25	Turkey	314

	1971			1976	
1	United States	5125	1	Sweden	9030
2	Sweden	4439	2	Switzerland	8871
3	Canada	4373	3	Canada	8409
4	Switzerland	3958	4	United States	7912
5	W Germany	3537	5	Norway	7774
6	Denmark	3494	6	Denmark	7594
7	Luxembourg	3251	7	W Germany	7247
8	Norway	3241	8	Australia	6763
9	France	3089	9	Belgium	6713
10	Australia	3081	10	Iceland	6611
11	Iceland	3028	11	France	6552
12	Belgium	2983	12	Netherlands	6501
13	Netherlands	2812	13	Luxembourg	6276
14	New Zealand	2596	14	Finland	5951
15	*United Kingdom*	*2497*	15	Austria	5407
16	Finland	2476	16	Japan	4922
17	Austria	2222	17	New Zealand	4126
18	Japan	2152	*18*	*United Kingdom*	*3914*

	1971			1976
19 Italy	1888		19 Italy	3041
20 Ireland	1526		20 Spain	2887
21 Greece	1247		21 Ireland	2509
22 Spain	1232		22 Greece	2404
23 Portugal	782		23 Yugoslavia	n.a.
24 Yugoslavia	754		24 Portugal	1628
25 Turkey	347		25 Turkey	1000

SOURCE: OECD National Accounts

Table 1·4: ECONOMIC AND INDUSTRIAL LEAGUE TABLES: BRITAIN AND COMPETITORS

1970 = 100

1 Output per man hour worked in manufacturing

	1971	1972	1973	1974	1975	1976	1977
Japan	104	114	133	136	131	148	158
Germany	104	111	117	121	126	135	139
France	105	114	121	125	121	135	139
Italy	103	113	124	122	122	140	*
Canada	107	111	117	119	121	125	131
US	106	110	113	116	118	124	127
UK	*105*	*112*	*118*	*119*	*119*	*124*	*121*

2 Wage costs per unit of output

	1971	1972	1973	1974	1975	1976	1977
US	101	103	107	113	121	124	132
Germany	107	109	114	123	127	126	132
Canada	102	106	110	122	139	153	162
France	106	109	117	135	163	169	185
Japan	111	118	126	163	194	186	192
UK	*109*	*113*	*121*	*150*	*196*	*220*	*246*
Italy	110	111	126	156	198	208	*

*Comparable figure not available

3 Unemployment – % rate standardised according to international definitions

	1971	1972	1973	1974	1975	1976	1977
Japan	1·2	1·4	1·3	1·4	2·0	2·1	2·1
Germany	0·8	0·8	0·8	1·5	3·6	3·6	3·5
France	2·9	2·9	2·6	2·7	4·1	4·6	5·2
US	5·7	5·4	4·7	5·4	8·3	7·5	6·9
Italy	3·4	3·9	3·7	3·1	3·6	6·4	7·5
UK	*3·8*	*4·1*	*2·8*	*2·9*	*4·4*	*6·9*	*7·6*
Canada	6·3	6·3	5·6	5·4	6·9	7·1	8·1

4 Industrial production

	1971	1972	1973	1974	1975	1976	1977
Canada	106	113	122	127	121	127	132
Japan	103	110	127	123	110	125	127
US	102	111	120	120	109	120	127
France	104	112	120	123	114	124	126
Italy	100	104	115	119	108	122	121
Germany	102	106	113	111	105	113	116
UK	*100*	*102*	*111*	*108*	*103*	*104*	*106*

5 Consumer prices

	1971	1972	1973	1974	1975	1976	1977
Germany	105·3	111·1	118·8	127·1	134·7	140·8	146·3
US	104·3	107·7	114·4	127·0	138·6	146·6	156·1
Canada	102·9	107·8	116·0	128·6	142·5	153·2	165·4
France	105·5	117·7	119·9	136·3	152·5	166·8	182·7
Japan	106·3	111·5	124·5	153·4	171·4	187·5	202·8
Italy	105·0	110·9	122·4	146·2	171·3	199·6	236·6
UK	*109·5*	*117·0*	*126·7*	*147·0*	*182·5*	*211·4*	*245·2*

6 Unit value of exports of manufactures

	1971	1972	1973	1974	1975	1976	1977
Germany	108	117	147	172	195	195	214
France	105	115	143	163	197	193	208
Japan	104	116	141	181	182	177	203
UK	*106*	*116*	*127*	*153*	*177*	*175*	*202*
Italy	106	114	126	154	180	166	194
US	102	104	113	137	159	170	179

(no figures available for Canada)

SOURCE: retabulated from NIESR

Table 1·5: BALANCE OF PAYMENTS, QUARTERLY, SINCE 1970

£ million
seasonally adjusted

		Exports	Imports	Visible balance	Invisibles	Current balance
1970	1	2004	1934	+ 70	+195	+265
	2	2009	2060	− 51	+184	+133
	3	1927	2019	− 92	+170	+ 78
	4	2181	2133	+ 48	+171	+219
1971	1	2066	2119	− 53	+194	+141
	2	2331	2234	− 97	+192	+289
	3	2348	2171	+ 177	+213	+390
	4	2316	2257	+ 59	+179	+238
1972	1	2245	2351	− 106	+206	+100
	2	2357	2465	− 108	+221	+113
	3	2108	2412	− 304	+201	−103
	4	2739	2923	− 184	+179	− 5
1973	1	2747	3107	− 360	+156	−204
	2	2921	3360	− 439	+358	− 81
	3	3133	3760	− 627	+361	−266
	4	3314	4241	− 927	+556	−371
1974	1	3606	4923	−1317	+390	−927
	2	4154	5519	−1365	+433	−932
	3	4379	5608	−1229	+445	−784
	4	4399	5682	−1283	+361	−922
1975	1	4664	5608	− 944	+379	−565
	2	4632	5289	− 657	+324	−333
	3	4828	5802	− 974	+354	−620
	4	5337	5965	− 628	+445	−183
1976	1	5642	6180	− 538	+448	− 90
	2	6242	7149	− 907	+517	−390
	3	6429	7573	−1144	+633	−511
	4	7103	8085	− 982	+568	−414
1977	1	7502	8449	− 947	+442	−505
	2	7930	8694	− 764	+400	−364
	3	8540	8486	+ 54	+429	+483
	4	8204	8159	+ 45	+306	+351

source: *Economic Trends*

Table 1·6: INCOMES POLICIES UNDER CONSERVATIVES AND LABOUR

CON

November 1972 90-day freeze (with right to extend by up to 60 days) imposed after breakdown of tripartite talks on voluntary controls. Pay and many prices frozen (but not fresh food or food dependent on imported materials); dividends pegged.

April 1973 Phase Two: pay limit of £1 per week per head plus additional 4% average for each group of workers. (Government hoped this would be allocated with bias towards low paid.) Top limit on any rise: £250. Prices to rise only when explained in terms of 'allowable costs' which are defined; but fresh food, etc, still outside controls. Price rise reporting system: toughest for largest firms. Profits and dividends to be curbed. Pay Board and Price Commission established with direct power to make rulings (unlike Labour's of 1964 which had only advisory role). Its work to be governed by a pay and price code.

November 1973 Phase Three: variable pay limit: 7% across group or £2·25 per head weekly with ceiling raised to £350. Further 1% rise allowed for removal of obstacles to economic use of manpower: also exemptions for move to equal pay and rewards for working 'unsocial hours'. 'Threshold' provision for rises, where negotiated, of 40p when index rises 7 points and further 40p for every point thereafter. Price reporting system stepped up.

LAB

July 1975 £6 ceiling on all rises; no rise at all above £8500. Price code will stop excessive settlements being passed on in higher prices. Cash limits on bills in public sector. Sanctions in private sector: those paying above agreed rate can be denied aid under Industry Act, refused contracts etc. 10% limit on dividend increases; council rent increases pegged to 60p per week, food subsidies increased, price controls tightened. Reserve powers to make the system statutory if the voluntary agreement fails to work; these were not published (and were never used).

June 1976 Pay rise ceilings of £250 for those below £50 a week, 5% on those between £50 and £80 a week, maximum 4% on all higher levels. Linked with 'conditional' tax changes in Budget (see above). Dividend control maintained.

July 1977 'Phase Three': no agreement with TUC, but TUC stands by rule that no one should have more than one increase within 12 months. Government sets 10% target ceiling for pay increases (expected out-turn is between 13% and 15%). Promises to back it by standing firm by 10% in public sector, using sanctions on private employers who pay more.

Table 1·7: INCOMES POLICIES: BEFORE AND AFTER

Movements in earnings and prices for 12 months before and 12 months after the start of the Conservative Phase One and the Labour Phase One

CON	PRICES		EARNINGS	
	Before	After	Before	After
1971	Nov 71 = 100	Nov 72 = 100	Nov 71 = 100	Nov 72 = 100
Dec	100·5	100·5	100·9	99·9
1972				
Jan	101·1	101·2	101·9	100·5
Feb	101·5	101·8	not available	101·2
Mar	101·9	102·4	105·0	102·3
Apr	102·9	104·4	105·9	103·5
May	103·4	105·1	106·9	104·8
Jun	104·1	105·7	107·8	106·5
Jul	104·4	106·1	108·7	107·9
Aug	105·2	106·4	109·7	108·3
Sep	105·7	107·4	113·0	109·6
Oct	107·2	109·5	115·0	110·9
Nov	107·6	110·3	116·6	112·4

LAB	PRICES		EARNINGS	
	Before	After	Before	After
	July 74 = 100	July 75 = 100	July 74 = 100	July 75 = 100
1974				
Aug	100·1	100·6	102·5	101·0
Sep	100·2	101·4	104·2	102·7
Oct	103·2	102·9	105·7	103·4
Nov	105·0	104·1	110·7	105·1
Dec	106·6	105·4	114·8	107·3
1975				
Jan	109·3	106·8	113·7	107·4
Feb	111·1	108·2	115·7	107·8
Mar	113·3	108·7	117·3	109·7
Apr	117·7	110·8	118·7	109·6
May	122·6	112·0	120·0	112·2
Jun	125·0	112·6	121·9	111·5
Jul	126·3	112·9	127·6	113·9

SOURCE: Department of Employment Gazette

Table 1·8: PRICES, WAGES AND THE COST OF LIVING
1970=100

	Hourly earnings	Retail prices	Food prices	Housing inc rent+ rates	Personal disposable income per head	Real personal disposable income per head
1971	112·7	109·5	109·4	110·7	110·9	102·4
1972	129·7	117·0	117·1	124·9	127·6	110·4
1973	146·2	126·8	131·7	140·1	146·0	117·9
1974	175·7	147·0	153·3	166·1	172·4	119·7
1975	222·6	182·6	188·0	209·4	213·9	119·9
1976	248·0	211·4	218·6	237·7	245·8	119·6
1977	268·7	245·3	254·2	265·1	279·9	118·1

SOURCE: NIESR, *Economic Trends*

Table 1·9: THE SHRINKING OF THE POUND
Sterling exchange value, last day of each year, against other leading currencies

	US $	French franc	Italian lira	Deutschmark
1971	2·5522	13·3125	1515·00	8·3395
1972	2·3481	12·0150	1367·25	7·5150
1973	2·3235	10·9138	1411·50	6·2788
1974	2·3495	10·4137	1525·50	5·6537
1975	2·0233	9·0375	1382·87	5·2987
1976	1·7020	8·4487	1489·00	4·0162
1977	1·9185	9·0075	1672·00	4·0135

SOURCE: Bank of England *Quarterly Bulletin*

Table 1·10: THE 1976 STERLING CRISIS
£ against US dollar, state of reserves in millions US dollars. 1976 (end of month figures)

	£=US $	Reserves		£=US $	Reserves
January	2·0292	6785	July	1·7842	5370
February	2·0253	7024	August	1·7764	5029
March	1·9160	5905	September	1·6680	5158
April	1·8410	4848	October	1·5860	4703
May	1·7590	5423	November	1·6537	5156
June	1·7847	5312	December	1·7020	4129

Table 1·11: HOW COMMODITY PRICES WENT THROUGH THE ROOF
World commodity prices, indexed from 1970 value=100

1971	1972	1973	1974	1975	1976	1977
105	116	168	295	300	385	431*

*Department of Industry projection

SOURCE: *Economic Trends*

Table 1·12: THE SHRIVELLING POUND IN YOUR POCKET

Purchasing power of the £ as against 1950, 1960 and 1970

	Against £1 in 1950	Against £1 in 1960	Against £1 in 1970
1966	59p	82p	
1967	57p	80p	
1968	55p	76p	
1969	52p	72p	
1970	49p	68p	100p
1971	44p	62p	91p
1972	41p	58p	85p
1973	38p	53p	78p
1974	33p	46p	67p
1975	26p	37p	54p
1976	23p	32p	47p
1977	20p	27p	40p

SOURCE: *Economic Trends*

Table 1·13: PERCENTAGE OF AVERAGE WAGE (MANUAL WORKER, FULL TIME, TWO CHILDREN UNDER 11) REQUIRED TO BUY CERTAIN GOODS IN OCTOBER 1967 AND OCTOBER 1977

	Oct 67	Oct 77
Pint of beer	0·7	0·7
Bottle of whisky	14·0	7·6
20 cigarettes	1·2	1·0
Large loaf	0·4	0·4
Pint of milk	0·2	0·2
1 lb sirloin beef	1·9	2·5
1 lb beef sausages	0·7	0·7
1 kWh electricity	0·05	0·05
1 therm gas	0·7	0·4
Bus fare, Westminster to Putney	0·5	0·8
Cheapest stamp	0·1	0·15

SOURCE: written answer to the Member for Putney
31 January 1978

Table 1·14: INTEREST RATE CHANGES FROM 1970 (%)

1970		1974		1977	
5 March	7·5	4 January	12·75	28 January	12·25
15 April	7	1 February	12·5	25 February	12
1971		5 April	12·25	25 March	10·5
1 April	6	11 April	12	1 April	9·5
2 September	5	24 May	11·75	7 April	9·25
1972		27 September	11·5	15 April	9
22 June	6	1975		22 April	8·75
13 October	7·25	31 January	11	29 April	8·25
27 October	7·75	28 February	10·5	13 May	8
8 December	8	26 March	10	5 August	7·5
22 December	9	25 April	9·75	12 August	7
1973		30 May	10	9 September	6·5
19 January	8·75	25 July	11	16 September	6
23 March	8·5	31 October	12	7 October	5·5
13 April	8	28 November	11·5	14 October	5
19 April	8·25	22 December	11·25	25 November	7
11 May	8	1976		1978	
18 May	7·75	30 January	10	6 January	6·5
22 June	7·5	27 February	9·25	11 April	7·5
20 July	9	26 March	9	5 May	8·75
27 July	11·5	30 April	10·5	12 May	9
19 October	11·25	28 May	11·5	8 June	10
13 November	13	24 September	13		
		29 October	15		
		26 November	14·75		
		31 December	14·25		

SOURCE: *Economic Trends*

Table 1·15: END OF YEAR INTEREST RATES 1971–6 (%)

	1971	1972	1973	1974	1975	1976	1977
US	4·5	4·5	7·5	7·75	6	5·25	6
Japan	4·75	4·25	9	9	6·5	6·5	4·25
Belgium	5·5	5	7·75	8·75	6	9	9
France	6·5	7·5	11	13	8	10·5	9·5
Germany	4	4·5	7	6	3·5	3·5	3
Italy	4·5	4	6·5	8	6	15	11·5
Netherlands	5	4	8	7	4·5	6	4·5
Sweden	5	5	5	7	6	8	8
UK	5	9	13	11·5	11·25	14·25	7

SOURCE: *International Financial Statistics*

Table 1·16: RISE AND FALL OF THE MONEY SUPPLY 1968–78

M1 consists of the notes and coins held by the public together with the sterling current accounts of the UK private sector with banks. M3 adds in deposit accounts, and accounts denominated in foreign currencies; it includes deposits owned by the public as well as the private sector.

Figures show change since previous quarter: seasonally adjusted.

		M1	M3			M1	M3
1968	I	30	298	1973	I	−10	1565
	II	149	425		II	772	1322
	III	163	304		III	−562	2184
	IV	140	258		IV	610	2318
1969	I	−158	266	1974	I	−359	1131
	II	−160	169		II	342	593
	III	48	197		III	389	1145
	IV	297	209		IV	1065	1352
1970	I	40	249	1975	I	293	340
	II	322	596		II	364	544
	III	81	345		III	793	1629
	IV	387	396		IV	565	389
1971	I	412	707	1976	I	614	634
	II	94	315		II	439	1593
	III	295	408		III	821	2063
	IV	110	792		IV	−78	71
1972	I	407	1104	1977	I	611	383
	II	457	1555		II	740	1581
	III	133	976		III	1373	713
	IV	507	1651		IV	1466	1557

SOURCE: *Economic Trends*

2   Public Spending

Public expenditure in the United Kingdom doubled in the 9 years from 1964 to 1973. By the end of 1977 it had doubled again. The figures were, of course, grossly swollen by inflation, but even in real terms the expansion was phenomenal – both under the Conservative government of 1970 (with Mrs Thatcher at Education and Sir Keith Joseph at Health the biggest spenders of all) and under the Labour governments of Harold Wilson and James Callaghan.

That a Labour government should go further than a Conservative government in expanding public expenditure was to be expected: Labour's view of life puts greater faith in collective effort, much less in individual provision, than the Conservatives'. Indeed, for a large part of the Labour Party – the 'social democratic' wing, associated with Anthony Crosland's 'The Future of Socialism', the classic document of Labour revisionism which first appeared in 1956 – the spending of public money for the public good is very much what the Labour Party is about. The difficulty of the Labour governments of 1974 – as of the Labour governments of 1964 and 1966 – was that they had to tailor their spending plans to a context of contraction rather than expansion, in which it became increasingly hard to see how Labour's plans could be paid for without additional demands on a public which – in the eyes of many on the Croslandite wing of the party – was already paying rather more tax than it could equably tolerate.

This tension between Labour's anxiety to fulfil its honoured role as provider for those who cannot provide for themselves and its simultaneous concern to demonstrate sound financial management of a mixed economy runs through the whole record of Denis Healey's term at the Treasury. The requirements of financial confidence drove the government repeatedly to trim (even at times to butcher) its public spending ambitions, while the need to win support for the counter-inflation policy, and alleviate the strains on household incomes which would otherwise fuel excessive wage demands, drove it repeatedly to introduce subsidies and remove them, to hand out reliefs and then take them back.

In his first budget (26 March 1974) Healey estimated the Public Sector Borrowing Requirement (PSBR), the difference between what the government spends and lends and its income from taxation and other sources, as likely to reach £2733 million. By November, that total had almost doubled, mainly because of tax changes and subsidies judged to be necessary in the interests of the counter-inflation policy. In the same November statement, however, the Chancellor added further government commitments which brought the new projected total up to £6300 million. When he delivered his April 1975 budget he estimated the likely out-turn at £7600 million. (In the event it turned out to be higher still: it was finally calculated at £7957 million – almost three times the estimate he had made a year before.)

Cuts in public spending, the Chancellor announced, surveying this record in his 1975 budget, were inevitable, and he outlined a programme of cuts designed to reduce the borrowing requirement by £1000 million in 1975–6 and £3000 million in 1976–7. But to avoid the wasteful disruption which was always involved in short-term reductions, he said, he would get his savings in the new financial year through tax increases and pitch his spending cuts, which were said to be worth £901 million, into 1976–7.

The Chancellor's difficulties are well illustrated by what happened to the policy on food subsidies. The Labour government had inherited subsidies on two commodities – milk and butter. The wide range of subsidies introduced when Labour came to office in 1974 (see tables 2·5 and 8·3) as a contribution to the counter-inflation drive were pruned in the 1975 budget as a contribution to the reduction of the PSBR. But this was in turn rescinded in July as part of the government's attempt to get a settlement with the unions on Phase One of the incomes policy.

The Public Expenditure White Paper of 19 February 1976 foreshadowed a further assault on subsidies, and the programme of spending cuts announced on 22 July 1976 in an attempt to halt the flight from the £ contained an announcement that the promised phasing out of food subsidies would be accelerated. A further acceleration of the phasing-out process was announced in the post-IMF cuts of December 1976. But on 15 July 1977 – again as part of the counter-inflation strategy – the Chancellor announced that the level of subsidy for 1977–8, originally fixed at £43 million, was now to be raised to more than five times that figure.

The Conservative conviction that the level of public spending would have to be drastically reduced and the level of subsidy sharply cut was echoed even by some members of the Labour government. A series of articles in the *Sunday Times* by two Oxford economists, Robert Bacon and Walter Eltis, documented and popularised the view that the inadequate performance of British industry over the years was in no small part due to the pre-emption of manpower and resources by the unproductive public sector. The reorganisation of local government and the National Health Service was generally believed (and not unreasonably: see table 9·5 on p. 107) to have led to a proliferation of bureaucrats with no compensating gains for consumers, taxpayers and ratepayers. In January 1976, Roy Jenkins, the Labour Home Secretary, noting the calculation that public expenditure now accounted for 60% of the gross domestic product, said: 'I do not think that you can push public expenditure significantly above 60% and maintain the values of a plural society with adequate freedom of choice.' (In fact, this 60% was a somewhat dubious indicator: it included transfer payments which while reducing the freedom of choice of some enhance the freedom of choice of others.)

The problems were precisely stated in the Public Expenditure White Paper of 1976 which rescinded plans made the previous year for a progressive increase in public spending and replaced them by a projection of declining public expenditure from 1975–6 to 1978–9. 'In the last three years,' it said, 'public expenditure has grown by nearly 20% in volume while output has risen by less than 2%. The ratio of public expenditure to gross domestic product has risen from 50% to 60% . . . As recovery proceeds, we must progressively reduce the deficit . . . more resources, capital as well as manpower, will be needed for exports and investment . . .'

Cuts made in previous budgets had, once more, been offset by spending increases, especially on employment measures, on the regeneration of industry, on higher social security benefits (especially to pay for the unprecedented levels of unemployment) and on counter-inflation measures. The estimates for the coming year and the year beyond it set out in this White Paper were therefore in fact still higher, despite this scaling down, than they had been in the White Paper before it. The real cuts were to come at the end of the period, rather than at the beginning.

The White Paper infuriated the Conservatives, who accused the Chancellor of once more doing too little too late, and dismayed the Labour left: the Tribune Group put out a statement rejecting the politics, the economics and the philosophy of the White Paper, saying it implied unacceptable levels of unemployment stretching through to the eighties. One minister (Joan Lestor) resigned. The right course for Labour, they said, was not to follow the Tories down their chosen road of public spending cuts followed by still higher unemployment, but to adopt the left solution of rebuilding Britain's depleted industrial base behind walls of trade protection. In a debate on the White Paper on 10 March, 37 Labour MPs (see table 20·2) abstained and the government was defeated. The debate was on a formal motion for the adjournment, but a vote of confidence followed in which Labour's rebels backed the government, though continuing to denounce the cuts.

The same White Paper developed a strategy which was to bring the government real success in the control of public spending, to an extent which even the Conservatives (though they said it had been their idea first) came to salute. Already, a system of cash limits, which cut off money once a target figure had been passed, had been applied to local authorities through the Rate Support Grant. Now cash limits were extended to cover three-quarters of government spending (though some sectors, like social security benefits, had to be exempted).

No changes in spending plans were made in the 1976 budget,

but the continuing fall of the £, and the growth of the PSBR (once more inflated by additional spending decisions, mainly on benefits, employment, and industrial aid) forced the government to introduce on 22 July 1976 a package of cuts worth about £1000 million. The cuts were needed, the Chancellor explained, to make room for Britain's recovery: 'unless the fiscal deficit falls steadily over the next three years as expansion proceeds, the financing of the public sector will pre-empt private savings which productive industry is likely to require on a substantial scale to finance stockbuilding and investment: or it will lead to excessive growth in the money supply which would refuel inflation'. The cuts did little to hold the £, however, and another, more spectacular round of cuts was introduced on 15 December 1976 as part of the deal which landed the IMF standby. A further scaling down of spending plans in the Public Expenditure White Papers of January and February 1977 set off a further Labour revolt and threatened the government's survival.

The subsequent recovery of the economy encouraged the government to attempt some minor refurbishing of its spending programmes in the Chancellor's statements of 15 July and 26 October 1977. The Public Expenditure White Paper of January 1978 was also held to be expansionary, though estimates varied as to how much. Although no round of cuts from Barber's onwards had achieved the savings set out for it, the cash limits system was agreed to have put the tightest rein ever devised on the spending of public money, and in 1977–8 there was as substantial an undershooting of the PSBR projection as there had been overshooting in previous years. Even if the cuts were condemned by some on the Opposition side as cosmetic rather than real, there was plenty of evidence, from schools starved of money for materials, from hospitals unable to open new wards for lack of staff and resources, from personal social services in undisguised decline, to show that the impact on the ground had been a real one. Nor was it clear that the resources made available by public sector cuts had been taken up in the private sector in the way the government had hoped. It was widely noted, too, that in so far as public expenditure cuts added to unemployment, this led to greater public spending on job creation schemes, social security benefits, and reduced receipts through taxation and insurance contributions. Indeed, a significant proportion of the PSBR which had terrified so many at home and abroad had gone on paying for the recession – a process which even more stringent cuts, such as the Opposition continued to demand, would only make worse.

Table 2·1: THE MAIN COMPONENTS OF PUBLIC SPENDING

showing proportion of total public spending taken by each service

1961		1966		1971		1977	
1 Defence	16·7	1 Social security	17·8	1 Social security	18·6	1 Social security	19·2
2 Social security	15·6	2 Defence	15·2	2 Education	12·5	2 Education	12·5
3 Education	9·7	3 Education	11·8	3 Defence	11·9	3 NHS	10·6
4 NHS	8·9	4 NHS	9·5	4 NHS	9·7	4 Defence	10·6
5 Housing	5·3	5 Housing	6·8	5 Housing	5·6	5 Housing	8·9

SOURCE: National Income and Expenditure (*Blue Book*)

Table 2·2: EXPANSION OF THE PUBLIC SECTOR

	All Public spending as proportion of GDP at factor cost	Public spending on goods and services as proportion of GDP	Proportion of all jobs in public sector	Public sector investment as proportion of all investment
1966	46·2	21·6	23·8	46·4
1967	50·1	22·9	24·8	48·9
1968	51·0	20·4	25·7	46·6
1969	50·3	22·2	25·8	43·4
1970	50·6	22·5	26·2	43·5
1971	50·0	22·5	27·1	42·2
1972	50·1	22·8	27·4	39·2
1973	51·1	23·4	27·2	39·9
1974	57·3	25·5	27·5	40·7
1975	59·0	26·9	29·2	42·4
1976		26·2	29·6	42·6

SOURCE: *Blue Book*, written answers

Table 2·3: TOTAL GOVERNMENT EXPENDITURE (*1*)
PUBLIC SECTOR BORROWING REQUIREMENT (*2*)

	(*1*) £ million	(*2*) £ million
1966	14,448	961
1967	16,672	1863
1968	18,290	1279
1969	18,954	−466
1970	20,706	− 17
1971	23,199	1373
1972	26,254	2047
1973	30,500	4168
1974	39,188	6336
1975	51,410	10,515
1976	58,506	9512

SOURCE: *Blue Book*

Table 2·4: PUBLIC SPENDING CUTS 1975–8

15 April 1975: £901 m off 1976–7 programme

	£ million		£ million
Defence	−110	Other environment	−85
Overseas services	− 12	Law, order, protective services	−27
Ag, fish and forestry	−152		
Trade, industry, employment	− 3	Education, libraries, science and arts	−86
Natd industries	−100	Health, personal social services	−75
Roads, transport	− 91		
Housing	−115	Other public services	−17
Common services	− 12	Northern Ireland	−16

22 July 1976: £952 m off 1977–8 programme

	£ million		£ million
Defence	−100	Other environment	−81
Overseas services	− 5	Education, libraries, science and arts	−30
Ag, fish, food, forestry	−105		
Trade, industry, employment	−105	Health, personal social services	−70
Natd industries	−157	Social security	−21
Roads, transport	− 87	Northern Ireland	−35
Common services	− 10		

15 December 1976: £1016 m off 1977–8 and £1513 m off 1978–9

	1977–8	1978–9
	£ million	£ million
Defence	−100	−200
Overseas aid	− 50	− 50
Food subsidies	−160	− 57
REP	−150	−170
Refinancing of fixed rate credits	−100	−200
Industrial training at colleges of further education	− 10	− 10
Natd industries	−110	−130
Roads	− 75	− 50
Housing	− 20	−300
Regional water authorities	− 75	−130
Environmental services	− 50	− 50
Community land acquisition	− 35	− 35
Courts	− 2	
Education building	− 22	− 11
Other education	− 20	− 30
Health and personal social services	− 10	− 20
Other NHS	− 5	− 5
Northern Ireland	− 5	− 10
Property Services Agency	− 27	− 45
Civil Service	− 30	− 10

Table 2·5: THE RISING TIDE OF SUBSIDY

| | CENTRAL | | | | | | | | LOCAL | | | | | |
	Housing	Agriculture, food, fish, forestry	Nationalised transport	Compensation for price restraint	Employment premiums	Aid to coal industry	Other	ALL CENTRAL	Housing	Transport	Other	ALL LOCAL	OVERALL TOTAL	% of all govt spending
1967	129	247	162		152	9	21	720	67	2	12	81	801	6·2
1970	210	232	92	40	141	12	36	763	98	4	11	113	876	5·3
1971	247	295	84	45	129	10	25	835	82	5	9	96	931	5·1
1972	281	271	119	51	114	169	64	1069	56	10	9	75	1144	5·3
1973	324	287	151	233	114	161	89	1359	78	19	15	112	1471	6·1
1974	553	787	317	638	139	190	95	2719	148	95	25	268	2987	9·6
1975	772	1378	468	262	238	127	146	3391	210	196	30	436	3827	9·2
1976	1109	851	476	10	234	65	235	2980	225	225	33	483	3463	7·1

(figures in £ million)

SOURCE: Economic Trends, November 1977

3 Taxation

A vote in the committee on the Finance Bill on 14 June 1977, though overshadowed at the time by other more glamorous government defeats, made what could well turn out to be a profound change in the psychology of British tax-raising and tax-paying. Until then, chancellors of all parties had enjoyed the enviable advantage of being able to increase their revenue year by year without any public announcement or even any conscious decision. Inflation, acting as the Chancellor's silent henchman, saw to that. People at the bottom of the scale, clutching newly-won pay rises, found them instantly eaten away by the obligation to start paying tax. Elsewhere, right up the ladder, a sizeable slice of every increase went to swell the taxman's coffers. Thus a 'neutral' budget – a budget which neither increased taxes nor decreased them, even by a penny – became, in effect, a tax-raising budget eating into spending power by the very act of not raising thresholds and allowances to match the rate of inflation.

What the Finance Bill committee now simply, but radically, did was to limit the Chancellor's little game by insisting that from now on personal allowances (though no others) must rise in line with inflation. (The Chancellor was at least given the right to come to the Commons and propose that allowances should not so rise, though the Liberals unsuccessfully moved an amendment which would have denied him even that.) But even then, a tax increase would have to be a *publicly announced* tax increase, an act of commission rather than omission, instead of the fruits of a surreptitious pact with inflation.

The justification of that can be seen in the spectacular increase in the Chancellor's tax haul over the years charted in table 3·4. As table 1·1 shows, some of this was due to announced increases in taxation, but even in years when taxes were ostensibly cut revenues kept soaring. The result was a burden on some taxpayers which no one would consciously have wished, and a well-attested popular revolt, whose political consequences confirmed Conservative preconceptions, set the Liberals crusading, and caused the Labour Party to re-examine its commitments to high public spending. As the Prime Minister told the Parliamentary Labour Party on 13 March 1978, when some MPs were arguing for public spending increases rather than tax cuts in the coming budget: 'If you want to retain power, you have got to listen to what people – our people – say, and what they want, and that is to pay less tax.'

It was also argued that the British taxpayer now carried heavier burdens than his counterparts almost anywhere in the world. But this is disputable. The burden of over-all taxation in Britain, according both to Treasury figures and figures kept by the EEC, was in 1975 still lighter than that in the Netherlands or Denmark, especially when social security payments, heavier in most other countries than in Britain, were counted in (see table 3·1). It was the level of *direct* taxation, rather than taxation over-all, which put Britain in a top place in the European league – especially at the very highest rates, as indicated in table 3·2.

Both Liberals and Conservatives demanded that Labour should make still bigger cuts in taxation by switching more of the burden on to indirect taxes. The Prime Minister and Chancellor appeared not unaverse to this, despite the old Labour belief that direct taxes, which are *progressive* (that is to say, taking a higher proportion of income from the rich than the poor) are preferable to indirect taxes, which cause the highest and lowest in society to pay the same impost on each packet of cigarettes and pint of beer. What stood in the way of change was the government's commitment to keep down inflation. Increases in VAT and duties on beer and cigarettes – being, also, unindexed – actually fell behind the rate of inflation so that, although this was rarely acknowledged, they were cheaper in real terms after four years of Labour government than at the beginning (see table 1·13).

Despite the growing doubts in the Labour Party in the mid-70s about the wisdom of imposing such high levels of taxation, it was clear that the combination of inflation and high tax levels had taken the country some way towards that redistribution of incomes to which the party was committed. It might not amount to what the October 1974 manifesto called 'a fundamental and irreversible shift in the balance of wealth and power in favour of working people and their families'. It was still very possible in Britain to find people who were extremely rich and people who were lamentably poor. More continued to be spent in clubs and race courses in an hour than was spent in some households in a week. But there had been a distinct closing (see table 3·5) of that divide through the tax and benefits system.

Table 3·1: TAXES AS % OF GROSS NATIONAL PRODUCT
at factor cost inclusive and exclusive of social security contributions

	1969		1972		1975		1975 incl SSC based on EEC tax statistics
	INC SSC	EXC SSC	INC SSC	EXC SSC	INC SSC	EXC SSC	
Canada	36·7	33·3	37·6	34·3	37·7	33·6	
Denmark	42·0	39·9	51·8	49·3	50·4	49·4	49·8
France	40·7*	25·9*	40·1	25·0	41·2	24·5	41·9
Italy	33·4*	20·5*	33·2	20·0	34·0	18·7	34·4
Netherlands	43·1	27·5	47·9	30·6	53·1	32·1	53·3
Sweden	44·5	35·7	50·5	40·4	52·2	42·0	
US	31·1	25·2	33·3	26·4	32·5	24·6	
UK	*42·7*	*37·1*	*38·4*	*32·4*	*40·8*	*33·5*	*40·3*
Belgium	38·0	27·2	39·5	27·3	44·7	30·9	45·7
Germany	40·0	29·0	40·0	27·6	41·9	27·8	41·9
Ireland	34·0	31·3	36·7	33·4	n.a.	n.a.	
Japan	20·8	17·0	22·0	17·8	22·4	17·0	

* = 1970 figures. Figures below line compiled on different accounting basis from those above

SOURCE: *Economic Trends*, December 1977

Table 3·2: TOP MARGINAL RATES OF INCOME TAX IN EEC COUNTRIES 1977 (%)

UK	83 (98 on investment income)
Belgium	72
Italy	72
Netherlands	72
Denmark	61·1
Ireland	60
Luxembourg	57
Germany	56
France	54 (60 on investment income)

SOURCE: written answer

Table 3·3: HOW THE TAX THRESHOLD FELL

Income tax threshold as percentage of median earnings:

1971–2	64·5
1972–3	68·6
1973–4	58·6
1974–5	59·5
1975–6	50·0
1976–7	50·6

SOURCE: *Social Trends*

Table 3·4: THE CHANCELLOR'S TAX HAUL 1967–77
(£ million)

	1967-8	1968-9	1969-70	1970-1	1971-2	1972-3	1973-4	1974-5	1975-6	1976-7
Income tax	3826·4	4337·2	4899·9	5728·3	6449·0	6475·3	7135·8	10,238·7	15,053·9	17,012·8
Surtax	241·9	224·2	255·4	240·3	349·1	340·9	307·3	185·8	108·8	62·2
Profits tax	31·8	8·2	2·1	2·3	2·0	0·8	1·0	1·0	0·7	0·2
Corporation tax	1221·0	1345·8	1686·5	1589·0	1557·6	1532·7	2262·2	2849·7	1997·3	2654·9
Capital Gains	15·5	46·8	126·8	138·8	155·5	208·4	323·6	380·4	387·1	323·4
Estate Duty	331·3	379·2	365·5	356·3	452·4	458·5	412·2	337·8	212·5	124·4
Capital Transfer									117·7	259·2
Stamp duty	97·1	124·1	120·2	116·2	166·3	227·6	190·3	197·4	281·1	271·6
Special charges		66·0	19·7	3·4	1·8	1·2	0·9	0·4	0·3	0·2
Development land										1·1
Other	0·1									
Beer	390·2	405·8	450·5	466·9	480·0	491·7	365·1	450·1	651·5	807·4
Wines, spirits	358·1	372·2	413·2	464·2	524·0	581·8	588·3	682·9	909·5	1137·8
Tobacco	1044·7	1105·0	1143·0	1139·8	1124·0	1182·6	1084·9	1337·4	1676·8	1873·9
Protective duty	214·0	214·0	226·2	262·8	269·3	348·5	437·1	500·5	512·8	675·0
Betting	67·9	99·7	119·1	130·4	155·0	171·3	185·4	238·4	264·9	284·2
Purchase tax	748·5	972·1	1111·6	1270·7	1429·0	1387·4	379·5	1·2	1·3	(—)
VAT							1447·4	2496·5	3395·0	3778·4
Motor duties	269·0	393·1	416·7	421·2	473·3	485·0	533·5	532·1	780·7	845·9
SET	1063·8	1362·7	1888·1	1989·6	1323·7	993·5	45·0	2·0	0·1	
Total tax*	10,819·2	12,887·8	14,733·4	15,294·5	16,256·0	16,467·4	17,431·4	22,131·8	28,116·6	32,455·9
+ broadcasting revenue, interest, dividends and other income: Overall Revenue	11,227·3	13,363·4	15,266·6	15,842·8	16,931·8	17,178·1	18,226·4	23,570·1	29,417·2	33,777·9

* including some minor categories not listed above.

Table 3·5: REDISTRIBUTIVE EFFECTS OF TAX AND BENEFITS 1971 AND 1976

This shows the income, before and after all tax and benefits, of each of ten income groups. The main figures show income; the italic figures beneath them show income as a proportion of the average.

Group	1971 Before	1971 After	1976 Before	1976 After
I	23	557	33	1493
	1·28	*36·1*	*0·87*	*44·5*
II	258	695	409	1654
	14·3	*45·0*	*10·8*	*49·3*
III	777	932	1277	2142
	43·1	*60·4*	*33·8*	*63·8*
IV	1195	1139	2376	2470
	66·3	*73·8*	*62·8*	*73·6*
V	1531	1299	3180	2891
	85·0	*84·0*	*84·1*	*86·2*
VI	1827	1502	3877	3276
	101·4	*97·3*	*102·5*	*97·7*
VII	2115	1701	4585	3716
	117·4	*110·2*	*121·3*	*110·8*
VIII	2472	1965	5420	4087
	137·2	*127·3*	*143·3*	*121·9*
IX	3015	2243	5683	4820
	167·3	*145·3*	*174·1*	*143·7*
X	4813	3405	10,066	6985
	267·1	*220·5*	*266·2*	*208·3*

SOURCE: *Economic Trends*, February 1978 (with additional calculations) which see for details of sampling and method

Table 3·6: PROPORTION OF WEALTH OWNED BY MOST WEALTHY OWNERS

The most wealthy	1961	1966	1971	1974
1% owned:	28·4	23·6	20·4	18·4
2% owned:	36·7	31·0	27·7	24·9
5% owned:	50·6	43·7	40·1	36·7

SOURCE: *Social Trends* (derived from Inland Revenue)

4 Energy

The discovery of rich reserves of gas and oil under the North Sea, and the abrupt quadrupling by Arab exporters of the price of oil, led to a radical reconstruction of British energy policy in the early seventies. In the sixties, the main – and agreed – theme of energy policy had been the running down of the contribution to be made by coal, with a programme of pit closures which cut the number of jobs in the industry by half between 1964 and 1974. In the 6 years of the 1964–70 Labour governments, the closures proceeded unabated: the number of producing collieries was almost halved in that period. The policy of moving out of coal looked all the more persuasive as a result of the North Sea discoveries and the progressive uprating of their estimated yield. Though North Sea gas claimed far less attention than North Sea oil it was already making a powerful contribution to the national economy by the mid-seventies (see table 4·1).

The increase in world prices of oil upset all previous calculations. The importance of indigenous supplies was suddenly enhanced – which meant that our North Sea resources became all the more precious and that our home-based coal industry began to look worth perpetuating on a wider scale than before. This sense of the new economic power with which the oil crisis had endowed them undoubtedly helped to explain the readiness of the miners to embark on a confrontation with the Conservative government in the winter of 1973–4.

Accordingly, the role of coal in future energy plans ceased to decline, new pits were plotted, and new efforts made to increase the lagging production records of the mining industry. A series of planned productivity deals failed to gain acceptance, but in 1977 the official National Union of Mineworkers' rejection of a deal of this kind was followed by a wave of local settlements which finally began to get productivity moving. The necessity of squeezing every possible penny out of North Sea resources in oil, where operations were predominantly in the hands of private sector companies, as well as in gas, where there was a state monopoly buyer, became more acute. Three Bills designed for this purpose were introduced by the Labour government. The Offshore Petroleum Development (Scotland) Bill, which got its second reading on 19 November 1974, empowered the government to acquire land in Scotland for oil-related purposes, including the building of platforms. The Oil Taxation Bill introduced a Petroleum Revenue Tax (PRT) initially fixed at 45% of North Sea profits, payable before the computation of revenue for Corporation Tax. This was in addition to the 12·5% royalties on wellhead value which companies already had to pay.

The same bill closed the loophole which allowed companies

to offset North Sea profits against losses elsewhere. The legislation was inspired by the findings of an all-party select committee of the Commons in 1973 which said that under existing arrangements the United Kingdom would not obtain either for the Exchequer or for the balance of payments anything like the share of the 'take' of oil operations which other countries were obtaining for oil in their territories. The report was accepted by the Conservative government which promised legislation on much the same lines as Labour's bill.

A third bill, however, was much more contentious and was opposed in Parliament by both Conservatives and Liberals. The Petroleum and Submarine Pipelines Bill established a British National Oil Corporation to take charge of the State's interests in North Sea oil development. Unlike commercial competitors it was exempt from PRT. The bill gave the Secretary of State wide powers of control over rates of development and depletion and over the construction and operation of pipelines. The Corporation was also to be the State's agent in negotiating participation arrangements both with existing and future North Sea contractors.

The second reading on 30 April 1975 was opposed by Conservatives and Liberals; the government had the support of the Scottish National Party, despite its complaints that it brought too meagre a benefit to Scotland. The Conservative spokesman called the powers given to the Secretary of State 'one of the most sweeping assumptions of dictatorial power by any government in this country outside wartime'.

The Conservatives argued that state control and interference would inhibit the successful exploitation of the oilfields and thus diminish rather than increase the ultimate benefit to Britain. The Liberals also attacked the extension of nationalisation and bureaucratic control involved in the new government strategy. For the SNP, the main grievance was the government's refusal to award a major share (or indeed all) of the revenue from resources under waters off Scotland's shores to Scotland rather than to the United Kingdom as a whole.

The Treasury estimated in August 1977 that the total revenue from royalties, PRT and Corporation Tax between 1970 and 1980 might be around £5000 million at 1976 prices, rising to an annual revenue of £3500 million by the mid-eighties. They put the net improvement on the balance of payments as rising from £900 million in 1976 to £4900 million in 1980 and £7500 million in 1985 (all at 1976 prices). Britain was expected to be self-sufficient in oil some time during 1979.

Meanwhile, popular concern grew about the increasing role

assigned to nuclear power in Britain's energy future. It came to a head in the autumn of 1977 during a long inquiry before Mr Justice Parker into plans by British Nuclear Fuels Limited (BNFL) for a thermal oxide reprocessing plant (THORP) at Windscale in Cumbria. The opponents were not concerned with the THORP plan alone, important though that was: they saw the final judgement on the Windscale case as potentially opening the way to a new and infinitely dangerous generation of nuclear technology. Next in line would be a decision on a commercial prototype fast-breeder reactor, able to use uranium 60 times more efficiently than a conventional reactor; that in turn could lead on to a full programme of fast-breeder reactors. It was argued that nuclear technology was inherently unsafe because of the vast potential effect of any accident – though it was maintained on the BNFL side that the risks attached were no greater than with conventional forms of energy and indeed often less. It was also argued that the spread of nuclear technology might put weapons of unprecedented power into the hands of terrorists if security arrangements were anywhere less than perfect.

All these issues had been examined by a committee under Sir Brian Flowers which reported on 22 September 1976. This counselled governments to proceed with caution. 'The dangers of plutonium in large quantities in conditions of increasing world unrest are genuine and serious,' it said. 'We should not rely for energy supply on a process that produces such a hazardous substance as plutonium unless there is no reasonable alternative. The abandonment of nuclear fission power would, however, be neither wise nor justified. But a major commitment to fission power and a plutonium economy should be postponed as long as possible. There should be increasing support for the development of other energy sources including energy conservation, combined heat and power systems, and fusion power.' The security safeguards which plutonium demanded had weighed especially heavily with them: 'the unquantifiable effects of the security measures that might become necessary in a plutonium economy should be a major consideration in decisions on substantial nuclear development'. That was not to say that the government would necessarily be wrong to proceed with the development of a commercial fast-breeder reactor (CFR 1); it was simply to say that it should not take this step without taking full account of their report's conclusions.

The Parker inquiry – the widest and most exhaustive of its kind which had yet been staged – found in favour of the THORP project, and its conclusions were rapidly accepted by the government. This led to protests and demonstrations outside Parliament, and to a Liberal move within it to reverse the government decision. On 15 May 1978 the Liberal leader, David Steel, moved that the Order sanctioning the development should be withdrawn. He was defeated by 224 votes to 80 on a division which cut across all party lines and united in the 'anti' lobby some of Labour's farthest left with some of the Conservative farthest right. The 'anti' vote (adding in tellers) comprised 46 Labour MPs, 18 Conservatives, 11 Liberals, three each from the Scottish and Welsh Nationalists and one Scottish Labour member.

The vote on the government side comprised (including tellers), 143 Labour, 82 Conservative and one Ulster Unionist. (Full voting figures are in table 20·1). Fewer than half of the 635 MPs voted. The debate about alternative sources of energy, which had attracted great political attention in France with the rise of the Ecologist Party, had still in the late seventies yet to get much of a hold on the collective imagination of Westminster.

Table 4·1: ENERGY CONSUMPTION: THE DECLINE OF COAL
Million tons of coal or coal equivalent. The figures in italics indicate the percentage of all consumption for which each source accounts.

	Coal	Petroleum	Natural gas	Nuclear electricity	Hydro electricity	Total
1951	206·2	25·4			1·0	232·6
	88·7	*10·9*				
1956	214·0	38·5			1·3	253·8
	84·3	*15·2*				
1961	190·0	72·2	0·1	1·1	2·1	265·5
	71·6	*27·2*				
1966	174·0	113·0	1·2	7·8	2·3	298·3
	58·3	*37·9*				
1971	137·1	148·8	28·4	9·7	1·7	325·7
	42·1	*45·7*	*8·7*	*2·9*	*0·5*	
1976	120·1	132·1	57·9	12·7	1·9	324·7
	37·0	*40·7*	*17·8*	*3·9*	*0·6*	
1977	120·4	134·2	61·3	14·1	2·0	332·0
	36·3	*40·4*	*18·5*	*4·3*	*0·6*	

SOURCE: *Economic Trends*

5   Industry

Despite vast government involvement and the injection of huge sums of public money (or perhaps, on some readings, precisely *because* of it), and despite the official adoption of an industrial strategy which – against much Labour tradition – resolutely declared its intentions to put the regeneration of British industry at the very top of the government's list of priorities, the state of British industry at the start of 1978 was not very much less woebegone than it had been when Labour came to power.

Output had still not returned to the levels of the three-day week. Productivity – the rate of output per man or woman at work – advanced only sluggishly, and fell humiliatingly short of the performance of most of our competitors. Investment failed – at least until 1977 – to respond adequately to the battery of incentives set out for it, just as it had long failed to respond to the inducements held out by the Heath government, including British entry to the EEC. The Labour Party tended to blame the financial institutions for failing to provide the money that was needed, and argued that only a greatly expanded system of state financing could achieve what was needed: but some independent investigations suggested that some institutions had money hanging about only waiting for takers to come forward.

Meanwhile the level of exports, once the worst of the recession was over, began to look disquietingly low and the level of imports disquietingly high. The first tentative signs of expansion brought the problems which had haunted every British bid for growth in two decades: the indicator which accelerated fastest tended to be that for imported goods. And though some of these were clearly needed as components in the industrial recovery, others simply established the long-standing preference in domestic markets for imported products. That, with the usually anecdotal yet impressively consistent evidence of sales efforts abroad hampered by low reliability and inability to meet delivery dates, strengthened the impression that British industry still had far to go to match the productivity and the over-all efficiency of many of our competitors.

Government policies of intervention were of two kinds: direct, through State participation or actual take-over, and indirect, through an accumulating range of schemes of public assistance to the private sector.

At the heart of the government's operations was the National Enterprise Board (NEB), set up under the Industry Act of 1975 to take over the government's existing holdings and add new companies to them. The aim was to buy into profitable areas of manufacturing industry, not just to bail out firms in trouble. It was also seen as a weapon against monopoly and a safeguard against the passing of companies of strategic importance under foreign control. But the weight of the NEB commitment to companies in trouble made the balance between the profitable and the loss-making enterprises in the NEB stable rather different in practice from what the manifesto had envisaged.

The biggest lame duck of all to come the NEB's way was British Leyland, the only substantial British-owned company left in the motor industry, employing more than 130,000 people and affecting the livelihoods of thousands more when it ran into deep trouble in 1974. The British Leyland Bill, which got its second reading on 21 May 1975 (the Conservatives, 8 Liberals and 3 Ulster Unionists voted against it), enabled the government to mount a £2800 million rescue plan based on the report of a team under Lord Ryder which set out a strategy designed to recapture for British Leyland a 33% share of the home car market. This target was condemned as unrealistic by the Conservative opposition, and that verdict was later endorsed both by the report of a Commons select committee chaired by the Labour backbencher Pat Duffy and by the findings of an inquiry carried out by the government's 'think tank' (Central Policy Review Staff).

The government was hardly out of the Leyland crisis when it found itself required to save the US-owned Chrysler company, where the management was threatening a total shut-down of operations with the loss of 27,000 jobs. After a tough debate in the Cabinet – so copiously leaked that it was later re-enacted by a team of journalists on Granada Television – the government agreed to spend up to £162·5 million to save the company, though in this case, the NEB, which was up to its neck in the affairs of the rival Leyland company, was not involved. Other companies partly or wholly acquired by the NEB included Rolls-Royce (formerly Rolls-Royce 1971, the subject of a Conservative rescue attempt under Heath), Ferranti, the machine tool company Alfred Herbert and International Computers, where NEB went into partnership with Plessey.

The 1975 Industry Act which set up the NEB also proposed a system of planning agreements under which companies would make available information about their plans to the government and in some cases to the unions in return for government assistance. The original intention of Labour's policy-makers had been that the planning agreement system should be compulsory, but it was introduced on a voluntary basis and in the event there were hardly any volunteers. By the end of 1977 only one agreement had been concluded: with Chrysler.

The 1975 Act had also maintained and strengthened powers of intervention and assistance originally established in the

84

Conservative Industry Act of 1972, and these were invoked by the then Industry minister, Tony Benn, in a series of operations leading to the setting-up of workers' cooperatives in companies which had run into trouble. In several cases – Scottish Daily News, Norton Villiers Triumph Meriden, Kirkby Manufacturing and Engineering Ltd (IPD) – the money was given against the advice of a watchdog body (the Industrial Development Advisory Board) set up under the 1972 Act to advise the Secretary of State on the commercial chances of such enterprises. The IDAB had also warned that Chrysler was unlikely to succeed.

The one major nationalisation project – apart from the Leyland take-over – carried out by the Labour government was the nationalisation of the aerospace and shipbuilding industries. This was done through the passing of the Aircraft and Shipbuilding Nationalisation Bill, but only after the government had to agree to the deletion of ship-repairing companies in order to get its legislation through by the end of the 1976–7 session. Conservatives and Liberals opposed the bill at all stages. No action was taken on Labour's long-standing commitment to nationalise all ports. A private bill to enable the British Transport Docks Board to acquire Felixstowe docks (thus effectively nationalising them) was lost in the Lords. The leadership also resisted pressure from the party to legislate to take banks and insurance companies into public ownership. One substantial exercise in denationalisation occurred when a block of shares acquired by British Petroleum during a rescue operation for Burmah Oil was sold as part of the post-IMF operation to reduce the borrowing requirement.

In general, this Labour government, much to the dismay of its left wing, was in business to amend the mixed economy rather than radically to transform or to replace it. It was committed, in the words of its 1974 White Paper on the Regeneration of British Industry, to a private sector which was 'vigorous, alert and profitable'. The relationship it sought with those areas of industry not directly under its control was set out in an agreement reached with leaders of industry and of the unions at Chequers on 5 November 1975. This listed among the reasons for past unsatisfactory performance – along with low and inefficiently deployed investment, inadequate manpower policies, and low productivity – the continual shifts in direction between one government and another, denying industry the continuity it needed to succeed, and the pre-emption by the public sector and personal consumption of resources necessary to industrial reconstruction.

The agreement led to the identification of 30 sectors of British industry especially deserving government attention and aid – either because they were intrinsically likely to succeed, or because government aid could make the difference between success and the lack of it, or because they were – like the motor components industry – vital to the success of other sectors.

The new industrial strategy was taken as a repudiation both of Labour's previous overriding concern with the social services and the social wage, and of unselective aid and aid concentrated on the saving of 'lame ducks'. The Conservatives, while not condemning the strategy out of hand, were deeply sceptical, and when only a month later the government intervened to rescue Chrysler they called it a straight reversal of the agreement reached at Chequers.

Both within the strategy and outside it, the government continued to spend vast sums on industrial aid. Although some forms of assistance, such as the Regional Employment Premium (now considered to be undesirably indiscriminate, and terminated in the post-IMF cuts in 1976), disappeared, additional aid for industry – quite apart from schemes designed to encourage employment – were repeatedly announced by ministers.

Increasing attention was also paid by all parties to the potential contribution of small businesses. This had long been a Liberal theme, and it became still more so as the party grew more attracted to the teachings of E. F. Schumacher whose book *Small is Beautiful* provided a convenient slogan for the widespread repudiation in the seventies of much of the 'bigger is better' thinking of the sixties. The Conservatives too had long regarded themselves as natural champions of small business, but now Labour also sought to appear in that light. The Chancellor's successive Budgets were increasingly provided with new reliefs and inducements, and a Cabinet minister, Harold Lever, was given special responsibility for acting as the friend of small business and devising new forms of assistance. Small business was also seen as an essential component in the drive to regenerate dying inner city areas. All such changes, however, were condemned by the Opposition as falling short of what was needed. The Conservatives said the right solution would be greater tax relief and less government interference. For industry and business of all sizes, the party was now once more committed to the non-interventionist doctrines it had brought into power in 1970 – only to throw them overboard when great companies like Rolls-Royce and the Clyde shipyards ran into trouble. The Conservatives said they would scrap the NEB, dismantle subsidies and move to a system of incentives and the freeing of British industry from price and profit controls.

In fact, however, tax on companies had been alleviated since the early days of the Labour government, partly because the government had become genuinely alarmed by the crisis of liquidity which engulfed many companies in 1974 under the joint influence of record inflation and tight price control, driving a record number into bankruptcy (see table 5·3). Recognising that companies' paper profits had become artificially swollen by stock appreciation, the Chancellor in his November Budget introduced a measure of tax relief on stock appreciation which he later extended and then made permanent.

In the same Budget, Healey announced that the price code was to be relaxed to allow more room for company profits, which had now reached a new low (see table 5·2). For the rest of his term, he combined assurances to the unions of continuing price control with progressive relaxations to ensure that the Price Code did not inhibit profitability altogether; and increasingly the government's system of price regulation came to bite less on individual price decisions and much more on investigating cases where firms might be exploiting a monopoly or near-monopoly situation in their markets to the detriment of the consumer. Indeed, the Prices Secretary, Roy Hattersley, published an article in the *New Statesman* in praise of competition – not normally a virtue much celebrated in the Labour Party.

After four years of government commitment to the regeneration of British industry, however, it remained clear that British industry was still far from having been regenerated. The government maintained that its strategy was making progress, but that it was bound by its nature to take time to get results. The Labour left argued that the weaknesses of British industry were so deep-seated, and the vulnerability of British industry to the challenge of imports so acute, that industry could only be rebuilt behind tariff walls. This was the essence of the Alternative Strategy adopted by the Tribune Group of left-wing Labour MPs, and argued by some in Cabinet: it took much of its theory from the work of a group of economists based in Cambridge whose chief spokesman was a former Treasury economist, Wynne Godley. While both the government and the Opposition repeatedly declared themselves hostile to protectionism, a variety of protectionist measures was in fact adopted, particularly to help the textile and footwear trades; while it could also be argued that several government subsidy schemes to industry, particularly in development areas, amounted to a kind of home market protection. By 1978, even once-ardent exponents of unfettered free trade like the Trade Minister, Edmund Dell, were committed to some kind of planning of the trading pattern, such as the French President, Giscard d'Estaing, had already advocated for some time.

Table 5·1: FT INDEX OF ORDINARY INDUSTRIAL SHARES 1971–7

	1971	1972	1973	1974	1975	1976	1977	1978
Jan	340·7	488·6	489·9	324·8	183·7	397·0	374·7	482·3
Feb	330·9	495·1	453·6	316·5	262·6	404·2	397·8	457·9
Mar	322·8	506·8	445·5	297·5	292·6	404·7	418·2	454·9
Apr	354·6	522·3	464·1	290·0	314·9	406·0	415·1	
May	369·2	533·7	457·4	296·6	339·0	406·6	456·7	
Jun	374·8	499·6	464·9	267·5	332·6	378·6	450·5	
Jul	416·8	502·7	431·2	254·8	304·4	383·8	443·1	
Aug	405·3	524·4	422·8	222·9	298·3	368·1	478·6	
Sep	442·9	392·4	418·0	203·5	328·9	344·0	522·8	
Oct	412·4	481·5	434·7	199·4	341·9	293·6	511·9	
Nov	414·3	491·6	401·5	181·0	367·9	301·0	480·5	
Dec	455·5	508·4	329·9	160·1	365·8	328·6	481·6	

SOURCE: *Economic Trends*

Table 5·2: PROFITABILITY OF INDUSTRIAL AND COMMERCIAL COMPANIES; PRE-TAX PROFITS AS PROPORTION OF NATIONAL INCOME

1960	14·6
1970	9·6
1971	9·9
1972	9·8
1973	8·6
1974	5·2
1975	3·8
1976	4·2

Written answer.
SOURCE: Commons *Hansard* 10 November 1977

Table 5·3: BANKRUPTCIES

	England and Wales:		Scotland:	
	Debtors adjudged bankrupt	Liabilities £ thousands	Sequestrations	Liabilities £ thousands
1970	4622	21,775	84	1545
1971	4353	29,284	64	843
1972	3860	20,237	75	1206
1973	3363	19,102	47	968
1974	5191	41,681	63	1619
1975	6676	81,553	89	3461
1976	6681	76,692	80	3171

SOURCE: *Annual Abstract*

Table 5·4: INVESTMENT IN PLANT AND MACHINERY AT CURRENT PRICES IN THE PRIVATE AND PUBLIC SECTORS

showing percentage change on previous year in *constant* prices (excluding effect of inflation).

	Pri	%	Pub	%	Total	%	Pri as % of total
1966	1651		1099		2750		60·0
1967	1668	+ 0·9	1217	+ 9·7	2885	+ 4·5	57·8
1968	1835	+ 6·7	1159	− 8·9	2994		61·3
1969	2116	+11·9	1081	−10·7	3197	+ 3·0	66·2
1970	2467	+ 7·8	1191	+ 0·8	3658	+ 5·4	67·4
1971	2575	− 4·1	1363	+ 3·6	3938	− 1·6	65·4
1972	2611	− 4·2	1384	− 5·6	3995	− 4·7	65·4
1973	3166	+13·1	1651	+ 9·5	4817	+11·9	65·7
1974	3935	+ 7·3	1865	− 3·8	5800	+ 3·6	67·8
1975	4402	−11·3	2394	+ 2·4	6796	− 7·1	64·8
1976	5260	− 0·6	2856	− 1·3	8116	− 0·8	64·8

SOURCE: National Income and Expenditure (*Blue Book*)

6   Labour

In 1963 the Macmillan government was stirred to a programme of reflation and regional regeneration by a rise in unemployment to a national total of half a million. In 1972, the Heath government reversed its previous commitment to cautious advance and went bravely for expansion after unemployment moved up to the million mark (and the subsequent Labour protest led to the suspension of a Commons sitting). But in the mid-seventies, all such landmarks were left far behind. Unemployment, and under a Labour government, surged steadily on to a million and a half, and then, stubbornly, lodged there.

Labour had come back to office in 1974 on a pledge to get the nation back to work, and the government had since repeatedly affirmed its belief that deliberately to keep men out of work as a weapon of economic management was wholly repugnant to it. There were some on its own benches who saw no way in which budgets like that of 1975 could reduce unemployment rather than increasing it. But the government was faced with a problem of a peculiarly vicious kind. It could, and often did, introduce programmes of palliative measures (table 6·5) but at best these would hold back unemployment rather than cure it.

The classic road back to full employment lay through reflation and increased activity throughout the economy. But that suffered from two, perhaps incurable, defects. There was no way, on the government's calculations, that it could be done without bringing back a ferocious inflation. And, in any case, it was no longer certain that expansion and investment would bring back the jobs which had been lost; for increasingly much of the most effective industrial investment created relatively few new jobs – perhaps even removed jobs that were there already.

So, though the unions and the left clamoured continually for a job-producing reflation, the government did not give it to them, believing the side-effects of the cure might well prove worse than the original disease. Elsewhere, however, the Wilson and Callaghan governments gave the unions a great deal of what they wanted. The strategy for the return to power worked out by Labour and the unions in opposition years had been built around a close and continuing collaboration – a Social Contract, as it came to be called – between them. If jobs could not be re-created, it was all the more urgent to remedy what both agreed were other legitimate grievances.

Much of Labour's major legislation was asked for, and part-inspired by, organised labour. The bills included:
The Trade Union and Labour Relations Bill, 1974.

Designed to reverse most of the Conservative Industrial Relations Act of 1971, it abolished the National Industrial Relations Court and the system of formal union registration (with non-registered unions debarred from the rights which registered unions enjoyed). It restored old rights to picket peacefully and to organise closed shops, and reinstated legal immunities for unions acting in contemplation or furtherance of a dispute. But the Conservatives' procedures on unfair dismissal were retained and strengthened. The Bill was amended in committee and in the Lords but when Labour got a parliamentary majority at the October election it used it to reverse most changes through the Trade Union and Labour Relations Amendment Bill. This Bill failed in its final stages because of an unresolved dispute between the two Houses over the issue of the closed shop in newspapers, but was put through in the 1975–6 session under the Parliament Act.
The Employment Protection Bill, 1975.

Based on a 20-point TUC plan for action, it put the newly

created Advisory Conciliation and Arbitration Service (ACAS), carrying out duties previously exercised direct by the Department of Employment, on a statutory footing and empowered it to intervene where disputes occurred over issues of trade union recognition. It gave added responsibilities, among them the issuing of a code of practice on the disclosure of information by companies to unions. It gave employees the right to a day's pay even when work was not available, and ensured pregnancy and maternity leave for women, whose jobs must also be left open for them. Unions were given the right to be consulted about expected redundancies and large firms required to notify the Secretary of State that they were coming. Though the Conservatives opposed this legislation, saying it gave the unions many new privileges with no compensating obligations, their spokesman, James Prior, said they would perpetuate ACAS and did not oppose the information clauses.

The Health and Safety at Work Bill, 1974.

It was based on the report of a committee under Lord Robens and was similar to a bill drafted by the Conservatives. It established a commission and executive with responsibilities for ensuring and policing standards in workplaces.

The Dock Work Regulation Bill, 1975.

This was designed to meet long-standing grievances of dockworkers about erosion of dock work open to them, though other sectors of the union movement were critical and amendments to meet their objections were made in committee. The bill established a five-mile cargo handling zone around sea and water fronts in which certain categories of work, including warehousing, storage, packaging and cold storage would be reserved for dockworkers. In committee it was established that where such work was of long standing and there was no direct connection with the docks the reservation should not apply. The Lords however struck out the provision for a cargo handling zone of five miles and substituted a 'definable dock area' of half a mile. The change was endorsed in the Commons when two Labour MPs, John Mackintosh and Brian Walden, deliberately abstained to ensure its success.

The government had promised legislation to introduce worker participation into company boardrooms. A committee under Lord Bullock recommended a form of board on which employers and employees would have equal representation with a chairman and other members from a 'neutral' source holding the balance. This proposal was vehemently opposed by the

Confederation of British Industry (CBI) and extensive divisions appeared in the trade union movement about its merits. Opposition parties also made clear they could not accept legislation on these lines. The Prime Minister, who had announced as soon as the report was published that he was not in favour of legislation which a successor government would feel bound to overthrow, saw no way of legislating on the lines Bullock recommended. The government abandoned plans for early legislation and introduced a consultative Green Paper designed to encourage worker participation in management on a flexible basis rather than compelling it. A White Paper based on a staged progress towards industrial democracy was published on 23 May 1978. The Conservatives described it as a great improvement on Bullock, but the general reaction in industry was unfavourable. It was said to contain, even now, too great a degree of compulsion, and to put too much additional power in trade union hands.

The early stages of the Labour incomes policy were a time of rare tranquillity in industry. In 1972, more than 23 million days had been lost through disputes. In 1974, more than 14 million were lost; by 1976 the toll was down to 3,284,000, though later tensions developed – particularly over eroded differentials – which set the figures climbing again. By comparison with the record of some countries, or with the record of days lost through illness and injury, the totals remained modest. But even then – the Conservatives argued – there was still much room for improvement. Conservative backbenchers condemned the payments received by strikers' families – in some cases by strikers themselves – and front-bench spokesmen said there ought to be a shift of responsibility for paying men on strike from the taxpayer to the unions involved.

In general, the Conservatives (echoed to a lesser extent by the Liberals, especially the former leader Jo Grimond) were disturbed by the government's relationship with the unions, which they saw as one of spineless subservience. A formidable group within the party, including some of the shadow cabinet, hankered for a return to the strategy of 1971, when the party introduced its Industrial Relations Act in a bid to bring trade union power under closer control and greater legal restraint. But another group, led by the employment spokesman, James Prior, warned the party against taking that course and successfully argued that the next Conservative government should keep its trade union legislation to a minimum. Prior also insisted – successfully, though against impressive odds – that the Conservatives should avoid any commitment to outlawing the closed shop – a stand which earned him some unpopularity in his party and led members of the National Association for Freedom, a pressure group particularly hostile to some aspects of trade union activity, to call for his resignation. Prior also took a conspicuously cautious line over the dispute at Grunwick, a film-processing company in north-west London, where mass picketing was staged after a dispute over union recognition, and did not join those on the Conservative benches who wholly identified themselves with the Grunwick management and the NAF campaign mounted on its behalf.

The official policy of the party was to maintain close links with the unions, and to consult constructively with them, without, they said, allowing the unions to continue to dictate events. The Conservative leader, Mrs Thatcher, also held out to the unions the hope that the return of a Conservative government would mean the lifting of restraints on free collective bargaining. At the same time, the party had not repudiated all forms of incomes policy and made it clear it would seek to control public sector wages through its role as employer (see also p. 52 above).

Table 6·1: UNEMPLOYMENT IN THE UK 1972–8
percentage rates seasonally adjusted excluding school leavers

	1972	1973	1974	1975	1976	1977	1978
Jan	3·9	3·2	2·4	3·0	5·0	5·6	5·9
Feb	4·0	3·0	2·5	3·1	5·1	5·6	5·9
Mar	4·0	2·9	2·5	3·2	5·2	5·5	5·9
Apr	4·0	2·8	2·5	3·4	5·3	5·5	5·9
May	3·8	2·7	2·5	3·6	5·3	5·5	5·8
Jun	3·7	2·7	2·5	3·8	5·3	5·7	5·7
Jul	3·7	2·6	2·5	4·1	5·4	5·9	
Aug	3·7	2·5	2·6	4·2	5·5	5·9	
Sep	3·7	2·4	2·7	4·4	5·5	6·1	
Oct	3·6	2·3	2·7	4·6	5·5	6·0	
Nov	3·5	2·2	2·8	4·8	*	6·0	
Dec	3·3	2·2	*	5·0	5·6	6·0	

* No count made because of industrial dispute

SOURCE: Department of Employment *Gazette*

Table 6·2: WORKING DAYS LOST THROUGH STOPPAGES, IN THOUSANDS

	Number	% official	% change on previous year
1966	2398	48·9	− 18·0
1967	2787	14·1	+ 16·2
1968	4690	46·9	+ 68·3
1969	6846	23·6	+ 46·0
1970	10,980	30·2	+ 60·4
1971	13,351	74·2	+ 23·4
1972	23,909	76·2	+ 76·4
1973	* 7197	27·9	− 69·9
1974	*14,750	47·7	+104·9
1975	6012	19·1	− 59·2
1976	3284	14·4	− 45·4
1977	9985		+204·0

*counting affected by industrial dispute

SOURCE: Department of Employment *Gazette*

Table 6·3: DAYS LOST THROUGH DISPUTES

International comparisons (per thousand employed)

	1970	1971	1972	1973	1974	1975	1976*
Australia	1040	1300	880	1080	2670	1390	1490
Belgium	830	720	190	520	340	340	na
Canada	2190	800	1420	1660	2550	2750	2270
W Germany	10	340	10	40	60	10	40
France	180	440	300	330	250	390	420
Ireland	490	670	600	410	1250	810	840
Italy	1730	1060	1670	2470	1800	1640	2200
Japan	200	310	270	210	450	390	150
Netherlands	140	50	70	330			10
Sweden	40	240	10	10	30	20	10
UK	740	1190	2160	570	1270	540	300
US	2210	1600	860	750	1480	990	1190

*preliminary figures

SOURCE: Department of Employment *Gazette*, December 1977 (which gives additional countries)

Table 6·4: EMPLOYEES KILLED IN INDUSTRIAL ACCIDENTS IN BRITAIN

	1970	1971	1972	1973	1974	1975	1976
All	911	839	784	826	753	730	646
Mining	91	72	64	80	48	64	50
Building	138	144	132	148	113	119	116

SOURCE: *Annual Abstract*

Table 6·5: THE GOVERNMENT'S JOB SAVING PROGRAMMES

Cumulative total of jobs estimated to have been provided through special government schemes, according to latest available information at 25 April 1978

Temporary Employment Subsidy: 408,187 workers at gross cost £347 m
TES Supplement: 65,520 workers at gross cost £16 m
Youth Employment Subsidy: 45,909 young people assisted
Small Firms Employment Subsidy: 6,680 extra jobs in special development areas

Job Release Scheme: 24,847 approved applications
Job Creation Programme: 139,939 jobs
Work Experience Programme: 51,553 places

Estimated expenditure on these schemes plus additional training programmes, April 1975 to March 1978: £580 m
Estimated expenditure for year 1978–9: £530 m

Estimated expenditure on additional schemes for 1978–9 (Youth Opportunities Programme, Special Temporary Employment Programme, Short-time working scheme): £135 m

SOURCE: information supplied by Department of Employment

7 Transport

Roads

The great motorway building era in Britain, which had begun under Harold Macmillan in 1959, came abruptly to an end under the Labour governments of the middle seventies, halted mainly by a succession of cuts in the public spending programme – though also by a rising tide of public opposition to the destruction of urban and rural Britain which big road building had involved.

Successive inquiries into major road schemes were badly disrupted or even prevented altogether by the activities of protest groups – symbolised by the ubiquitous freelance crusader John Tyme – complaining that the proceedings were unjust, undemocratic, weighted in Whitehall's favour. The result was an anguished re-thinking in Whitehall, designed, as much as anything, to split off those liberal-minded persons who sympathised with allegations that the scales were tilted from the minority who were fanatically opposed to road building of all kinds and who would have continued to protest even if the procedures had been beyond rational criticism.

Meanwhile, however, with revenue declining and costs soaring, plans for filling out the road network were progressively reduced. In December 1973 the Conservative Chancellor, Anthony Barber, knocked £212 million out of the roads and transport budget as part of his £1200 million programme of cuts.

A further £91 million was removed in the public spending cuts of April 1975, another £87 million in the cuts of July 1976, and two more slices of £75 million and £50 million in the post-IMF reductions of December 1976. A transport White Paper in June 1977 put a ceiling of £380 million a year on motorway and trunk-road spending – helping to make possible a £150 million increase in spending on rural bus services, fast disappearing in some parts of the countryside.

The two imperatives – spending cuts and public opposition – came together in two further White Papers published on 5 April 1978. One proposed reforms in the roads inquiry procedures. From now on, inspectors would no longer be appointed by the Department of the Environment – the very department whose schemes were under scrutiny – but by the Lord Chancellor's office. Much more official information – especially about alternative routes – would be made publicly available. The other White Paper set out a road building programme for the straitened seventies, with 34 schemes worth some £90 million disappearing altogether from the programme while others were substantially modified. This scaling down of the network was in line with the report of a committee under Sir George Leitch which had questioned the necessity to go on building roads on the assumptions which had been formed in the late fifties and sixties. In particular, it challenged the contention that road building was an essential lure to bring industry out into the regions.

Road Safety

A bill to make the wearing of seat belts compulsory was introduced in 1976 and given a second reading on 3 March by 249 to 139. Opponents of the bill, from all parties, condemned it as an invasion of personal freedom. The bill was not completed by the end of the session and no time was found for it later, despite the government's initial claim that it would save 1000 lives and 11,000 serious injuries a year. No action was taken on the report of a committee on drink and driving under Frank Blennerhasset QC which recommended greater powers for the police to stop drivers suspected of drunken driving. (The effects of Labour's 1967 breathalyser legislation seemed by now to be wearing off.) The committee had called for improvements in breath-testing techniques and the search for these was said to be holding up legislation.

Railways

Despite a developing government determination to cut the high level of taxpayers' aid, the rail network which Labour inherited largely survived. Contingency schemes for a further reduction in passenger services were devised, and in some cases leaked to newspapers, but were not implemented. The transport Green Paper of 1976, following lines developed by Anthony Crosland while at the Department of the Environment, threatened hefty reductions in the subsidies on commuter services, which it called 'regressive', on the assumption that middle-class Britain commuted more often than working-class Britain; but (especially after its repudiation by Labour's National Executive) the full rigours of the Green Paper were avoided. The main casualty of the spending cuts was the plan to build a rail link to the Continent through the Channel Tunnel: Labour scrapped the Chunnel on 20 January 1975 (the decision was approved in an emergency debate on the same day by 294 votes to 218). The other major transportation epic abandoned by Labour was the scheme for a third London airport on Maplin Sands off the Essex coast, 'frozen' in March 1974 and dispensed with entirely on 18 July.

Table 7·1: PUBLIC EXPENDITURE ON ROADS

(1) – Total expenditure (£ million)
(2) – Expenditure as proportion of total public spending
(3) – Expenditure as proportion of GNP

	1	2	3
1966	471	3·3	1·4
1967	560	3·4	1·6
1968	608	3·3	1·6
1969	685	3·6	1·7
1970	807	3·9	1·8
1971	839	3·6	1·7
1972	917	3·5	1·7
1973	1094	3·6	1·7
1974	1201	3·1	1·6
1975	1562	3·0	1·7
1976	1625	2·8	1·5

SOURCE: National Income and Expenditure (*Blue Book*)

Table 7·2: PUBLIC EXPENDITURE ON TRANSPORT AND COMMUNICATIONS

(1) – Total expenditure (£ million)
(2) – Expenditure as proportion of total public spending
(3) – Expenditure as proportion of GNP

	1	2	3
1966	373	2·6	1·1
1967	455	2·7	1·3
1968	644	3·5	1·7
1969	433	2·3	1·1
1970	478	2·3	1·1
1971	555	2·4	1·1
1972	701	2·7	1·3
1973	686	2·2	1·1
1974	1396	3·6	1·9
1975	1535	3·0	1·6
1976	1141	2·0	1·0

SOURCE: National Income and Expenditure (*Blue Book*)

Table 7·3: ROAD AND RAIL TRAVEL

	Miles of motorway	Vehicles on road (thousands)	Private cars (thousands)	Deaths on road	Rail miles open for passenger traffic
1960	95	9,440	5526	6970	13,653
1966	631	13,286	9513	7985	10,220
1967	761	14,096	10,303	7319	9939
1968	906	14,447	10,816	6810	9526
1969	964	14,751	11,228	7365	9430
1970	1057	11,950	11,515	7499	9148
1971	1270	15,478	12,062	7699	9053
1972	1669	16,117	12,717	7763	9056
1973	1754	17,014	13,497	7406	8984
1974	1883	17,252	13,639	6876	8983
1975	2026	17,500	13,747	6366	9019
1976	2226	17,811	14,029	6570	9004
1977				6611*	

*provisional

SOURCE: *Annual Abstract*

8 Agriculture

The political debate on agriculture was increasingly dominated in the mid-seventies by the effects of British membership of the EEC. The result was to bring the parties rather closer together than had usually been the case in agriculture, with the Conservatives in general endorsing the robust national line taken by John Silkin, the combative anti-marketeer who became Labour's agriculture minister in September 1976.

The Conservatives, certainly, condemned the outcome of Labour's early price reviews, arguing that Labour was giving too much weight to the short-term interest of the consumer and too little to the needs of the producer (which, in time, would work against the interests of the consumer too). They also complained of the effects of Labour's tax innovations, notably the Capital Transfer Tax, as well as the threatened Wealth Tax, on farming. But all parties were united in their dissatisfaction with the Common Agricultural Policy of the Community (CAP), because of its alleged inefficiencies, inequities and detrimental effects on Britain.

What did disturb the tranquillity, though, and set the parties at their traditional loggerheads was the dispute over the green £. This was an artificial rate of currency for EEC farm transactions, designed to preserve an element of stability in these transactions while the real £ went up and down (mainly, of course, down). The effect was to cushion the British consumer, who paid in green £s, against the full effects of depreciation, and to set up a hefty EEC subsidy to keep prices of exports to Britain – and so, prices in the shops for the British consumer – down.

The perpetuation of the green £ at a rate which was growing increasingly unrealistic was opposed both within the EEC and by the British farming community, whose income too was suffering because of it. The British government stolidly resisted all pressure for devaluation until January 1978, when it announced its intention to devalue by 5%.

The Conservatives and Liberals, however, felt this was not large enough to protect farm incomes. The Conservatives tabled a Commons amendment demanding a 7·5% devaluation, while the Liberals asked for 10%. The Conservative amendment was carried on 23 January 1978.

Although the EEC had favoured devaluation, the figure on which Westminster had decided was not to their liking at all, especially with the coming year's farm budget in the making. There were fierce protests from Britain's partners in the Nine, who saw British farmers escaping from the framework of the EEC farm budget; to which Silkin blandly replied that he could not allow the verdict of the House of Commons to be flouted.

The Conservatives were wholly opposed to Labour's legislation to do away with 'tied cottages' in agriculture through the

Rent (Agriculture) Bill of 1976 which gave security of tenure to agricultural as to other tenants. The Conservatives called the bill unnecessary, undesirable, and uncertain in effect. The Liberals voted with the government to provide a second reading majority of 33 (291 to 258) on 4 May.

The issue which caused most anguish in this area, though, was fishing. The government became involved in a bitter dispute with Iceland and an awkward one with the EEC. On 15 July 1975, Iceland announced its intention to extend its limits from 50 to 200 miles. The coming of the 200-mile limit had by now begun to look more or less inevitable; the Americans were already on the road to it, and the Conservatives had been pressing for Britain to set a 200-mile limit of its own. But Britain refused to be bound by Iceland's unilateral initiative. There was a series of skirmishes at sea between Icelandic and British boats, and attempts at a negotiated settlement broke down with Iceland severing diplomatic relations and threatening to leave NATO. An interim agreement under which only 24 trawlers a day would be allowed inside the 200-mile mark and conservation restrictions would have to be observed was signed by the Foreign Secretary, Anthony Crosland, on 1 June 1976. It meant, he said 'painful structural changes' for the industry.

Meanwhile, a second dispute had developed between Britain and her partners in the Nine over EEC plans for its own 200-mile limit. Britain supported the concept of 200-mile limits but opposed the stipulation that member states of the EEC should be allowed to reserve limits of no more than 12 miles for their own exclusive use. Both Britain and the Republic of Ireland now demanded that exclusive limits should be set at 50 miles (the British fishing industry had asked for 100). Crosland now threatened that Britain would impose a 200-mile limit unilaterally, and appropriate legislation was promised in the Queen's Speech. The wrangling continued into 1978, with Silkin telling the EEC that, failing agreement, Britain must adopt her own solutions. The Conservative spokesman endorsed this line.

This dispute re-opened old arguments about the terms on which Britain had entered the EEC. Its negotiators had accepted the 12-mile figure in the hope that something better could be contrived later. (It was largely because of its failure to get better undertakings on this score that Norway decided against EEC membership.) Labour now blamed this dispute on the earlier weakness of the British negotiator, the Conservative Geoffrey Rippon.

Table 8·1: PUBLIC EXPENDITURE ON AGRICULTURE, FISHERIES, FORESTRY AND FOOD

(1) – Total expenditure (£ million)
(2) – Expenditure as proportion of total public spending
(3) – Expenditure as proportion of GNP

	1	2	3
1966	307	2·1	0·9
1967	365	2·2	1·0
1968	396	2·2	1·0
1969	391	2·1	1·0
1970	398	1·9	0·9
1971	497	2·1	1·0
1972	455	1·7	0·8
1973	515	1·7	0·8
1974	1066	2·7	1·4
1975	1701	3·3	1·8
1976	1199	2·0	1·1

SOURCE: National Income and Expenditure (*Blue Book*)

Table 8·2: SELF-SUFFICIENCY IN AGRICULTURE
Proportion of UK food supplies produced at home

	Current price basis	Constant price basis
1966–7	51·8	50·8
1967–8	52·4	51·6
1968–9	52·1	51·5
1969–70	53·0	52·4
1970–1	53·2	53·5
1971–2	53·6	53·9
1972–3	54·6	54·0
1973–4	54·5	56·0
1974–5	52·0	56·5
1975–6	53·7	52·2

SOURCE: *Annual Abstract*

Table 8·3: FOOD SUBSIDIES 1974–7

£ million

	1974	1975	1976	1977*
Milk	278	359	229	156
Butter	43	89	67	14
Cheese	22	64	49	17
Bread	41	83	58	19
Flour	2	8	8	3
Tea	10	30	24	
Total	395	632	435	209

*estimated

SOURCE: *Social Trends* (derived from Department of Prices)

9   Health and Welfare

In 1974 the Labour government pledged that it would improve and expand both the National Health Service and the social services. By 1978, however, the NHS was tottering even more precipitously towards collapse. Cutbacks in spending meant that personal social services had barely been able to maintain past standards and, despite considerable increases in social security benefits, poverty had increased with more and more people drawing means-tested benefits – mainly because of rising unemployment.

In the 1978 Budget, the government promised pensions of £19.50 for single people and £31·20 for married couples. But the most significant development in this area was the introduction of a completely new pensions scheme, piloted through by Barbara Castle as Social Services Secretary. This threw out Conservative pensions proposals of 1973 which, said Mrs Castle, would have meant means-tested supplements for millions of pensioners well into the next century. The new system replaced flat-rate benefits by earnings-related pensions which would mature over a period of 20 years.

The politics of stringency threw Labour left-wingers and the Conservatives into an occasional unholy alliance. On 5 December 1974, Labour backbenchers helped defeat the government when it tried to stop a relaxation of the earnings rule for pensioners – an estimated increase in public expenditure of £240 million between 1975 and 1978 and £225 million from 1980. The government did, however, have a majority of 35 against a Conservative attempt to abolish the earnings rule completely. And in 1976, three Labour MPs voted with the Conservatives in committee against a proposal to cut unemployment benefit for occupational pensioners.

The Conservatives remained committed to a tax credits scheme, and with child benefit the government appeared to have adopted one plank of this philosophy. Child benefit was designed to replace the existing dual system of family allowances payable to the mother and child tax allowances on the fathers' income by an all-in, tax-free benefit payable to the mother. It was due to be introduced in 1977, and Conservatives and the Labour left forged another alliance in the uproar that ensued when the government reneged on its commitment and decided to phase in the benefit over three years instead. The reason given was that the transfer from 'wallet to handbag' would have seriously strained pay policy because of its drastic reduction in take-home pay.

With the rapid increase in the numbers of elderly and disabled people, more emphasis was placed on assisting disability. A non-contributory invalidity pension and an invalid care allowance were introduced, as well as a mobility allowance for the disabled and a scheme under which disabled people could lease adapted cars from a charitable organisation.

The Conservatives' approach was dominated by the complaint that too many people were drawing benefits and that the system was riddled with abuse. Working people, they said, resented the fact that many were better off on supplementary benefit. The government was perpetually on the defensive, insisting that there were no large-scale abuses. But it was obvious that, in some cases at least, low wages did furnish invidious comparisons with benefits. The poverty trap did not ease up. In 1974, the Finer committee reported that there were some 620,000 one-parent families, with 1,080,000 children between them, many living in dire poverty. It recommended a new benefit for such families as well as a unified system of family law but its expensive proposals, like so many other social reforms, fell by the wayside.

The fiercest ideological battles between the parties took place over the stricken body of the NHS. Mrs Castle was constantly involved, throughout her period of office, in acrimonious disputes with the medical and nursing professions and with the parliamentary Opposition.

The continuing row was over a muddled combination of three things: doctors' and nurses' dissatisfaction with their pay, Labour Party (and health workers') opposition to private practice within the NHS, and concern over the crumbling fabric of the service itself. All this was conducted against the upheaval of the NHS reorganisation – resulting from the 1973 Conservative legislation – which Labour had opposed on the grounds that it was undemocratic but now said it was too late to alter.

Hospital consultants took the unprecedented step of working to contract and GPs threatened to resign from the health service. The issue of low pay became confused with that of clinical independence, which the doctors felt was threatened by the government's attitude towards private practice. Nurses and junior doctors also took industrial action for better pay and conditions, which they got.

The political issue came to a head over pay beds. The government put up their charges and announced that they would be removed completely from the NHS, which provoked a storm of opposition from doctors and Conservatives. Compromise proposals to phase out pay beds gradually while making sure that the private sector could cushion the change were worked out by Lord Goodman and enshrined in the Health Services Act. Despite assurances by David Ennals, the new Social Services Secretary, that the government was not waging war on private practice, the bill was denounced by the Conservatives for failing to put patients before politics. Patrick Jenkin, the Opposition spokesman, alleged that the abolition of pay beds meant throwing away revenue of £30 million to £40 million per year. The bill was given a second reading by 289 to 269. On second reading, five Scottish National Party and two Plaid Cymru members supported the government, while the Liberals and 8 United Ulster Unionists voted with the Conservatives. Labour Party conferences, however, repeatedly called for an end to all private health schemes.

In 1974, Mrs Castle reiterated Labour's policy goal of a free health service. The ensuing years, however, saw prescription charges rise, although more people became exempt from them. Doctors' requests for an immediate injection of £500 million into the NHS were turned down, although the Prime Minister assured them that the service would not be allowed to collapse. But inflation dealt the already ailing NHS a severe blow. Waiting lists reached record levels, extending for years in many specialities. The lists grew because of more demand for better facilities, a large increase in the numbers of the elderly and handicapped, higher costs, drastic public expenditure cuts – and because of the consultants' work-to-contract. Furthermore, old and out-of-date buildings and equipment were not renewed.

Meanwhile, the glaring inequalities within the NHS were recognised by the Resources Allocation Working Party, set up by the Department of Health, which decided to redistribute part of the cash allocation from the wealthier to the poorer health service regions. This policy was adopted in 1976, although the concept of a 'wealthy' region was somewhat academic; none could afford any cash reductions.

The one major welfare reform that met with the unqualified approval of the Conservatives was the Children Act 1975. This gave new rights to children and to foster and adoptive parents, and diminished the rights of natural parents, in an attempt to put the welfare of the child first.

Table 9·1: PUBLIC SPENDING ON THE SOCIAL SERVICES

(1) – Total expenditure, £m, on all social services including education
(2) – As proportion of total public spending
(3) – As proportion of GNP

	All services			Health service			Social security benefit		
	1	2	3	1	2	3	1	2	3
1966	5904	40·9	17·6	1375	9·5	4·1	2577	17·8	7·7
1967	6609	39·6	18·7	1524	9·1	4·3	2900	17·4	8·2
1968	7390	40·4	19·6	1656	9·1	4·4	3340	18·3	8·9
1969	7919	41·8	19·9	1733	9·1	4·4	3571	18·8	9·0
1970	8861	42·8	20·2	1980	9·6	4·5	3921	18·9	8·9
1971	9924	42·8	20·0	2248	9·7	4·5	4308	18·6	8·7
1972	11,658	44·4	21·0	2597	9·9	4·7	5111	19·5	9·2
1973	13,119	43·0	20·2	2939	9·6	4·5	5528	18·1	8·5
1974	16,219	41·4	21·6	3847	9·8	5·1	6835	17·4	9·1
1975	21,975	42·7	23·4	5181	10·1	5·5	8906	17·3	9·5
1976	26,337	45·0	23·9	6182	10·6	5·6	11,233	19·2	10·2

SOURCE: National Income and Expenditure (*Blue Book*)

Table 9·2: HEALTH SERVICE CHARGES TO USERS

	All services £ million	% of cost of all services found from charges
1966–7	60	3·9
1967–8	63	3·8
1968–9	80	4·4
1969–70	93	4·8
1970–1	107	4·5
1971–2	131	4·9
1972–3	149	4·8
1973–4	165	4·6
1974–5	180	3·8

SOURCE: DHSS Health and Personal Social Services Statistics

Table 9·3: WEEKLY RATES OF PRINCIPAL BENEFITS AT 31
DECEMBER EACH YEAR (5)

	Unemploy- ment benefit £	Retirement pension (couple) £	Industrial injury (full rate) £	Family allowance (2nd child) £	Family income supplement (1 child) £
1970	5·00	8·10	7·75	0·90	
1971	6·00	9·70	8·75	0·90	4·00
1972	6·75	10·90	9·50	0·90	5·00
1973	7·35	12·50	10·10	0·90	5·00
1974	8·60	16·00	11·35	0·90	5·50
1975	11·10	21·20	13·85	1·50	7·00
1976	12·90	24·50	15·65	1·50	8·50
1977	14·70	28·00	17·45	*	8·50

*replaced by child benefit

SOURCE: *Annual Abstract*

Table 9·4: EARNINGS, PRICES AND PENSIONS 1968–77

Index 1970=100

	Weekly earnings	Prices	Single pension	Married pension
1968	83·2	89·3	90·0	90·1
1969	89·7	93·9	100·0	100·0
1970	100·0	100·0	100·0	100·0
1971	111·3	109·5	120·0	121·7
1972	125·1	117·0	135·0	134·6
1973	142·5	126·8	155·0	154·3
1974	167·5	147·0	200·0	197·5
1975	212·3	182·6	232·0	259·3
1976	245·4	211·4	306·0	302·5
1977	270·4	245·3	350·0	345·7

SOURCE: *Annual Abstract*, NIESR

Table 9·5: HEALTH SERVICE STAFF AND PRACTITIONERS

(1) – Total
(2) – Percentage increase on previous year

All health service staff and practitioners:

	1971	1972	1973	1974	1975
(1)	799,673	831,753	843,119	859,468	914,068
(2)		4·0	1·4	1·9	6·4

of whom:

Administrative and clerical:

	1971	1972	1973	1974	1975
(1)	78,796	83,708	87,406	94,798	105,781
(2)		6·2	4·4	8·5	11·6

Medical staff:

	1971	1972	1973	1974	1975
(1)	30,482	31,952	33,329	34,338	36,217
(2)		4·8	4·3	3·0	5·5

Total personal social services staff:

	1971	1972	1973	1974	1975
(1)	122,600	135,600	151,162	166,197	179,070
(2)		10·6	11·5	9·9	7·7

Percentage increase by grades 1971–5:

Medical staff	18·8	Administrative and clerical	34·2
Dental	26·8	Ambulance	12·2
Nurses, midwives	18·1	Ancillary and other	1·4
Professional and technical	17·9	Doctors	5·9
Works maintenance	9·7	Dentists	7·2

SOURCE: DHSS Health and Personal Social Services Statistics

Table 9·6: INFANT MORTALITY

Death of infants under one year, per thousand live births.

	All UK	England + Wales	Scotland	N Ireland
1936	62·1	58·7	82·3	76·9
1941	63·3	60·0	82·7	76·6
1946	42·7	42·9	53·8	54·0
1951	31·1	29·7	37·4	41·2
1956	24·4	23·8	28·6	28·9
1961	22·1	21·4	25·8	27·5
1966	19·6	19·0	23·2	25·5
1971	17·9	17·5	19·9	22·7
1976*	15·7	14·2	14·8	18·3

* Provisional

SOURCE: *Annual Abstract*

Table 9·7: WAITING LISTS AND BED AVAILABILITY, NHS
(England and Wales)

	waiting list 31 Dec	per thousand population	average daily available beds
1966	510,422	11·31	434,846
1967	509,537	11·22	434,378
1968	505,107	11·07	432,140
1969	532,370	11·62	428,737
1970	525,926	11·44	423,621
1971	493,371	10·70	419,612
1972	479,199	10·35	412,664
1973	508,617	10·96	403,526
1974	517,424	11·14	396,235
1975	588,483	12·67	387,632
1976	607,141	13·08	383,132
1977 Sept	591,096		

SOURCE: DHSS

10   Housing

It has become accepted that, on paper at least, there is now no housing shortage in Britain, with about 500,000 more houses in the country than households. Housing problems, however, hardly diminished after the Labour Party came to power in 1974. The queues of the homeless stretched ever longer; although the number of sub-standard houses had fallen considerably in the past 25 years, there were still about 2·7 million households living in unsatisfactory conditions or sharing. The inner cities still presented a dismal picture of decay and neglect; and the construction industry suffered from a severe recession resulting in many lay-offs and bankruptcies.

The situation seemed to be stagnant despite a massive increase in expenditure. Between 1974 and 1976 expenditure on housing increased by 30% – but nevertheless fewer houses were built and rehabilitated than between 1971 and 1974 because of a mixture of rent freezes, soaring interest rates and bureaucratic tangles. The financial crisis meant that interest rates reached record levels and local authority mortgages were cut back, despite an October 1974 Labour manifesto commitment to expand them.

Ideological differences between Labour and the Conservatives were most clearly expressed by the swing back from private to public housing as soon as Labour took office. In 1974, the number of private house starts almost halved from the previous year. The Conservatives had pushed the private share of new housing up considerably; under Labour, the public sector was given an equivalent boost. Much of Labour's programme was also devoted to municipalisation of private houses and increased rent subsidies for council tenants. The Conservatives supported council house sales, a major extension of home ownership and an arrest to the decline of the privately rented sector.

However, the government gradually leaned towards a two-party consensus on housing finance. It had begun by repealing parts of the Conservative Housing Finance Act 1972, which gave help only selectively, and returned to a wider system of subsidies. The Conservatives alleged that this was backtracking to a system of 'indiscriminate' subsidies which would do nothing to meet the pressing need for houses. But a more permanent and satisfactory system was obviously needed. Anthony Crosland, then Environment Secretary, accordingly set up a Housing Finance Review, saying that the subject had become a 'dog's dinner' of muddled practice.

In a consultative document setting out the results of the review, the government significantly omitted any proposals to cut mortgage tax relief, a policy adopted by the Labour Party Conference 1976. Instead, it proposed local strategy and investment programmes embracing both public and private sectors, recognising a strong desire for home ownership. It promised special help for first-time buyers – later enshrined in the Home Purchase Assistance and Housing Corporation Guarantee Bill – a tenants' charter and more help for housing associations. The faint praise offered by Michael Heseltine, the Conservative spokesman, was suitably damning: 'The Green Paper is a damp squib, but at least it splutters in the right direction.'

The biggest clash between the parties, however, occurred over the introduction of the Rent Act 1974 which greatly increased security of tenure for unfurnished tenants. Hugh Rossi, the Conservative housing spokesman, denounced this for creating 'chaos and uncertainty', and from the creation of the act the argument raged over whether or not it had significantly contributed to the decline of the privately rented sector – a decline from about 52% of the housing market in 1951 to 15% in 1976. In spite of Conservative allegations, the government insisted that the trend had been irreversible.

Nevertheless, the government did admit that the Rent Acts were a mess. Crosland commented that they had become 'an impenetrable jungle which daunt the responsible and the irresponsible alike'. And in a consultation paper, the government acknowledged criticism of the Rent Acts for inhibiting the full use of the existing stock of houses and for causing frustration and anxiety to landlords and tenants.

Meanwhile, the policy of renovating old houses continued. The Housing Act 1974 followed Conservative proposals to establish Housing Action Areas which, like General Improvement Areas, were eligible for grants. However, after 1974 there was a drastic slump in the level of improvement grants, mainly because the government had tightened up regulations to prevent people from improving second houses.

As homelessness grew, so the issue became a political football, with the Liberals forcing a measure through as part of the Lib-Lab pact against strenuous efforts by the Conservatives to water it down. The Housing (Homeless Persons) Act, sponsored by the Liberal MP Stephen Ross, defined the homeless in priority need and set out the duties of housing authorities to meet the problem. The most important Conservative amendment re-introduced the element of discretion that the bill had originally been intended to remove.

Conservatives mounted vigorous opposition to the Community Land Act, a measure to compel local councils to municipalise most development land. Although it subsequently proved to be a paper tiger, since councils had no money with which to implement it, the bill created sufficient alarm to draw more than 1000 amendments and the Liberals voted against it on its second reading. Curiously, though, the government's revised policy on inner cities drew its fiercest attack for not pumping in sufficient money from the ranks of the Conservative Party in the person of Peter Walker. The Inner Urban Areas Act gave local authorities powers to support the creation of new employment opportunities and to improve the environment in the industrial areas. It was planned to spend about £1000 million on the projects over the next decade, but Walker said that the proposals were 'relatively small chicken-feed' compared with what was needed and that in two or three years' time the plight of the inner cities would be even worse.

Table 10·1: PUBLIC EXPENDITURE ON HOUSING

(1) – Total expenditure (£ million)
(2) – Expenditure as proportion of total public spending
(3) – Expenditure as proportion of GNP

	1	2	3
1966	979	6·8	2·9
1967	1129	6·8	3·2
1968	1157	6·3	3·1
1969	1208	6·4	3·0
1970	1315	6·4	3·0
1971	1307	5·6	2·6
1972	1498	5·7	2·7
1973	2346	7·7	3·6
1974	4110	10·5	5·5
1975	4322	8·4	4·6
1976	5190	8·9	4·7

SOURCE: National Income and Expenditure (*Blue Book*)

Table 10·2: NEW MORTGAGE COMMITMENTS (£m)

	Total	Average price of new dwellings on which mortgages are completed	
		1966=100	1970=100
1966	1223	100·0	
1967	1649	106·1	
1968	1480	118·3	
1969	1580	119·9	
1970	2188	127·6	100·0
1971	3013	140·8	110·4
1972	3802	176·9	138·7
1973	3254	246·2	193·0
1974	3115	284·8	223·3
1975	5302	312·8	245·2
1976	6089	335·7	263·2

SOURCE: *Economic Trends*

Table1 10·3: HOUSING STARTS, GREAT BRITAIN 1966–76

	Total thousands	% change	Private	% of all	Public	% of all
1966	379·3		193·4	51·0	185·9	49·0
1967	447·5	+18·0	233·6	52·2	213·9	47·8
1968	394·4	−11·9	200·1	50·7	194·3	49·3
1969	343·4	−12·9	166·8	48·6	176·6	51·4
1970	318·9	− 7·1	165·1	51·8	153·8	48·2
1971	344·3	+ 8·0	207·4	60·2	136·9	39·8
1972	351·0	+ 1·9	228·0	65·0	123·0	35·0
1973	328·5	− 6·4	215·7	65·7	112·8	34·3
1974*	252·7	−23·1	105·9†	41·9	146·8	58·1
1975	323·0	+27·8	149·1	46·2	173·9	53·8
1976	325·6	+ 0·8	154·7	47·5	170·9	52·5

* The lowest figure since 1951
† The lowest figure since 1953

11   Education

Ever since the war, an expanding education service had been seen as a prerequisite of social progress. The total education bill doubled between 1966 and 1972, from about £1·7 million to £3·4 million, and doubled again between 1972 and 1976, reaching a total of £7·3 million. All parties assumed that more meant better. The change was therefore all the more dramatic when public expenditure cuts under the Labour government savaged the education service and shattered Labour's election promises of expansion.

Primary, secondary and higher education were all hit. The university building and other higher education programmes were cut. The 1976 Public Expenditure White Paper revealed that education expenditure was planned to fall in real terms for three years after 1976–7. Instead of the promised attention to nursery education, the capital nursery allocation was to be reduced by nearly 70% between 1974–5 and 1978–9.

As if this wasn't bad enough, severe fluctuations in demographic projections created additional confusion. It had been assumed that the school population would continue to rise until 1990. This was then held to be wrong; the peak of about 9 million schoolchildren had been reached, it was thought, and numbers were expected to decline sharply to about 7 million in the late

1980s. But then again, in the first four months of 1978, the birth rate increased leading to new hopes that drastic school closures and teacher unemployment might still be avoided.

Reductions in public expenditure, however, coupled with the fact that increases in teachers' salaries slowed down any drift away from the profession, did create serious teacher unemployment anyway, with many colleges of education closed down.

There was great suspicion among the universities that the Labour government was biased against them – a suspicion shared by the Conservatives. The universities were badly hit by the denial to them of full inflationary increases in government grants, and their concern was given added point by the suggestion made by Reg Prentice, then Education Secretary, that they should sell their treasures. The Conservatives accused the government of trying to destroy the universities' freedom by suggesting they ought to adjust their admissions to meet national manpower needs. Morale in the universities was further undermined by the long-running dispute over university teachers' pay. Even when it was settled, in 1978, the issue remained a rancorous one with the university teachers still feeling that justice had not been done. It was a situation which the Conservatives compared unfavourably with the pay rises agreed with non-university teachers.

There were, however, two main areas in education where the parties clashed. The first was that of education standards on which the Conservatives sustained an unremitting attack, claiming that the government was more interested in its 'doctrinaire' policies than in standards of teaching. Norman St John-Stevas, the Opposition spokesman, said: 'We should be getting on with the job of improving schools, not discussing systems.' Standards in the basic skills of reading, writing and arithmetic, as well as the problems of discipline, vandalism and truancy, came under fire.

The Labour government was forced to take serious notice of these criticisms when the William Tyndale junior school in north London ran into trouble. After parents and teachers at the school expressed grave concern about the informal teaching methods being used, the headmaster and some teachers were suspended (and later sacked). Five school managers resigned, and an independent inquiry condemned a number of teachers for being more concerned with ideologies than with the children in their care.

As a result of this seminal episode, the Prime Minister launched the Great Debate into educational standards, expressing his concern about informal methods of teaching and saying that there was a case for a common core curriculum. He came close to the Conservative demands for the reintroduction of national standards although the Education Secretary, Shirley Williams, maintained that there was no question of the government wanting to control the curriculum.

But by far the most important and acrimonious inter-party dispute concerned the imposition of comprehensive schooling on recalcitrant local authorities. The Conservatives, while saying they did not oppose comprehensives in principle, had allowed local authorities to choose their own systems. (Comprehensive education continued to spread during the Heath government's period in power.) The incoming 1974 government reverted to previous Labour policy to end selection at eleven-plus, and told councils to submit their plans for comprehensive systems to the Department of Education. Seven councils refused; and so the government, supported by the Liberals, introduced the Education Bill forcing them to do so. The Conservatives vehemently opposed the move, saying that the bill embodied all the worst dogmatism of the socialist attitude to education.

Meanwhile Tameside Council in Greater Manchester, newly under Conservative control, was defying the government's education policy in a move which became of great constitutional importance. The Education Secretary, then Fred Mulley, used his powers under the 1944 Education Act to direct Tameside to comply. This enraged the Conservatives, with St John-Stevas commenting: 'The government has once again shown its contempt for constitutional processes and parliamentary democracy.' The matter went to the House of Lords which upheld Tameside and ruled that Mulley had misdirected himself. The issue was, however, by then academic since the Education Act was passed shortly afterwards.

The Conservatives protested even more bitterly over the decision to abolish grants to direct grant schools, forcing them to choose between independence and the State comprehensive system. Two-thirds of the direct grant schools chose independence; the majority of those that opted to join the State system were Roman Catholic. St John-Stevas called the affair 'an unprecedented step of educational vandalism' and re-affirmed the party's promise to restore the direct grant list. Yet grassroots pressure inside the Labour Party, as expressed in Labour's Programme 1976 and approved by conference, went further than the government in reiterating the long-term aim of abolishing all fee-paying in schools.

Table 11·1: PUBLIC EXPENDITURE ON EDUCATION

(1) – Total expenditure (£ million)
(2) – Expenditure as proportion of total public spending
(3) – Expenditure as proportion of GNP

	1	2	3
1966	1700	11·8	5·1
1967	1893	11·4	5·4
1968	2096	11·5	5·6
1969	2250	11·9	5·6
1970	2532	12·2	5·8
1971	2899	12·5	5·8
1972	3414	13·0	6·2
1973	3949	13·0	6·1
1974	4601	11·7	6·1
1975	6561	12·8	7·0
1976	7340	12·5	6·7

SOURCE: National Income and Expenditure (*Blue Book*)

Table 11·2: PROPORTION OF PUPILS STAYING ON AT SCHOOL

	After 16	After 17	After 18
1958	15·3	7·8	2·8
1963	20·4	10·1	3·7
1968	28·2	14·8	5·3
1973	33·5	18·6	6·2
1974	25·7	17·7	6·1
1975	26·0	17·4	5·7

SOURCE: *Annual Abstract*

Table 11·3: THE SPREAD OF COMPREHENSIVE SCHOOLING 1971–8 (ENGLAND AND WALES)

(proportion of pupils in each type of school)

Maintained secondary schools

	1965	1971	1972	1973	1974	1975	1976
Middle schools deemed secondary		1·8	2·3	3·7	4·6	5·4	5·7
Comprehensive	8·5	35·9	41·1	47·0	57·4	64·3	70·0
Modern	55·2	37·0	33·4	28·7	23·0	18·2	15·0
Grammar	25·5	18·2	16·6	14·8	11·0	9·0	7·5
Technical	10·8	1·2	1·0	0·8	0·6	0·5	0·4
Others		5·9	5·5	5·1	3·3	2·6	1·5
Totals (*thousands*)		3143·9	3251·4	3362·6	3723·7	3826·6	3935·5
Assisted and independent schools (*thousands*)		293·5		297·1	302·4	327·2	328·7

SOURCE: *Social Trends*

115

12   Law and Order

The Conservatives continued during the mid-seventies to make the running on the issue of law and order, with frequent charges that the government was doing too little to stem the rising tide of crime. At party conferences, they called for more police and more public support for them, stiffer penalties and a tougher approach to young offenders. Their traditional grouse, however, developed new political overtones. Their conferences painted dire pictures of workers being beaten up by pickets, of direct action by totalitarian Trotskyites, of law and order being undermined by marches and demonstrators. They accused the government of condoning violence at the Grunwick film-processing plant in Willesden, London, where several MPs had joined the picket. And the Clay Cross issue still festered. In an act passed in 1975, the government exempted councillors at Clay Cross, in Derbyshire, who had rebelled against the 1972 Conservative Housing Finance Act, from any further surcharges arising from the rebellion. This was despite previous advice from Sam Silkin, later to become Labour's Attorney-General, that: 'An Act of Indemnity passed for this purpose would, in my opinion, contravene all constitutional practice and would set a dangerous precedent.' The act was seen by Conservatives as a measure that clearly condoned law-breaking, and led Lord Hailsham to complain in the conference law and order debates of a new element of political crime.

Silkin further drew Conservative fury when he refused to take action against Post Office workers who were blacking mail to South Africa and, later, to the Grunwick factory. The Conservatives again accused him of sanctioning law-breaking, but Silkin maintained that he had to balance the need to uphold the law against any repercussions to the public resulting from his moves. An attempt by the National Association for Freedom to force him to act failed when the House of Lords ruled that Silkin was the sole guardian of the public interest.

Meanwhile, the Home Secretary was resisting pressure from his own left wing to ban marches and demonstrations by the extreme right. Violent clashes on such occasions, however, only led him to reiterate that the National Front should be dealt with by the race relations laws, not by the Public Order Act. After the violence of Lewisham, where opponents of the Front clashed with the police, the Conservatives called for new ground rules to deal with demonstrations including the passing of exemplary sentences. Merlyn Rees consistently refused to ban any marches, maintaining that this was a decision for the police; and in London, the police did eventually ban marches and demonstrations for two months in order to stop a National Front march through Ilford before the by-election. Here, Conservatives supported Rees; Whitelaw warned against the danger of turning evilly disposed minorities into martyrs by seeking to ban their lawfully-expressed views.

An all-party consensus was also reached on action against terrorists, although the Labour left later began to express strong reservations. A sustained campaign of violence on the British mainland by the IRA during 1974 culminated in the worst terrorist incident in British history when 21 people died in bomb explosions at two public houses in Birmingham. After this the Home Secretary, Roy Jenkins, introduced the 'draconian' measure of the Prevention of Terrorism Act which banned the IRA, gave the Home Secretary wide powers to exclude or expel suspected terrorists and gave the police equally sweeping powers of arrest and detention. Although these powers were unprecedented in peacetime, the bill passed through all its parliamentary stages in 18 hours. Later, however, left-wing MPs who were concerned about the threat to civil liberties forced a vote on the third reading of a bill bringing in even tougher measures, including a new offence of failing to disclose information about terrorists. The bill was passed by 118 votes to 11.

Conservatives kept up the pressure for the restoration of the death penalty. After the murder of the right-wing activist Ross McWhirter in 1975 Mrs Thatcher said: 'I personally believe that those who commit these terrible crimes against humanity have forfeited their right to live.'

However, many MPs, including some who were not ideologically opposed to hanging, feared an increase in violence and hostage-taking if it were reintroduced. In two debates, on 11 December 1974 and 11 December 1975, the Commons rejected the restoration of the death penalty for terrorist crimes, by 369 to 217 and 361 to 232. On both occasions there was – despite a free vote – a sharp division between Conservative and Labour opinion. The figures were:

Table 12·1: VOTING FOR THE RESTORATION OF THE DEATH
PENALTY

1974

	For	Against	DNV†	Total
Con	202	55	18	275
Lab	3	296	18	317
Lib	1	11	1	13
Nat	5	6	3	14
Others	8	3	1	12
Total*	219	371	41	631
		+ Speaker and 3 deputies		635

1975

	For	Against	DNV	Total
Con	216	48	12	276
Lab	3	296	16	315
Lib	3	8	2	13
Nat	5	7	2	14
Others	7	4	2	13
Total*	234	363	34	631
		+ Speaker and 3 deputies		635

† did not vote

* Totals include tellers

The Labour Party came to power committed to place more emphasis on non-custodial treatment and to reduce the prison population which stood at 37,000 in 1974. Jenkins warned that if the prison population should rise to 42,000 conditions would approach the intolerable and drastic action would become inescapable. In 1976 the prison population reached 42,006. No drastic action was taken and the numbers did not significantly fall, despite the introduction of community service orders, under which offenders could be required to perform a specific number of hours' service to the community.

The Conservatives kept up the attack on the government for 'softening' sentences rather than fighting the growing numbers of crimes of violence, criminal damage and juvenile offences. Whitelaw said in a speech in 1976: 'A government that cannot protect its own citizens from attack in the streets of its towns and cities, that cannot protect property from damage or homes from intrusion, has failed to live up to the basic duties of government.'

While the government came under fire from the left for not channelling enough funds to make the Children and Young Persons Act 1969 work, the Opposition claimed that the Act was not tough enough, with Whitelaw calling for severe discipline for young offenders on the line of army 'glasshouses'. The undermanning of the police was another serious bone of contention between the two parties. The Conservatives said in *The Right Approach* that the police represented one of the few areas where an increase in public spending was essential. When Jenkins introduced his Police Bill, with its proposals to set up an independent machinery to hear complaints about the police, Ian Gilmour, then Shadow Home Secretary, condemned it as 'grotesquely ill-timed' when the police were fighting a desperate battle to maintain law and order. The bill was given an unopposed second reading. Nevertheless, morale in the police forces was bad, with talk at one time of a strike over pay. Because of the degree of unrest, the government announced that the scope of the Edmund-Davies inquiry into police procedure would be widened to include police pay.

Table 12·2: PUBLIC EXPENDITURE ON POLICE AND PRISONS
£ *million*

	Police	Prisons	Total	Proportion of total public expenditure
1966	241	34	275	1·9
1967	272	39	311	1·8
1968	296	48	344	1·9
1969	322	56	378	2·0
1970	375	65	440	2·1
1971	439	76	515	2·2
1972	479	89	568	2·1
1973	558	107	665	2·2
1974	695	148	843	2·1
1975	909	193	1102	2·2
1976	1137	234	1371	2·3

SOURCE: National Income and Expenditure (*Blue Book*)

Table 12·3: CRIME, ENGLAND, WALES AND SCOTLAND 1969–76

(thousands)

	Crimes reported	% increase	Persons found guilty	% increase	Crimes of violence	% increase	Murders* England and Wales	Murders Scotland
1969	1654·7		1800·1		23·1		69	22
1970	1735·6	4·9	1875·0	4·1	25·4	10·0	91	25
1971	1846·4	6·4	1893·6	1·0	28·5	12·2	85	40
1972	1868·6	1·2	2025·7	7·0	30·6	7·4	88	33
1973	1825·7	−2·3	2143·9	5·8	35·5	16·0	82	33
1974	2155·6	18·1	2154·1	0·5	35·6	0·3	154	35
1975	2338·1	8·5	2209·5	2·6	38·6	8·4	96	37
1976	2400·3	2·7	2275·9	3·0	40·7	5·4	91	41

*offences 'decided by the court to be murder'

120

Table 12·4: POLICE ESTABLISHMENT AND STRENGTH

	Establishment	Strength	% shortfall
1969	119,055	101,071	15·1
1970	119,556	103,232	13·7
1971	120,454	106,409	11·7
1972	122,216	109,594	10·3
1973	124,401	110,619	11·1
1974	127,614	112,449	11·8
1975	129,152	118,028	8·6
1976	130,043	120,218	7·6

SOURCE: *Annual Abstract*

13 Race and Immigration

Immigration blew up into a major issue between the political parties at the beginning of 1978, paradoxically at a time when the figures showed that the rate of immigration into Britain had considerably slowed down. Nevertheless, the issue had been simmering more and more uneasily for years, an unease not dispelled by the operation of the 1971 Immigration Act which had originally been opposed by the Labour Party on the grounds that it was unnecessary. Neither race nor immigration had been a major issue in either election in 1974.

Both main parties assumed that good race relations depended on strict immigration control – an assumption rejected by the Labour left, who at the 1976 Party conference, called for the repeal of both the 1971 and the 1968 Immigration Acts. The Liberals, too, embraced a more open policy at their 1976 conference where they called for the removal of all restrictions on the entry of United Kingdom passport holders and unrestricted entry for dependants and fiancés of those already settled in the UK.

In the first couple of years of the new Labour administration the Home Secretary, Roy Jenkins, did three things to liberalise the immigration rules. He announced an amnesty for those who had entered illegally before 1 January 1973, the date that the new Immigration Act came fully into force, if they had been exempt from removal before this. He commented: 'I have had to balance the risk of encouraging the smuggling of immigrants against the need to allay the widespread apprehension within

121

the immigrant communities which the continued exercise of these retrospective powers would be likely to cause.' But it was attacked by the Opposition. James Prior, then Conservative Home Affairs spokesman, said that the amnesty would be unfair to legal immigrants and that 20,000 people, rather than the Home Secretary's estimate of 9–11,000, would benefit.

Jenkins's other liberal measures were to increase the number of UK passport holders from 3500 to 5000, to avoid a repetition of a crisis similar to the expulsion of the Uganda Asians, and to give Commonwealth or foreign husbands of British women the same right of entry as wives of British men.

The Conservatives denounced this last measure as being abused and called for it to be ended. The race and immigration climate then changed significantly for the worse with three separate events. The Home Office admitted an error in its immigration statistics, having underestimated the flow of immigrants in 1973 by about 60,000 – a fact seized upon by Enoch Powell. Alex Lyon, a junior minister at the Home Office, was sacked and there were some suggestions that this was because of his relatively liberal views. And then Powell obtained a copy of the Hawley report. This, compiled by a senior Foreign Office civil servant, alleged that there was an illegal immigrant industry and enumerated a number of other abuses. In vain did Alex Lyon claim that Hawley had been misled. The Conservatives pressed for accurate figures; William Whitelaw, the Shadow Home Secretary, said that British people wanted to know that there would be an end to all immigration; Jenkins was urged to tighten up control. Racial tension increased, with the murder of an Indian youth in Southall, London, in June 1976.

In 1977 the Home Secretary, now Merlyn Rees, did tighten up the rules again. Husbands of British women who married overseas would only be admitted for up to 12 months before being considered for settlement – an attempt to stop 'marriages of convenience'. The move was welcomed by Whitelaw, but he said that by itself the move did not go far enough.

Meanwhile, race relations were being acknowledged as a problem requiring new legislation. Concern was growing over discrimination in housing, education and employment. The Race Relations Act, an attempt to remedy this, was a most complex measure of 80 sections which tried to tread the tightrope between improving society and protecting individual freedom. Drafted along the lines of the Sex Discrimination Act, it created a new body, the Commission for Racial Equality, whose main task was to tackle wide patterns of discrimination.

The Conservatives broadly supported the measure (although a handful voted against it on second reading – see table), but the toughest opposition came from the House of Lords, most of whose many amendments were thrown out by the Commons. A major controversy erupted over the removal of the necessity to prove an intention to stir up racial hatred, with Whitelaw warning of 'dangerously arbitrary powers'. Another furore developed over the outlawing of discrimination in clubs, with Whitelaw commenting: 'It represents a completely revolutionary attitude to the private life of the citizen.'

The government, however, was coming under increasing attack from its own left wing over delays and restrictions in its immigration policy and over its insistence that good race relations depended on immigration control. Early in 1978 the Prime Minister told some reporters in Bangladesh that immigration was 'a problem for us, not for you'. Within days of his remark, immigration had blown up into a major election issue. Margaret Thatcher warned on television that Britain might become 'swamped' by peoples of a different culture. Conservatives, she said, wanted an end to immigration to maintain good race relations and to preserve 'fundamental British characteristics'. There was an immediate furore, with Labour and Liberal MPs denouncing her as a racialist and for attempting to steal the National Front vote.

In this highly charged atmosphere, the report of the Select Committee on Race Relations and Immigration achieved a heightened significance. The committee of five Labour and five Conservative MPs agreed that immigration needed to be tightened up, that a quota should be introduced for the Indian subcontinent, that there should be 'internal controls' and that all major immigration should be clearly stopped. The Labour left denounced the Labour members of the committee and the Home Secretary criticised the report. The Conservatives, however, said the report would not sufficiently cut back immigration and proposed a register of dependants and quotas to limit immigration from everywhere except the EEC.

Meanwhile, the Home Office had produced a discussion document on nationality law which said that the present citizenship of the United Kingdom and colonies should be replaced by British citizenship for those with close ties with the UK, and British overseas citizenship for other citizens of the United Kingdom and colonies. This suggestion was attacked by the Liberals who maintained that there should only be one class of citizen and that there should be no discrimination on grounds of race or sex. The Conservatives called for a new nationality

123

Table 13·1: IMMIGRANTS BY COUNTRY OF LAST RESIDENCE

*United Kingdom
thousands*

Country of last residence[1]	1966	1967	1968	1969	1970	1971	1972	1973	1974	1975	1976	1966–76
Commonwealth	113	132	138	119	125	118	134	109	97	109	95	1288
Old Commonwealth	36	46	50	46	54	52	50	50	40	43	40	507
Australia	20	28	27	26	32	32	32	32	23	26	25	302
Canada	9	10	12	13	15	13	11	11	7	7	7	118
New Zealand	7	8	10	7	8	7	7	7	10	10	8	88
New Commonwealth	76	86	88	73	70	66	84	59	57	66	55	780
African Commonwealth	21	18	23	17	20	27	45	23	19	22	18	252
Indian sub-continent[2]	27	40	40	32	28	24	23	17	16	20	16	282
West Indies	15	13	11	10	8	9	6	5	4	5	4	86
Other Commonwealth	14	15	14	14	15	9	11	14	18	19	18	160
Foreign	107	93	84	87	101	82	88	87	87	88	85	987
EEC[3]	37	30	27	29	32	21	24	24	29	23	25	301
Rest of Europe	25	21	17	18	23	17	17	15	14	13	11	191
USA	23	22	19	20	23	22	20	20	19	17	16	222
South Africa	7	6	6	6	7	8	8	9	6	8	9	80
Other foreign countries	15	14	14	13	16	14	18	20	19	28	23	193
Total	219	225	222	206	226	200	222	196	184	197	180	2275

[1] Excluding movement between the United Kingdom and the Irish Republic
[2] Including Pakistan
[3] Denmark is included in the European Economic Community (EEC) from 1973

SOURCE: OPCS Demographic Review

act to 'allay fears about immigration' but were not specific about its shape.

Table 13·2: HOUSING AMENITIES BY COLOUR, GREAT
          BRITAIN
(sample basis)
% of sample with

bath or shower	White	Coloured
Sole use	92	76
Shared use	3	16
None	5	8
inside W/C		
Sole use	91	75
Shared use	1	7
None	8	18

SOURCE: Social Trends, derived from general household survey of 1975–6

Table 13·3: MPs VOTING AGAINST SECOND READING, RACE
          RELATIONS BILL

      Budgen, Con, Wolverhampton SE;
      Molyneaux, UUUC, Antrim S;
    *Powell, UUUC, S Down;
      Ridley, Con, Cirencester;
    *Ross, UUUC, Londonderry;
      Stokes, Con, Halesowen;
      Stott, Lab, Westhoughton;
      Winterton, Con, Macclesfield.
Tellers: *Bell, Con, Beaconsfield;
      *Stanbrook, Con, Orpington.

* also opposed Sex Discrimination Bill

14   Social Reform

The years following 1974 were distinguished more by the number of social reforms that didn't take place than by those that did. The government's most notable failure was to reform the Official Secrets Act 1911, which it had promised in its October 1974 manifesto following the Franks report on official secrecy. The manifesto said that Section 2, the 'catch-all' clause, would be replaced by a measure which would impose a burden on public authorities to justify the withholding of information. The stated aim was to make the process of government more open to the public.

Secrecy, however, remained the order of the day, despite pressure from MPs of all parties for reform. The long-promised bill to reform the Official Secrets Act never materialised, despite a series of leaks which brought it into disrepute. The most spectacular of these was the leak to the magazine *New Society* of Cabinet documents about the government U-turn over child benefits. Despite the subsequent police investigation – which failed to discover the culprits – Michael Foot, Leader of the House of Commons, used the occasion to criticise the act for being like an 'unruly eiderdown' that flopped over everything.

Richard Crossman made a significant, if posthumous, contribution to the row with the publication of his *Diaries* which contained confidential details of government and Cabinet administration. The Attorney-General tried unsuccessfully to ban serialisation of the book in the *Sunday Times*, and the Radcliffe Committee recommended that restrictions should survive on the publication of information 'destructive of the confidential relationships on which our government system is based'. The Prime Minister, Mr Callaghan, made a modest contribution to open government by proposing that government sources should publish background information (though several requests by newspapers for such information subsequently failed); but he decided that Cabinet committees should remain secret.

The secrecy debate reached its peak with the deportation of Philip Agee, the former CIA agent, and Mark Hosenball, an American journalist on the London *Evening Standard*. The charges against them were never revealed in detail, but they were charged under Section 1 (the 'spy' clause) of the act for obtaining and disseminating information harmful to security. The government won a debate on the issue, despite serious concern by many MPs that the two were ignorant of the charges against them and so were unable to cross-examine.

The 1970s saw a flurry of other recommendations for social reform, many of which were not put into effect. In 1974 the Phillimore committee on contempt of court recommended relaxation of the rules of *sub judice*. In 1975 the Faulks committee on defamation recommended a simplification of procedure and the abolition of the distinction between libel and slander. None of these recommendations found its way onto the statute book.

However, the Law Commission's recommendation to limit the offence of conspiracy simply to conspiracy to commit a criminal act was implemented in the Criminal Law Act. The main social reform of the period, however, concerned opportunities and equal treatment for women. The Sex Discrimination Act made it unlawful to discriminate on grounds of sex in the fields of employment, education, housing, goods and services, and created an Equal Opportunities Commission to investigate discriminatory practices. It went much further than the Conservative White Paper on the subject which had been produced in 1973, and it was broadly supported by all three parties – although the Opposition were concerned that it might lead to expensive, time-consuming bureaucracy (for MPs opposing the legislation, see table 14·4). It became effective on the same day as the Equal Pay Act 1970.

Rape became an issue of political significance when in 1975 the Law Lords ruled that a man could not be guilty of rape if he believed that the victim had consented. This provoked a storm of protest and led to the setting up of the Heilbron committee, which decided that the Lords had been correct in principle but that a rape complainant should be protected in a number of ways. The following year the Sexual Offences (Amendment) Act was passed, which prohibited the naming of the complainant or, before conviction, the defendant.

The battering of women by their husbands or lovers became recognised as a widespread and serious problem. The many refuges that sprang up were clearly not sufficient, and so the Domestic Violence and Matrimonial Proceedings Act, sponsored by Jo Richardson, Labour MP for Barking, was passed. This gave women who were not in the process of separating from their husbands the power to get injunctions against their spouses or co-habitees to prevent them from entering the house.

Abortion was an issue which refused to go away. Despite the fact that the Lane committee recommended in 1974 that the 1967 Abortion Act should be liberalised to reduce the glaring inequalities in the availability of abortion throughout the country – another reform that was not put into practice – there were two attempts to make the law far more restrictive. The first was a Private Member's Bill introduced by James White, Labour MP for Glasgow Pollok, which received a second reading on 7 February 1975 by 203 votes to 88. It was referred to a select committee and subsequently lapsed. The select committee proposed some measures to tighten up private abortion practice. However William Benyon, Conservative MP for Buckingham, then put forward his Abortion (Amendment) Bill, ostensibly to reduce 'abuse' in the private sector but which would have substantially restricted the working of the Act. The bill was given a second reading on 25 February 1977 by 170 votes to 132, but eventually failed because the government refused to give it sufficient time.

Table 14·1: VOTING ON THE ABORTION AMENDMENT BILLS

7 February 1975

	For	Against	DNV	Total
Con	98	4	173	275
Lab	92†	84†	142	318†
Lib	4	2	7	13
Nat	7	0	7	14
Other	4	0	8	12
Total*	205	90	337	632†
		+ vacant seats		1
		+ Speaker and deputies		3
				636†

* includes tellers

† A. Wilson (Lab, Hamilton) is recorded as having voted in both lobbies.

26 February 1977

	For	Against	DNV	Total
Con	113	21	143	277
Lab	50	111	149	310
Lib	2	1	10	13
Nat	4	1	9	14
Other	3	0	11	14
Total*	172	134	322	628
		+ vacant seats		3
		+ Speaker and deputies		4
				635

* includes tellers

Table 14·2: ABORTIONS ANNUALLY SINCE 1969 (ENGLAND AND WALES); DIVORCES; ILLEGITIMACY

	Total	Proportion performed within NHS	Proportion to non-residents of GB	Divorces (England, Wales and Scotland)	Illegitimate births as proportion of all live births (UK)
1969	54,819	61·5	n.a.	55,221	8·1
1970	86,565	55·1	11·9	62,509	8·0
1971	126,777	42·4	25·0	78,922	8·2
1972	159,884	35·7	31·6	124,180	8·5
1973	167,149	33·3	33·2	112,673	8·5
1974	162,940	34·6	32·2	120,245	8·7
1975	140,521	36·9	23·3	128,317	9·0
1976	127,904	39·1	20·3	134,823	9·0
1977	132,999	39·2	22·5		

SOURCE: Written answer 21 April 1978; *Annual Abstract*

Table 14·3: SEX DISCRIMINATION IN POLITICAL PARTIES: PROPORTION OF WOMEN CANDIDATES AND MPs AT GENERAL ELECTIONS

	1970				Feb 1974				Oct 1974			
	Con	Lab	Lib	Nat	Con	Lab	Lib	Nat	Con	Lab	Lib	Nat
Women candidates	26	29	23	10	32	40	40	10	30	50	49	9
% of all	4	5	7	15	5	5	6	8	9	5	8	8
MPs	15	10	—	—	9	13	—	1	7	18	—	2
% of all	5	3	—	—	3	4	—	14	3	6	—	14

Table 14·4: MPs VOTING AGAINST SECOND READING, SEX DISCRIMINATION BILL

Gow, Con, Eastbourne;
McCusker, UUUC, Armagh;
Morgan-Giles, Con, Winchester;
*Powell, UUUC, S Down;
*Ross, UUUC, Londonderry.

Tellers: *Bell, Con, Beaconsfield;
*Stanbrook, Con, Orpington.

* also opposed Race Relations Bill

15 Devolution and the Regions

In July 1966, Welsh Nationalists – Plaid Cymru – won their first Westminster seat in a by-election at Carmarthen. In November 1967, the Scottish Nationalists won Hamilton, their first seat since 1945, when R. D. McIntyre represented Motherwell for three months. But at the 1970 election, the party lost Hamilton and won only one seat – Western Isles – and many in the main parties began to think the Nationalist threat was dying away.

The reprieve did not last long. Opinion polls and by-elections showed a steady growth in SNP and Plaid Cymru support during the 1970 Parliament. The Plaid took 37% of the vote in a by-election at Merthyr Tydfil in April 1972 and in November 1973 Margo Macdonald won Glasgow Govan for the SNP. And this time the tide did not recede when a General Election came round. The Scottish Nationalists won 7 seats in February 1974 and Plaid Cymru two; in October, the SNP won 11 seats, pushing their share of the vote in Scotland up to 30% and relegating the Conservatives to third place, while the Plaid took a third seat with 10·7% of the Welsh vote (see Part III).

For some time now the major parties had been working on plans to give the Scots and Welsh more power to determine their own affairs. The Conservatives were early on the road with Edward Heath's 1968 proposals for a directly elected Scottish Assembly. In 1969 Labour set up the Crowther (later Kilbrandon) Commission on the Constitution, which reported, with a battery of majority and minority reports, in 1973.

The Liberals had long argued that nothing short of a federal solution was adequate to meet the demands of the Scots and the Welsh, and had been talking in terms of greater devolution within England too.

But the electrifying rise of the nationalists – especially the SNP – added a new urgency to their proceedings. The result was the domination of the Westminster legislative programme for two successive years (1976–7 and 1977–8) by massive devolution bills which, but for the eventual imposition of a timetable, would have happily been debated by a faithful but unflagging few until doomsday.

It began with a White Paper on 27 November 1975. There was to be one bill for both Scotland and Wales setting up a legislative assembly for Scotland and an executive assembly for Wales. The Scots would have an executive, headed by a chief executive, and would be given a wide range of legislative and executive powers over domestic services including health, social work (but not social security), schools (but not universities), housing (though with restrictions over rent control, in the interest of national counter-inflation policies), roads and transport, and Scotland's already distinctive legal system. The Assembly would be denied power over mainstream economic matters, over industry, and over the two development agencies which were the Scottish and Welsh counterparts of the NEB.

To the disgust of the SNP, whose slogan, Scotland's oil, exemplified the extent to which oil had given old dreams a new credibility, the Scottish Assembly was not to be assigned the revenues from the oil in Scotland's off-shore waters. The only revenue-raising power given to the Assembly was the right to levy a surcharge on rates. The Welsh Assembly was given responsibility for a wide range of services throughout Wales, many of them previously exercised by the Secretary of State through the Welsh office, though some were at present exercised by appointed bodies.

The proposals were debated on a 'take note' motion – that is to say, the Commons was not specifically asked to approve or reject – on 19 January 1976. The Conservatives were highly critical; for the Liberals, Jeremy Thorpe saw the proposals as a recipe for conflict – which a federal solution would avoid. Two ultra-devolutionist Labour MPs, Jim Sillars and John Robertson, attended the debate as members of their own newly-founded Scottish Labour Party, having left Labour in protest against the restricted scope of the proposed Scottish Assembly. An unofficial backbench division produced a vote in the government's favour of 295 to 37.

It soon became clear that the government would have to contend not only with Conservative opposition and a very ambivalent attitude among Liberals and Nationalists; it also had to deal with a determined group among its own backbenchers who were convinced that the proposals were unworkable, unnecessary and even potentially fatal to the unity of the UK. Opponents of the bill argued that devolution would be the beginning of a slippery slope that would lead eventually to independence. The government said that if legitimate demands were ignored the clamour for independence would become unstoppable. As the White Paper had put it, 'the status quo is not an option'.

The bill got its second reading on 16 December 1976 by 292 votes to 247. There had been changes since the White Paper: the Scottish and Welsh development agencies were now to be devolved, though within government guidelines. The rate surcharge – predictably unpopular – had been dropped, and not replaced. Doubts about whether the Assembly might be exceeding its powers on a given issue were now to be resolved by judges, not Westminster politicians. Demands that the settlements should be put out to popular referendum were, however, still unacceptable.

But that demand, too, was met before long as the government scraped around for a second reading majority. The referendum announcement helped to win over some waverers; a handful of Conservatives, angered by a Shadow Cabinet decision to impose a three-line whip, decided to defy it (the Shadow Scottish Secretary and his deputy resigned); and so the government got its second reading motion safely through. Later, on 15 February 1977, the referendum was approved by 231 to 24.

But a bigger test still was on the way. Unchecked, the debates on this bill were likely to last for ever: there had to be a time-table, a 'guillotine'. But the Tory devolutionists, whatever their feelings at second reading, were not going to vote for that; nor were the Liberals, who were still unhappy about the form of the bill; the Labour rebels were unpersuadable. On the night of 22 February 1977, the guillotine vote was lost by 312 to 283.

Table 15·1: *BREAKDOWN OF GUILLOTINE VOTE*

	For	*Against*	*DNV*	*Total*
Con	0	274	3	277
Lab	264	22	25	311
Lib	2	11	0	13
Nat	14	0	0	14
Other	5	7	2	14
Total*	285	314	30	629
		+ vacant seats		2
		+ Speaker and deputies		4
* Includes tellers				635

That killed the bill. The government discussed and pondered; examined and rejected a Conservative plea for a grand constitutional conference embracing all parties. On 26 July Michael Foot reported the government's conclusions. There would be two bills, not one. Detailed controls by London over the work of the assemblies would be relaxed. The Scottish executive members would become 'secretaries' headed by a First Secretary (not a Prime Minister, though the ultra-devolutionists still hoped that day would come). There would be a power of premature dissolution even though the assemblies were elected for a fixed term (a lesson, this, learned from debates on the abandoned bill). There was still no independent power (or duty) to raise revenue – but the Assembly would now be funded on a fixed percentage figure instead of by a process of annual general hassle.

The Liberals and Nationalists thought all this an improvement; moreover the Liberals were now committed through the Lib-Lab pact to backing the bills as the best available staging post on the road to federalism. So the government's chances of success the second time round looked brighter. The Conservatives, on the other hand, had hardened. A devolutionist Scottish shadow secretary, Alick Buchanan-Smith, had been replaced by the arch-opponent of devolution, Teddy Taylor. The Tory commitment to a directly elected assembly had been discreetly ditched. Instead, they were calling for a constitutional conference to start again from scratch. Better yet more delay, they said, than a hopelessly botched solution.

On 16 November 1977, the Scotland Bill was guillotined by 313 votes to 287.

Table 15·2: VOTING ON THE SCOTLAND BILL, NOV 77

	For	Against	DNV	Total
Con	0	270	10	280
Lab	285	9	14	308
Lib	12	1	0	13
Nat	14	0	0	14
Other	4	9	1	14
Total*	315	289	25	629
		+ vacant seats		2
		+ Speaker and deputies		4
* Includes tellers				635

The Wales Bill was guillotined on the same day by 314 votes to 287.

Table 15·3: VOTING ON THE WALES BILL, NOV 77

	For	Against	DNV	Total
Con	0	275	15	280
Lab	286	6	16	308
Lib	12	0	1	13
Nat	14	0	0	14
Other	4	8	2	14
Total*	316	289	34	629
		+ vacant seats		2
		+ Speaker and deputies		4
* Includes tellers				635

The opposition remained fierce, and had most of the debate. On 25 January 1978, dissident Labour MPs, joined by Conservatives, wrote into the bill a provision that the government would have to move for the dropping of the Scotland Act if fewer than 40% of the Scottish electorate voted 'yes' in the referendum – a stipulation which had not been observed, or even suggested, with the European referendum. A similar provision was later added for Wales (for an analysis of major votes on devolution, which includes a breakdown of MPs backing the 40% rule see table 15·6). The debate on devolution within Wales was less vivid than that in Scotland, partly because nationalist feeling and Nationalist voting was confined in Wales to precise areas of the country, not spread right across the board as in Scotland. (The SNP lost no deposits in 71 seats in October 1974; Plaid Cymru lost 26 out of 36.) As for the English, their mood was difficult to detect, let alone interpret. Much of the English hostility to Scottish devolution had come from the north-east and north-west, where it was feared that Scotland's gains might be bought at their expense; the Assembly would eat up money which might otherwise have gone to Merseyside or Tyneside.

But there seemed more interest in depriving the Scots of their devolution settlement than in devising devolution settlements for the English regions. The government dutifully presented on 9 December 1976 a White Paper on English devolution, but there was little to it: as Michael Foot sadly observed, England 'just wasn't interested'.

Yet the regional imbalance of the country remained as striking as ever. When governments moved in Britain to damp down an overheated economy, it was London, the south-east, the Midlands which were feeling the heat, not the north, Scotland, or Wales – let alone Northern Ireland, where unemployment was most intractable (see chapter 19). The array of incentives that governments had provided over the years had at best prevented the gap from widening: they had certainly not closed it. And now the two incentives which, according to an inquiry by the Trade and Industry sub-committee of the Expenditure Committee of the Commons in 1973–4, were actually most valuable in persuading industry into the economically backward regions were disappearing: good roads were to be built more sparingly, to save public money; the regional employment premium was now considered to be too indiscriminate and was being discontinued.

The difficulty of ironing out inequities at a time when no region was doing very well was illustrated by the painful progress of David Owen's scheme for adjusting the astonishing discrepancies between one health region and another – the so-called RAWP (Resources Allocation Working Parties). The anguished cries of those whose advantages were being reduced quite drowned any sound of public gratitude from those who stood to gain.

Table 15·4: UNEMPLOYMENT IN THE REGIONS
(annual averages)

1968		1972		1976	
1. South East	1·6	1. South East	2·1	1. South East	2·8
2. East Midlands	1·8	2. East Anglia	2·9	2. East Midlands	4·9
3. East Anglia	2·0	3. East Midlands	3·1	East Anglia	4·9
West Midlands	2·0	4. South West	3·5	4. Yorks & Humb	5·6
5. North West	2·4	5. West Midlands	3·6	5. West Midlands	5·9
6. South West	2·5	6. Yorks & Humb	4·2	6. South West	6·5
Yorks & Humb	2·5	7. North West	4·8	7. Scotland	7·0
8. Scotland	3·7	8. Wales	5·2	8. North West	7·1
9. Wales	4·0	9. North	6·3	9. Wales	7·5
10. North	4·6	10. Scotland	6·4	10. North	7·6
11. N Ireland	7·1	11. N Ireland	7·8	11. N Ireland	10·3
Average, England:	2·1		3·3		5·4
UK:	2·5		3·8		5·8

SOURCE: Retabulated from *Annual Abstract*

Table 15·5: INFANT MORTALITY BY REGION (1975)

Deaths of infants under 1, per thousand live births.

South West	14·4
Wales	14·5
East Anglia	14·7
North	14·9
South East	15·0
East Midlands	15·1
West Midlands	16·9
Scotland	17·2
Yorks and Humb.	17·3
North West	17·3
N Ireland	20·4

SOURCE: *Social Trends*

Table 15·6: KEY VOTES ON DEVOLUTION

X denotes a vote for the government, O a vote against.
S denotes Speaker or deputy.

The votes shown are:

SW2R	Second Reading, Scotland and Wales Bill, 16 December 1976
SWG	Guillotine, Scotland and Wales Bill, 22 February 1977
S2R (W2R)	Second Reading, Scotland Bill, 14 November 1977 (for Wales, Second Reading Wales Bill, 15 November 1977)
SG (WG)	Guillotine, Scotland Bill, 16 November 1977 (and Guillotine of Wales Bill on the same day)
SPR (WPR)	Vote on method of election to be used for the Scottish Assembly, 23 November 1977. A vote for the government denotes support for First Past the Post, and a vote against the government (symbol O) a vote for proportional representation. (And similar table on PR for Wales 1 March 1978.)
REF	Vote on insertion of a 'hurdle' in the referendum; for Scotland 25 January 1978. O under this heading denotes a vote for the hurdle. (Lists for the equivalent votes on Wales were not published at the time because of an industrial dispute.)

Records of voting by Scottish MPs:

LAB MP	Constituency	SW 2R	SW G	S 2R	S G	S PR	REF
Bray, J.	Motherwell	X	X	X	X	X	—
Brown, H. D.	Provan	X	X	X	X	X	X
Buchan, N.	Renfrew W	X	X	X	X	X	X
Buchanan, R.	Springburn	X	—	X	X	X	—
Campbell, I.	Dunbarton W	X	X	X	X	X	X
Canavan, D.	Stirling W	X	X	X	X	X	X
Carmichael, N.	Kelvingrove	X	X	X	X	X	X
Cook, R. F.	Edinburgh C	X	X	X	X	X	O
Craigen, J.	Maryhill	X	X	X	X	—	—
Dalyell, T.	W Lothian	O	O	O	O	O	O
Dempsey, J.	Coatbridge	X	X	X	X	X	—
Doig, P.	Dundee W	X	X	X	X	X	O
Eadie, A.	Midlothian	X	X	X	X	X	X
Ewing, H.	Stirling	X	X	X	X	X	—
Galpern, Sir M.	Shettelston	S	S	S	S	S	S
Gourlay, H.	Kirkcaldy	X	X	X	X	X	—
Hamilton, J.	Bothwell	X	X	X	X	X	X
Hamilton, W.	Fife C.	X	O	X	X	—	O
Hart, Mrs J.	Lanark	X	X	X	X	X	X
Hughes, R.	Aberdeen N	X	—	X	X	X	O
Hunter, A.	Dunfermline	X	X	X	X	X	—

LAB MP	Constituency	SW 2R	SW G	S 2R	S G	S PR	REF
Lambie, D.	Ayrshire C.	X	X	X	X	—	X
Mabon, Dr D.	Greenock	X	X	X	X	—	X
Mackenzie, G.	Rutherglen	X	X	X	X	X	X
Mackintosh, J.	Berwickshire	X	X	X	X	—	—
MacLennan, R.	Caithness	X	X	X	X	—	—
McCartney, H.	Dunbarton C	X	X	X	X	X	X
McElhone, F.	Queen's Park	X	X	X	X	X	X
McMillan, T.	Glasgow C	X	X	X	X	X	X
Millan, B.	Craigton	X	X	X	X	X	X
Miller, Dr M.	E Kilbride	X	X	X	X	X	—
Murray, R. K.	Leith	X	X	X	X	X	X
Ross, W.	Kilmarnock	X	X	X	X	X	X
Selby, H.	Govan	—	X	X	X	—	—
Smith, J.	Lanark	X	X	X	X	X	X
Strang, G.	Edinburgh E	X	X	X	X	—	X
White, J.	Pollok	X	X	X	X	X	X

CON MP	Constituency	SW 2R	SW G	S 2R	S G	S PR	REF
Buchanan-Smith, A.	Angus N	X	O	X	—	O	X
Corrie, J.	Ayrshire N	—	O	O	O	—	—
Douglas-Hamilton, Lord J.	Edinburgh W	—	O	O	O	O	O
Fairbairn, N.	Kinross	O	O	O	O	X	—
Fairgrieve, R.	Aberdeenshire W	—	O	—	O	O	—
Fletcher, A.	Edinburgh N	—	O	O	O	O	—
Galbraith, T.	Hillhead	O	O	O	O	—	O
Gilmour, Sir J.	Fife E.	—	O	—	O	—	O
Gray, H.	Ross & Cromarty	X	O	X	O	O	—
Harvie Anderson, Miss B.	Renfrew E	O	O	O	O	—	O
Hutchison, M. C.	Edinburgh S	O	O	O	O	X	O
Monro, H.	Dumfries	—	O	O	O	O	O
Rifkind, M.	Pentlands	X	O	—	O	O	—
Sproat, I.	Aberdeen S	O	O	O	O	X	O
Taylor, E.	Cathcart	O	O	O	O	X	O
Younger, G.	Ayr	—	O	—	O	—	—

LIB MP	Constituency	SW 2R	SW G	S 2R	S G	S PR	REF
Grimond, J.	Orkney & S	X	O	X	X	—	—
Johnston, R.	Inverness	X	O	X	X	O	X
Steel, D.	Roxburgh	X	O	X	X	O	X

NAT PARTY MP	Constituency	SW 2R	SW G	S 2R	S G	S PR	REF
Bain, Mrs M.	Dunbarton E	X	X	X	X	O	X
Crawford, D.	Perth & E	X	X	X	X	O	X
Ewing, Mrs W.	Moray & N	X	X	X	X	O	X
Henderson, D.	Aberdeenshire E	X	X	X	X	O	X
McCormick, I.	Argyll	X	X	X	X	O	—

NAT PARTY MP	Constituency	SW 2R	SW G	S 2R	S G	S PR	REF
Reid, G.	Stirling E	X	X	X	X	O	—
Stewart, D.	W Isles	X	X	X	X	O	X
Thompson, G.	Galloway	X	X	X	X	O	X
Watt, H.	Banff	X	X	X	X	O	—
Welsh, A.	Angus S	X	X	X	X	O	X
Wilson, G.	Dundee E	X	X	X	X	O	X

SCOT LAB MP	Constituency	SW 2R	SW G	S 2R	S G	S PR	REF
Robertson, J.	Paisley	X	X	X	X	—	—
Sillars, J.	S Ayrshire	X	X	X	X	O	X

Record of voting by Welsh MPs:

LAB MP	Constituency	SW 2R	SW G	W 2R	W G	W PR
Abse, L.	Pontypool	—	O	O	O	X
Anderson, D.	Swansea E	—	—	X	X	X
Callaghan, J.	Cardiff SE	X	X	X	X	X
Coleman, D.	Neath	X	X	X	X	X
Davies, D.	Llanelli	X	X	X	X	X
Davies, I.	Gower	—	X	X	X	X
Ellis, T.	Wrexham	—	X	X	X	—
Evans, F.	Caerphilly	—	O	O	O	X
Evans, I.	Aberdare	—	—	—	X	X
Foot, M.	Ebbw Vale	X	X	X	X	X
Hughes, C.	Anglesey	X	X	X	X	X
John, B.	Pontypridd	X	X	X	X	X
Jones, A.	Rhondda	X	X	X	X	X
Jones, B.	Flint E	X	X	X	X	X
Kinnock, N.	Bedwellty	—	—	—	X	X
Morris, J.	Aberavon	X	X	X	X	X
Padley, W.	Ogmore	X	X	X	X	X
Roderick, C.	Brecon	X	X	X	X	X
Rowlands, E.	Merthyr	X	—	X	X	X
Thomas, J.	Abertillery	X	X	X	X	X
Williams, A.	Swansea W	X	X	X	X	X

CON MP	Constituency	SW 2R	SW G	W 2R	W G	W PR
Edwards, N.	Pembroke	O	O	O	O	O
Gower, Sir R.	Barry	O	O	O	O	O
Grist, I.	Cardiff N	O	O	O	O	X
Meyer, Sir A.	Flint W	O	O	O	O	O
Morgan, G.	Denbigh	O	O	O	O	X
Roberts, M.	Cardiff NW	O	O	O	O	X
Roberts, W.	Conway	O	O	O	O	—
Stradling Thomas, J.	Monmouth	O	O	O	O	X

LIB MP	Constituency	SW 2R	SW G	W 2R	W G	W PR
Hooson, E.	Montgomery	X	X	X	X	O
Howells, G.	Cardigan	X	X	X	X	O

NAT MP	Constituency	SW 2R	SW G	W 2R	W G	W PR
Evans, G.	Carmarthen	X	X	X	X	O
Thomas, D. E.	Merioneth	X	X	X	X	O
Wigley, D.	Caernarvon	X	X	X	X	O

16   Europe

Labour came into power at the February 1974 election committed to a 'fundamental renegotiation' of the terms on which the Conservatives had taken Britain into Europe. To this they added a second pledge – to submit the results of the renegotiation to the people through a referendum. It had been the Labour anti-marketeers who wanted to break the European connection, who had first supported a referendum. In the event, however, it became the means by which the Prime Minister and his Foreign Secretary were able to mobilise a public endorsement for their policy of keeping Britain in – against the opposition of their own Labour Party which wanted the renegotiated terms rejected.

The Foreign Secretary, James Callaghan, set out the government's terms for continuing British membership in two speeches in Luxembourg – on 1 April and again on 4 June. The first confronted the rest of the Nine bluntly – rather too bluntly for some tastes – with the contents of Labour's February manifesto. This demanded:

Major changes in the Common Agricultural Policy (CAP) especially to perpetuate access to British markets for low cost producers outside.

Trade and aid policies designed to help not just 'associated overseas territories' in Africa but developing countries throughout the world.

'New and fairer' methods of financing the Community budget (aimed specifically at reducing Britain's contribution).

The retention by Parliament of the powers over the economy necessary for effective regional, industrial and fiscal policies.

Agreed controls on capital movements to protect the balance of payments and home-based employment.

Economic and monetary union: 'we would reject any kind of international agreement which compelled us to accept increased unemployment for the sake of maintaining a fixed parity, as is required by the current proposals for a European Economic and Monetary Union.'

No harmonisation of VAT requiring the taxation of necessities which the UK had decided to exempt.

The second Luxembourg speech was considered notably more conciliatory than the first and contained an assurance that the renegotiation demands would not in the British government's view entail any changes in the basic treaties of the Community.

Negotiations continued throughout the year and were concluded at the Dublin EEC summit of 10–11 March 1975. On 18 March Wilson told the Commons that the objectives of the renegotiation had been 'substantially though not completely achieved'. He would recommend the terms to the Cabinet. He listed the results of the renegotiation as follows:

CAP: would cease to be a threat to the world trade in food. Low cost producers outside Europe would have continued access to the British market.

The Budget: cuts had been agreed which would bring down the UK contribution by an estimated £125 million a year.

Economic and monetary union: progress had been tacitly abandoned.

Regional industrial and fiscal policy: there would effectively be no blocks on the UK's freedom of action, and where such obstacles might otherwise exist they would be removed by derogations.

Commonwealth and developing countries: Commonwealth sugar and New Zealand dairy products would be given more generous treatment.

VAT: the threat of harmonisation had receded.

Capital movements: exchange controls would be maintained as before.

When the terms were put to the Cabinet, 7 ministers opposed acceptance: Michael Foot, Tony Benn, Peter Shore, Barbara Castle, John Silkin, Eric Varley and William Ross. A statement by the first 5 of these on 23 March said the renegotiated terms fell short even of minimum requirements. They could not accept them on economic grounds when Britain's trade deficit with Europe was running at £2 billion a year (see table 16·5). And they could not accept on political grounds when the rights of the British people and its elected Parliament remained subordinate to a non-elected Commission and Council of Ministers in Brussels.

With divisions in the Cabinet, as in the party, clearly irreconcilable, Wilson had already announced that the usual doctrine of collective Cabinet responsibility would in this case be suspended. Ministers opposed to the renegotiated terms would be allowed to vote against them in Parliament and campaign against them in the country, though Ministers would be expected to uphold the majority line in dealing with Parliamentary business. (The unwillingness of Eric Heffer, Minister of State in the industry department, to accept this condition led to his dismissal.) The lapsing of collective responsibility was denounced by the Conservatives, who saw it as an open abdication of government authority. The Conservatives did not condemn the renegotiated terms out of hand, but said that the whole renegotiation process had essentially been fraudulent, since such improvements as had been obtained could have been obtained through routine bargaining processes without the melodrama and tension of renegotiation.

On 9 April, the Commons approved the government recommendation to stay in the EEC by 396 votes to 170.

Table 16·1: VOTING ON STAYING IN EEC

	For	Against	DNV	Total
Con	249	8	18	275
Lab	137	145	33	315
Lib	12	0	1	13
Nat	0	13	1	14
Other	0	6	6	12
Total*	398	172	59	629

+ vacant seats 2

+ Speaker and deputies 4

635

* Includes tellers.

Thirty-eight ministers voted against accepting the terms.

On the following day, the Commons approved the Referendum Bill on second reading by 312 votes to 248.

A special conference of the Labour Party on 26 April rejected the terms, approving a recommendation from the National Executive for withdrawal by 3,724,000 to 1,986,000.

141

The referendum was held on 5 June and resulted in a majority of over two to one in favour of staying in. Support was highest in the south and lowest in the regions most distant from London, with Northern Ireland showing only a narrow majority for continued membership. In general, the yes vote was distinctly higher in Conservative or Liberal dominated areas and lower in areas of Labour domination. The only areas voting against continued membership were Shetland and Western Isles.

Table 16·2: VOTING IN REFERENDUM, JUNE 1975

	% yes	% no	Turnout
England	68·6	31·4	64·6
Wales	64·8	35·2	66·7
Scotland	58·4	41·6	61·7
N Ireland	52·1	47·9	47·4
Total	67·2	32·8	64·5

After the result, the Prime Minister declared: 'The debate is now over.' Leading campaigners against British membership also accepted the verdict as final. Tony Benn said: 'I read the message loud and clear. When the British people speak, everyone – including ourselves – should tremble before their decision.'

In practice, though, Britain's future in Europe turned out to be far from tranquil. Britain remained a member of the Community, but a far from enthusiastic member, and there was a series of disputes with the Community which led some in Europe to conclude that perhaps de Gaulle had been right, and the British were inherently incapable of being good Europeans. John Silkin, appointed Agriculture Minister in September 1976, took a robustly combative line over successive issues in agricultural and fisheries policy (see also Part II ch. 8); there were wrangles over Britain's unwillingness to be represented by the EEC in a major international conference on energy in December 1975; over the siting of a nuclear fusion research centre (the Joint European Torus) which Britain argued – in the end, successfully – should be based at Culham in Oxfordshire; over the EEC requirement that tachographs should be installed in lorry-drivers' cabs; over the contents of ice cream; and over the alleged wish of the Community to get its hands on a greater share of North Sea oil, to eliminate the British Milk Marketing Board (which suddenly to its surprise found itself a much-loved British institution) and even to drive the British milkman off the streets.

Both major parties shifted to what might be called a 'minimalist' position, supporting continuing British membership but rejecting many of the supra-national and federalist ambitions of the founding fathers. Mrs Thatcher, much less of a European crusader than her predecessor Edward Heath, saw the community developing as 'a partnership of nation states each retaining the right to protect its vital interests, but developing more effectively than at present the habit of working together'.

This shift was nothing like enough, however, for the Labour anti-marketeers, mostly but not exclusively from the left of the party. Alarmed by what they saw as the unchecked drift of investment and jobs across the Channel and the steadily accumulating deficit on Britain's trade with the rest of the Nine (see table 16·5) they began in the spring of 1977 to revive the demand that Britain should leave the EEC. A resolution to this effect was passed by the Tribune Group in May, and resolutions on the same lines were prepared for the party conference in October.

The Prime Minister's response was to write to the general secretary of the party, Ron Hayward, a letter setting out the terms round which he believed the party might unite. Withdrawal, he said, would cause a profound upheaval not only to our relations with Europe but also to our relations with the rest of the world, particularly the United States. 'The best way forward for us,' he wrote, 'is to define the essential elements of a distinctive policy that will meet the legitimate concern and interests of the British people and will strengthen unity and democracy in Europe.' There were six areas which deserved attention: the maintenance of the authority of national governments and parliaments; the democratic control of Community business; the need in framing common policies to allow governments to attain their own economic, industrial and regional objectives; reform of the CAP; development of a Community energy policy compatible with national interests; and enlargement of the Community. (This last was supported by most minimalists, who believed that the wider and more diverse the Community became, the harder it would be to unify its national practices.)

The party accepted the Callaghan formula. But one element of the argument refused to lie down. The Labour Party remained opposed to the holding of direct elections for the European Assembly. At its 1976 conference, it voted against them by 4,016,000 to 2,264,000. The government ignored this vote – the Foreign Secretary had already made it clear that he regarded Britain as irrevocably committed – and a bill to authorise direct elections was produced in June 1977. It was given a second reading on 7 July by 394 votes to 147 but made no further progress. Reintroduced in the new session, it was again approved, this time by 381 votes to 98, on 24 November.

Table 16·3: VOTING FOR DIRECT ELECTIONS

	For	Against	DNV	Total
Con	229	16	35	280
Lab	132	74	102	308
Lib	11	0	2	13
Nat	9	3	2	14
Other	2	7	5	14
Total*	383	100	146	629

+ vacant seats 2
+ Speaker and deputies 4

* Includes tellers.   635

The bill now stipulated that elections should be held by a form of proportional representation – the Regional List system. This was for two reasons. The UK had made such slow progress that it was in danger of defaulting on the agreed date for elections, in the summer of 1978. If the traditional first-past-the-post system was used, boundaries would need to be drawn, which would rule out any chance of being ready on time. The regional list system required no drawing of boundaries. It was also necessary as part of the Lib-Lab pact since Callaghan had promised the Liberal leader David Steel to use his best endeavours to get a PR system adopted. His best endeavours however failed to persuade even some of his Cabinet colleagues, and Labour MPs were allowed a free vote. The result, on 13 December, was the adoption of an amendment favouring the use of first-past-the-post (see also, voting records table 20·1).

Table 16·4: VOTING ON THE REGIONAL LIST

	PR	FPP	DNV	Total
Con	61	198	22	281
Lab	147	115	46	308
Lib	13	0	0	13
Nat	2	0	12	14
Other	1	8	5	12
Total*	224	321	85	630

+ vacant seats 1
+ Speaker and deputies 4

* Includes tellers.   635

The Liberal Party Assembly the previous September had demanded that Labour support for PR should be regarded as a 'crucial indicator' of its commitment to the pact. In the event, only a minority of Labour MPs had voted for PR; 14 ministers, among them three Cabinet ministers, had been among those voting against it. But a special assembly of the party in January decided it would not be right to break off the pact on this score – especially since the electorate was unlikely to consider this an issue which demanded a General Election. The bill completed its Commons stages on 16 February 1978 and a new target date for European elections was fixed for June 1979.

Table 16·5: UK TRADE WITH EEC AND WITH OTHER SECTORS
(£m)

	EEC	Rest of Western Europe	N America	Oil exporters	Total
1970	+ 44	+178	−484	− 114	− 25
1971	− 185	+118	−172	− 188	+ 279
1972	− 584	− 37	− 79	− 131	+ 701
1973	−1182	−277	−278	− 329	−2354
1974	−2027	−352	−696	−2216	−5195
1975	−2405	− 55	−659	− 701	−3205
1976	−2082	+ 5	−805	− 697	−3510
1977	−1678	+236	−734	+ 893	−1612

(balance of payments basis)

SOURCE: Department of Trade and Industry

Table 16·6: ESTIMATED PAST AND FORECAST CONTRIBUTIONS TO EEC BUDGET 1973 TO 1982

£ million

	Gross contributions	Receipts	Net contributions
1973	181	79	102
1974	181	150	31
1975	342	398	− 56
1976	463	296	167
1977	750	335	415
1978	1090	450	640
1979	1225	450	775
1980	1315	455	860
1981	1280	460	820
1982	1290	465	825

SOURCE: Public Expenditure White Paper 1978

17 Foreign Policy

Foreign policy was little debated in the Commons in the mid-seventies and still less discussed outside – a mark, no doubt, of Britain's declining influence in the world. Both main parties remained committed to the Atlantic Alliance and British membership of the EEC (but see Part II ch. 16). The Conservatives under Mrs Thatcher took a notably more hostile line towards the Soviet Union, whose Press at one stage dubbed her the Iron Maiden. They were deeply sceptical about the agreement on détente reached at the Helsinki conference in 1975, arguing that the Soviet Union's record – as for instance, in its activities in Africa – clearly demonstrated its unreadiness to carry out in practice the obligations accepted in the Helsinki agreement.

Aside from Europe, the most demanding issue of foreign policy was southern Africa and especially Rhodesia. For a long period after the Unilateral Declaration of Independence in November 1965 the two great parties had taken a largely bi-partisan approach. A segment of the Conservative Party defended the Smith government and opposed the renewal of sanctions year by year – but they rarely mustered much over two dozen votes.

Britain's changed attitude towards southern Africa was dictated both by political judgement and by the shifts in our trading pattern which made countries of black Africa, as well as the Arab states of the Middle East, more important to us. The Conservatives were much more generally apprehensive than Labour about a progressive Russian (and, from Angola onwards, Cuban) infiltration of Africa. While some Conservatives deduced from this the need to shore up the white anti-Marxist regimes of South Africa and Rhodesia, Labour saw it as a warning not to become closely identified with white governments and so appear hostile to the aspirations of black Africa.

These tensions were to be seen at work in the reaction to the 'internal settlement' reached by Ian Smith and three black leaders in March 1978, and the attempts of the Patriotic Front of Joshua Nkomo and Robert Mugabe, backed by the presidents of surrounding black states, to persuade the West not to endorse it. The internal settlement came at the end of a long and convoluted series of attempts to find settlements, internal or external, for Rhodesia. One was under way soon after Labour returned to office in Britain: in the winter of 1974, the South

Africans, prompted by the withdrawal of Portugal from Mozambique and thereafter Angola, began putting pressure on Rhodesia to get talks under way. In December, the three principal black leaders, Nkomo, the Rev Ndabaninge Sithole and Bishop Abel Muzorewa, united their organisations in the African National Congress and began negotiations with Smith.

The new alliance was soon riven by disputes and after the failure of talks in a train above the Victoria Falls in August 1975 it broke up, with Muzorewa and Nkomo each trying to expel the other. Between December 1975 and March 1976 there were further talks between Smith and Nkomo during which a complicated system of inter-related voting lists was devised in an attempt to reassure white opinion, but the formula was not acceptable to Smith's Rhodesia Front Party and the talks collapsed. During 1976 guerrilla incursions into Rhodesia intensified. Mozambique closed the border: the success of the Russian-backed MPLA in Angola alarmed the white community in Southern Africa and the Conservative Party in Britain. In a debate in March Tory backbenchers called for the immediate lifting of sanctions and even for arms to be sent to the Smith government, but the front bench spokesman for the party resisted both demands and, like the government, urged a swift transition to majority rule.

On 22 March, the Foreign Secretary, James Callaghan, called for agreement on all the groups involved in deciding Rhodesia's future on the basis of majority rule within 18 months to two years, a bar on independence before then, and undertakings that the transition would be peaceful and not unduly protracted. In the autumn, the US Secretary of State, Henry Kissinger, working in close cooperation with Britain, produced a package based on a transition to majority rule within two years. A council of state was to be set up, with equal numbers of white and black members, under a white chairman, supervising a council of ministers who would draw up a new constitution.

Against most expectations, Smith accepted, largely it seemed because of accumulating evidence of rapid deterioration both in Rhodesia's military and its economic situation. (The economic depression which had hit so many countries had damaged the Rhodesian economy too and made its costly defence effort look hardly sustainable.) The outcome was a conference at Geneva from October to December, chaired by Britain, attended by the four principal black leaders: Nkomo and Robert Mugabe, who had united their forces in a Patriotic Front, Sithole and Muzorewa. The conference made virtually no progress, and the whole Rhodesian equation was further complicated on 9 January when the black African presidents agreed to endorse the Patriotic Front.

From now on Smith concentrated his efforts on an internal settlement with Muzorewa and Sithole. A revised set of proposals was put forward by the British in January, giving a central role to a resident commissioner backed by armed forces. A further joint British-US initiative produced proposals, published on 1 September, based on these principles:

1 The surrender of power by the illegal regime and a return to legality
2 An orderly and peaceful transition to independence in 1978
3 Free impartial elections on universal adult suffrage
4 Britain to establish a transitional administration
5 A UN presence, including a UN force, to be present throughout the transition
6 An independence constitution to be established, providing for a democratically elected government, abolition of discrimination, protection of individual human rights and independence of the judiciary
7 A development fund to revive the economy
It was stipulated that independence should come not less than 6 months after the return to legality.

Meanwhile, however, Smith had been working towards agreement with Muzorewa, Sithole and a black tribal leader long favourable to the Smith regime, Chief Chirau. On 1 March they announced agreement on an internal settlement based on a parliament of 100 members of which 28 would be white (20 of these seats to be filled by white electors only, the rest by all electors from a slate of white candidates). There would be an executive council of the Prime Minister (Smith) and the three black leaders, supervising a ministerial council working on cabinet lines and including equal numbers of whites and blacks. In exchanges in the British House of Commons on 9 March 1978, Callaghan and Margaret Thatcher agreed on the advisability of Nkomo and Mugabe becoming associated in the settlement. But there seemed little practical chance of that.

The problem for the Foreign Secretary, David Owen, was this. He feared that the internal settlement, with Nkomo and Mugabe excluded and hostile, might lead to an intensification rather than an end of the guerrilla war and to a possible widening of the conflict. If the British government were to be identified with the internal settlement in these circumstances it might appear in Africa as a defender of entrenched white interest, thus destroying its credit in much of the continent. Yet he was unwilling to write off the internal solution, as the front-line presidents wished him to do, as just another attempt by Smith to perpetuate white supremacy, this time with the aid of complaisant black leaders. Popular support for Muzorewa and Sithole – possibly greater support than there was for Nkomo and Mugabe: without elections there was no way of telling – was too deeply entrenched to be dismissed out of hand. His only hope, therefore, was to find some way of bridging the gap between the two sides and in some way associating Nkomo and Mugabe – or at least Nkomo – with the settlement.

As time went on, Owen came under fierce pressure from the Conservative Party to abandon this line in favour of endorsement of the internal settlement – which, it was pointed out, satisfied all the tests of the 'six principles' laid down by successive British governments except one – the test of popular opinion – which couldn't be taken yet. In a debate on 4 May 1978, the old bipartisan line seemed in danger of breaking as the Conservative front bench spokesman, John Davies, warned that the party might no longer be able to continue its support for sanctions now that Smith had reached this settlement. Conservative criticism of Owen's refusal to encourage the settlement reached a new peak of ferocity after a massacre of missionaries at Vumba in June 1978. Some Conservative backbenchers said the British government must share responsibility for their deaths.

Table 17·1: BRITAIN'S MAIN TRADING PARTNERS, 1968 AND 1976

(£m)

IMPORTS	1968		1976
1 US	1056·2	1 US	3042·8
2 Canada	513·9	2 W Germany	2755·0
3 W Germany	436·4	3 Netherlands	2425·1
4 Netherlands	393·1	4 France	2089·9
5 Sweden	314·5	5 Benelux	1300·2
6 France	312·6	6 Sweden	1186·7
7 S Africa	272·0	7 Canada	1159·9
8 Ireland	271·0	8 Italy	1103·8
9 Denmark	239·2	9 Iran	1046·6
10 Italy	235·9	10 Ireland	1006·2
11 Australia	211·0	11 Saudi A	977·8
12 New Zealand	196·7	12 Switzerland	961·7
13 Benelux	174·2	13 Japan	795·8
14 Norway	162·2	14 Denmark	704·9
15 Finland	160·7	15 USSR	645·1
16 USSR	158·1	16 Norway	623·0

EXPORTS	1968		1976
1 US	907·6	1 US	2447·7
2 W Germany	364·8	2 W Germany	1833·9
3 Australia	320·6	3 France	1708·8
4 Ireland	279·0	4 Netherlands	1498·8
5 Canada	268·7	5 Benelux	1400·5
6 S Africa	266·3	6 Ireland	1246·2
7 Sweden	263·7	7 Sweden	1045·0
8 Netherlands	256·1	8 Switzerland	1000·0
9 France	254·3	9 Italy	825·4
10 Benelux	244·0	10 Nigeria	773·9
11 Italy	178·8	11 Australia	687·6
12 Denmark	164·0	12 Denmark	654·6
13 Switzerland	141·6	13 S Africa	645·3
14 Norway	127·9	14 Canada	628·7
15 USSR	104·9	15 Iran	513·1
16 New Zealand	104·4	16 Norway	473·4

SOURCE: *Annual Abstract*

Table 17·2: OVERSEAS AID, BRITAIN AND OTHER COUNTRIES

(% of GNP)

	UK Official	Private	Total	Belgium	France	W Germany	Italy	Japan	Netherlands	Sweden	USA
1970	0·37	0·64	1·01	1·19	1·24	0·79	0·73	0·92	0·73	0·74	0·63
1971	0·41	0·64	1·05	1·09	1·00	0·88	0·85	0·96	1·63	0·69	0·67
1972	0·40	0·58	0·98	1·16	1·06	0·67	0·55	0·93	1·42	0·66	0·66
1973	0·37	0·24	0·61	1·10	1·10	0·52	0·46	1·42	1·03	0·73	0·64
1974	0·42	0·78	1·20	1·11	1·23	0·83	0·27	0·65	1·30	1·15	0·71
1975	0·38	2·11	2·50	1·36	1·16	1·17	0·95	0·59	1·56	1·09	1·15
1976	0·39	0·60	0·99	1·83	1·32	1·19	0·85	0·72	1·96	1·53	0·74
1977†	0·38*	—	—	0·46	0·63	0·27	0·09	0·21	0·85	0·99	0·22

* provisional
† official flows only

SOURCE: Overseas Development Ministry (OECD)

18   Defence

Labour came to office committed to reduce public spending on defence. The formula – less drastic than successive party conferences had asked for – was to reduce the proportion of the gross domestic product spent on defence to about that of other European countries (see table 18·3). A defence statement at the end of 1974, said to have been designed to meet this commitment, was attacked by the Conservatives on the grounds that its cuts imperilled national security, and by the Labour left on the grounds that it was not really cutting defence spending at all (it allowed for a rise on current levels of spending, but fixed this well below what had been planned in earlier defence reviews). The subsequent Labour years produced further rounds of cuts, each producing the same arguments. The Conservatives condemned the lot, saying that however stringent the economic circumstances which were forcing the government to cut spending they did not justify these reductions in Britain's security. Any future Conservative spending cuts, they promised, would exempt defence. The Labour left remained dissatisfied by the distance between the cuts the movement was demanding and the cuts which the Labour government was ready to offer.

The government's position, as spelled out in successive White Papers, was this. The NATO alliance – now overwhelmingly the focus of our defence effort – remained essential to our national interests. Disarmament could be pursued by various routes: there were the negotiations on a comprehensive test ban treaty, the Vienna talks on mutual and balanced force reductions, and the intermittent US-USSR dialogue on strategic arms limitation (SALT). Meanwhile, however, the West must remain vigilant and well-prepared about Soviet intentions, since their activities on the ground looked less pacific than much of what they usually said. The Warsaw Pact, said the 1975 White Paper, faced the NATO alliance with a marked superiority in manpower and conventional weapons. The 1976 White Paper reported that in conventional ground and air forces the imbalance in central Europe had moved further in the Warsaw Pact's favour, and the 1977 White Paper warned: 'Détente has reduced the political tensions between East and West but has not yet resulted in a lessening of military confrontation.' The 1978 White Paper found the capability of the Warsaw Pact forces 'formidable and growing'. 'On any view,' it said, 'Soviet forces have in many areas been strengthened in size and quality on a scale which goes well beyond the needs of any purely defensive posture.'

Yet even on this basis, Britain could not spend more than her troubled economy could reasonably provide. 'It would be wrong for Britain,' said the 1977 White Paper, 'to try to sustain a defence contribution out of all proportion to her economic strength. The attempt would in the long run have adverse effects on our security, since our ability to make an effective defence contribution depends on the strength of our economy.' Or as the Defence Minister, Fred Mulley, put it in October 1976: 'Just as it would be wrong to endanger national security in our concern with social justice, so it is no good having a defence policy which could bankrupt the society it is designed to defend.'

The first round of cuts, ordered by Defence Secretary Roy Mason in December 1974 and amplified in the Defence White Paper of 19 March 1975, was designed to save £4700 million over 10 years, so reducing the cost of the programme from 5.5% to 4.5% of GNP. Expected savings were to rise from £300 million in 1975–6 to £500 million a year by 1978–9 and £750 million by 1983–4. Service manpower would be reduced by 5000 for the Navy, 15,000 for the Army and 18,000 for the RAF, and 10,000 jobs in defence industries would have to go. Commitments were to be abandoned or reduced, especially in South-East Asia; the agreement with the South Africans for the use of the Simonstown base would be ended. Re-equipment plans in all three services would be sharply cut. When the plans were debated on 16 December 1974, 52 Labour backbenchers voted against them.

A further round of cuts was ordered in the 1975 Budget. These took an additional £110 million off the White Paper programme. In a debate on 7 May, 57 Labour MPs voted against the government in protest against the 'inadequate' extent of the cuts, but the Conservatives voted with the government, giving it a majority of 432.

The extent of these cuts caused consternation in NATO – as a report by a select committee in January 1976 warned the government – and the Chief of Defence Staff, Field Marshal Sir Michael Carver, said the services were now down to 'absolute bedrock'. But defence was again a casualty, along with so much else, in the Public Expenditure White Paper of February 1976, when additional cuts of £173 million in 1977–8 and £198 million in 1978–9 were ordered; in the July measures of the same year, when a further £100 million was docked from the 1977–8 programme; and in the post-IMF cuts of December 1976, which struck £100 million out of the programme for 1977–8 and £200 million out of that for 1978–9.

This last assault brought a public protest from NATO, whose secretary-general, Joseph Luns, wrote to the Defence Minister, Fred Mulley 'deploring' what had been done: 'it must be recognised that the present reduction cannot but be detrimental to the effectiveness of the United Kingdom's forces, in as much as previous cuts practically exhausted the possibilities of finding savings in areas which could be considered as not directly related to NATO . . . it is particularly disturbing that these negative developments coincide with a sharpened awareness in the Alliance of the unremitting effort made by the Warsaw Pact to improve its defensive posture and the implications of this for our future security.'

None of that cut much ice with the Labour Party. In October 1976, its conference endorsed a report from a sub-committee of the National Executive setting out ways of removing £1300 million from the defence budget by 1983–4. Denied publication under the official Labour Party imprint, as originally planned, it was later published in paperback by Quartet Books under the title, *Sense about Defence*.

In Parliament too the left was fighting for further cuts. On 14 December, 47 Labour MPs voted for a £272 million reduction in a £517 million defence supplementary estimate, and in January 1977 there was the largest defence revolt so far, when 76 Labour MPs backed a Tribune Group amendment declaring that its planned cuts of £300 million in defence spending over the next two years were too small. (For voting on this amendment, see the table of major Labour rebellions on pp. 174–7).

Table 18·1: PUBLIC EXPENDITURE ON DEFENCE

(1) – Total expenditure (£m)
(2) – Expenditure as proportion of total public spending
(3) – Expenditure as proportion of GNP

	1	2	3
1966	2202	15·2	6·6
1967	2406	14·4	6·9
1968	2436	13·3	6·5
1969	2286	12·1	5·7
1970	2459	11·9	5·6
1971	2760	11·9	5·6
1972	3090	11·8	5·5
1973	3410	11·2	5·3
1974	4132	10·5	5·5
1975	5214	10·1	5·5
1976	6176	10·6	5·6

SOURCE: National Income and Expenditure (*Blue Book*)

Table 18·2: THE DECLINE OF DEFENCE MANPOWER

thousands

	Royal Navy and Marines	Army	RAF	Total
1967	97·0	196·2	124·1	417·4
1968	95·1	189·4	120·3	404·8
1969	90·2	178·5	114·3	383·6
1970	86·0	174·0	113·0	373·0
1971	82·5	173·4	112·1	368·0
1972	82·4	178·3	110·7	371·4
1973	81·2	179·8	105·9	367·0
1974	78·3	171·7	99·2	349·3
1975	76·2	167·1	95·0	338·3
1976	76·1	169·8	90·7	336·6
1977	76·2	167·3	86·9	330·5

SOURCE: *Annual Abstract*

Table 18·3: NATO DEFENCE SPENDING

As proportion of GNP of each country (figures from International Institute for Strategic Studies)

	1970	1971	1972	1973	1974	1975	1976†
Belgium	2·6	2·1	2·0	2·7	2·8	3·0	3·0
Canada	2·1	1·9	1·9	2·0	2·1	2·2	1·9
Denmark	2·5	2·3	2·3	2·1	2·2	2·2	2·8
France	3·5	3·5	3·4	3·5	3·6	3·9	3·7
W Germany*	3·4	3·6	3·8	3·4	3·6	3·7	3·6
Greece	3·5	3·8	3·9	4·1	4·0	6·9	5·5
Italy	2·7	3·0	3·0	3·0	2·9	2·6	2·6
Luxembourg	0·9	0·9	0·9	0·8	0·9	1·1	1·2
Netherlands	3·5	3·4	3·3	3·3	3·4	3·6	3·4
Norway	3·5	3·4	3·3	3·2	3·1	3·1	3·1
Portugal	6·1	5·8	5·2	6·2	6·6	6·0	3·9
Turkey	3·5	3·8	3·6	4·1	3·7	9·0	5·6
UK	4·8	4·8	4·9	4·9	5·1	4·9	5·1
US	7·7	7·2	6·4	6·1	6·1	5·9	6·0

* Including aid to W Berlin.
† Provisional

SOURCE: The Military Balance (IISS)

Table 18·4: NATO DEFENCE SPENDING AT CONSTANT PRICES

Growth since 1970

Index: 1970=100

	1971	1972	1973	1974	1975	1976
Belgium	101·3	107·0	110·9	115·4	124·7	129·8
Canada	100·6	100·8	100·6	108·0	106·6	114·0
Denmark	109·4	108·9	103·6	113·2	122·9	121·3
France	99·8	99·2	101·1	108·1	112·5	116·5
W Germany	107·2	114·6	119·0	124·2	123·6	122·2
Greece	105·8	112·6	112·9	108·1	172·6	198·4
Italy	113·1	125·0	124·7	124·8	116·7	113·0
Luxembourg	101·6	112·9	124·1	133·5	141·8	151·9
Netherlands	104·7	108·2	110·0	117·9	120·7	118·1
Norway	102·5	102·6	103·3	106·0	115·0	115·3
Portugal	104·7	103·3	95·4	114·4	78·6	60·5
Turkey	114·3	123·6	131·1	147·0	259·8	253·2
UK	105·2	113·7	112·0	115·9	114·6	117·8
US	92·3	92·6	88·1	86·9	84·3	86·8

SOURCE: The Military Balance (IISS)

19   Northern Ireland

From the first outbreak of a new generation of troubles in August 1968, successive British governments had two aims in Northern Ireland: to reduce and eventually eliminate the levels of violence, and to construct new political institutions capable of taking the endemic hatred out of the province. They had limited success in the first objective, and virtually none in the second.

The level of killings reached its peak in 1972 (see table 19·1) and then declined, only to surge up again in 1976. During 1977 a period of peace set in which led to hopes that the worst of the troubles might be over: there was even a month in which no civilian was killed. But the respite did not last long. Though the level of violence which had prevailed in 1972 mercifully never returned, a steady succession of killings through the winter of 1977–8 demonstrated beyond doubt that the Provisional IRA was not finished yet.

Merlyn Rees, who had succeeded the Conservative Francis Pym as Northern Ireland Secretary, was determined that internment, introduced by the Conservative Home Secretary Reginald Maudling in August 1971, must be phased out. Despite much provocation, he persisted in this course and the last detainee was released on 5 December 1975. (1891 people had been held during the period of internment.)

Meanwhile, however, the Emergency Provisions Act, introduced in 1973 to provide special non-jury trials for alleged terrorist offences, was renewed by Labour and then redrawn – following the report of a committee under the former Lord Chancellor Lord Gardiner on the working of the legislation – in a new bill in 1975. (For Labour opposition to this legislation, see table 20·2.) A series of killings on the mainland, culminating in 20 deaths in Birmingham on 21 November 1974, led to the passage through the Commons on 27–8 November of a Prevention of Terrorism Act which banned the IRA in Britain, gave the government power to serve exclusion orders, empowered police arrests without warrants and extended, in this case, the time for which a suspect might be held while not yet charged. (See also Part II ch. 14.)

The February 1974 General Election had come at a very damaging time for Northern Ireland. The power-sharing Executive set up as a result of the Assembly elections of 28 June 1973 had taken office only a month earlier, and the return in the Westminster elections of MPs almost all of whom were wholly opposed to the power-sharing arrangement was a crucial blow to its chances of survival. The experiment lasted until May. What brought it down then was an Assembly vote in favour of the Sunningdale Agreement of the previous December, the terms of which had included the recognition of an 'Irish dimension' in the politics of the island and the setting up of a Council of Ireland as a bridge between North and South. A strike in protest against the Assembly vote was organised by a body calling itself the Ulster Workers' Council. The province was before long paralysed. The Executive reluctantly asked Rees to set some kind of dialogue going with the strikers. He refused. The Unionist members then left the Executive and power-sharing collapsed.

London responded by calling a constitutional convention to examine new political arrangements for the province. It was stipulated that the new arrangements would need to be based on power-sharing and that the Irish dimension must continue to be recognised. Elections for the convention took place on 1 May 1975 using the single transferable vote system of proportional representation. But the majority of the 78 seats – 46 in all – went to parties opposed to power-sharing, and the convention found itself quite unable to agree on any recommendations which fell within the lines laid down by London. In the end, the convention produced a report embodying the recommendations of its Unionist majority. These called for a form of devolved government on similar lines to the old Stormont, though with a system of committees designed to give a greater weight to the minority community. Inevitably, the British government saw nothing here on which a new pattern of devolved administration could be founded. The recommendations were rejected on the grounds that they were unlikely to mobilise a wide enough basis of consent – a view which the Conservative opposition at Westminster accepted. The Convention was dissolved on 5 March 1976, and Rees told MPs that no fresh initiative was contemplated at present. The continuation of direct rule was approved by the Commons on 2 July.

Roy Mason, who succeeded Rees as Northern Ireland Secretary when Callaghan became Prime Minister, also offered little in the way of political initiatives, concentrating his efforts on new security measures and attempts to bring investment and jobs into a region where by the summer of 1977 unemployment stood at $12·5\%$ (see also table 15·4). In May 1977 he successfully repelled a second strike led by 'loyalist' workers, who were demanding the end of direct rule and a major offensive against the Provisional IRA. Despite extensive intimidation, the majority of workers in the province refused to join the strike, and attempts to shut down electricity supplies – crucial to the success of the earlier strike – were this time a failure. The lack of any foreseeable alternative to direct rule led to reconsideration of Northern Ireland's representation at Westminster which during the life of Stormont had always been proportionately lower than for the UK as a whole. (In the October 1974 General Election, the average electorate for Northern Ireland constituencies was 86,377, compared with an average for all UK constituencies of 63,123.) An increase in Northern Ireland's representation from 12 to 17–18 seats was agreed by a Speaker's Conference which reported on 21 February 1978. During the summer of 1978, the Conservatives demanded an early implementation of this increase – before rather than after the coming election – and also condemned the government for failing to make progress on a scheme of local government for the province.

Table 19·1: DEATHS IN NORTHERN IRELAND

	Army	UDR	RUC	Civilian	Total
1969			1	12	13
1970			2	23	25
1971	43	5	11	114	173
1972	103	26	17	322	468
1973	58	8	13	171	250
1974	28	7	15	166	216
1975	14	6	11	216	247
1976	14	15	23	244	296
1977	15	14	14	69	112

Total since 1969: 1800

Voting Records

This sequence contains voting records of MPs who were still in the House until May 1978 on 8 occasions when voting cut across Party boundaries.

They are:

DP1 Motion for the restoration of the death penalty for terrorist offences, 11 December 1974

DP2 Motion for the restoration of the death penalty for terrorist offences, 11 December 1975

A1 James White's bill to amend the law on abortion: second reading, 7 February 1975

A2 William Benyon's bill to amend the law on abortion: second reading, 25 February 1977

In these votes, the symbol X denotes a vote for the bill or motion – i.e. *for* the amendment of the abortion law, and *for* the restoration of the death penalty.

The next three votes are on Europe.

R is the vote on the Prime Minister's motion seeking approval of the renegotiated terms of British membership of the EEC, 9 April 1975. DE is the vote on the second reading of the Direct Elections Bill, 24 November 1977. PR is the vote on the method of election. In each case, X is a vote for the government – i.e. for acceptance of the terms, for direct elections, and for proportional representation rather than first past the post.

W is the vote on David Steel's move to reject the order sanctioning development at Windscale (15 May 1978). Here X indicates a vote for the government and O a vote for rejection of the order.

S denotes a Speaker or deputy who does not vote. N denotes that a member was not an MP when this vote was taken (because he had left by then, or because he had not yet been elected).

Tellers are counted as voters throughout.

Table 20·1: VOTING RECORDS 1974-77

LAB MP	Constituency	D P1	D P2	A 1	A 2	EUROPE			
						D R	E	P R	W
Abse, L.	Pontypool	O	O	X	X	X	X	—	O
Allaun, F.	Salford E	O	O	—	O	—	O	O	—
Anderson, D.	Swansea E	O	O	X	O	X	X	X	X
Archer, P.	Warley W	O	O	O	—	—	X	X	X
Armstrong, E.	Durham NW	O	O	X	O	X	X	X	X
Ashley, J.	Stoke S	O	O	—	O	X	X	X	—
Ashton, J.	Bassetlaw	O	O	—	—	O	O	—	—
Atkins, R.	Preston N	O	O	X	—	O	O	O	—
Atkinson, N.	Tottenham	O	O	O	—	O	O	O	—
Bagier, G.	Sunderland S	O	O	—	—	X	X	O	X
Barnett, G.	Greenwich	O	O	O	O	O	—	X	X
Barnett, J.	Heywood	O	O	X	O	X	X	X	X
Bates, A.	Bebington	O	O	O	O	O	X	X	X
Bean, R.	Rochester	O	O	—	—	—	O	X	—
Benn, A.	Bristol SE	O	O	—	O	O	—	O	X
Bennett, A.	Stockport N	O	O	O	O	O	O	O	—
Bidwell, S.	Southall	O	—	O	O	O	O	O	O
Bishop, E.	Newark	O	O	—	X	X	X	X	X
Blenkinsop, A.	S Shields	O	O	—	—	X	X	—	O
Boardman, H.	Leigh	O	O	X	—	X	—	X	X
Booth, A.	Barrow	O	O	O	O	O	—	O	X
Boothroyd, Miss B.	W Bromwich W	O	O	—	O	X	X	X	—
Bottomley, A.	Middlesbrough	O	O	—	—	X	X	O	X
Boyden, J.	Bishop Auckland	O	O	—	—	X	X	—	—
Bradley, T.	Leicester E	O	O	—	—	X	X	X	—
Bray, J.	Motherwell	O	O	X	X	X	X	O	—
Broughton, Sir A.	Batley	O	—	—	—	X	—	—	—
Brown, H.	Glasgow Provan	O	O	O	O	X	X	X	X
Brown, R.	Newcastle W	O	O	—	—	X	X	X	X
Brown, R.	Hackney S	O	O	O	O	X	X	X	X
Buchan, N.	Renfrew W	O	O	—	—	O	—	O	O
Buchanan, R.	Glasgow S'burn	O	O	X	X	X	X	—	X
Butler, Mrs J.	Wood Green	O	O	O	O	O	—	O	O
Callaghan, J.	Cardiff SE	—	—	—	—	—	X	X	—
Callaghan, J.	Middleton	O	O	X	—	O	—	O	—
Campbell, I.	Dunbart'shire W	O	O	X	X	O	—	—	X

LAB MP	Constituency	D P1	D P2	A 1	A 2	EUROPE D R	P E R	W
Canavan, D.	Stirlingshire W	O	O	X	X	—	O	O	O
Cant, R.	Stoke C	O	O	—	—	X	X	X	—
Carmichael, N.	Glasgow K'grove	O	O	O	O	O	O	O	—
Carter, R.	B'ham Northfield	O	O	—	—	X	X	X	—
Carter-Jones, L.	Eccles	O	O	X	X	O	O	O	—
Cartwright, J.	Woolwich E	O	O	—	O	X	X	X	X
Castle, Mrs B.	Blackburn	O	O	—	O	O	O	O	O
Clemitson, I.	Luton E	O	O	X	X	O	—	O	O
Cocks, M.	Bristol S	O	O	X	X	O	X	X	X
Cohen, S.	Leeds SE	O	O	X	X	X	X	—	X
Coleman, D.	Neath	O	O	X	—	X	X	X	X
Colquhoun, Ms M.	Northampton N	O	O	O	O	O	O	X	O
Concannon, D.	Mansfield	O	O	—	—	—	X	X	—
Conlan, B.	Gateshead E	O	O	—	—	—	—	X	X
Cook, R.	Edinburgh C	O	O	O	—	O	O	X	O
Corbett, R.	Hem'l Hempstead	O	O	O	O	O	X	X	O
Cowans, H.	Newcastle C	N	N	N	—	N	O	X
Cox, T.	Tooting	O	O	X	X	O	—	O	X
Craigen, J.	Glasgow M'hill	O	O	X	X	X	—	X	X
Crawshaw, R.	Liverpool Toxteth	O	O	—	O	X	X	X	X
Cronin, J.	Loughborough	—	O	O	—	X	X	X	—
Crowther, S.	Rotherham	N	N	N	O	N	O	X	X
Cryer, R.	Keighley	O	O	O	O	O	—	O	—
Cunningham, G.	Islington S	—	O	O	O	O	O	O	—
Cunningham, J.	Whitehaven	O	O	—	—	X	X	—	X
Dalyell, T.	West Lothian	O	—	X	X	—	X	—	—
Davidson, A.	Accrington	O	O	—	—	—	—	X	X
Davies, B.	Enfield N	O	O	O	O	O	O	O	—
Davies, D.	Llanelli	O	O	—	—	O	—	X	X
Davies, I.	Gower	O	O	—	—	X	X	X	X
Davis, S. C.	Hackney C	O	O	—	O	O	—	X	X
Deakins, E.	Walthamstow	O	O	O	O	—	—	O	X
Dean, J.	Leeds W	O	O	—	—	—	O	O	—
De Freitas, G.	Kettering	O	O	O	O	X	X	X	X
Dell, E.	Birkenhead	O	O	—	—	X	X	X	X
Dempsey, J.	Coatbridge	O	O	X	X	O	X	O	—
Dewar, D.	Garscadden	N	N	N	N	N	N	N	X
Doig, P.	Dundee W	X	X	X	—	X	X	O	X
Dormand, J.	Easington	O	O	—	—	—	—	X	O
Douglas-Mann, B.	Mitcham	O	O	O	O	O	X	X	—
Duffy, P.	Sheffield A'cliffe	O	O	X	X	X	X	X	X
Dunn, J.	L'pool Kirkdale	O	O	X	X	X	X	—	—
Dunnett, J.	Nottingham E	X	X	—	—	X	X	X	X
Dunwoody, Mrs G.	Crewe	O	O	O	O	O	O	O	O
Eadie, A.	Midlothian	O	O	X	X	O	—	O	X
Edge, G.	Aldridge	O	O	—	O	O	—	X	O
Edwards, R.	Wol'rhampton SE	O	O	O	—	—	—	—	—

LAB MP	Constituency	D P1	D P2	A 1	A 2	EUROPE D R	E	P R	W
Ellis, J.	Brigg	O	O	O	O	O	O	O	O
Ellis, T.	Wrexham	O	O	—	—	X	X	X	X
English, M.	Nottingham W	O	O	X	X	O	X	O	—
Ennals, D.	Norwich N	—	O	—	O	X	X	X	X
Evans, A.	Caerphilly	—	O	—	—	O	—	O	X
Evans, I.	Aberdare	O	O	—	—	O	O	O	—
Evans, J.	Newton	O	O	X	O	O	—	O	X
Ewing, H.	Stirling	O	O	X	X	O	—	X	X
Faulds, A.	Warley W	O	—	—	—	—	X	X	—
Fernyhough, E.	Jarrow	O	O	—	—	O	O	O	—
Fitch, A.	Wigan	O	O	X	—	X	X	X	X
Flannery, M.	Sheffield H'b'gh	O	O	O	O	O	O	O	O
Fletcher, E.	Darlington	O	O	—	O	O	O	O	O
Fletcher, R.	Ilkeston	O	O	O	—	—	—	—	—
Foot, M.	Ebbw Vale	O	O	—	O	O	—	X	X
Ford, B.	Bradford N	O	O	—	—	X	X	—	X
Forrester, J.	Stoke N	O	O	O	—	O	O	O	X
Fowler, G.	Wrekin	O	O	O	O	X	X	X	X
Fraser, J.	Norwood	O	O	O	O	O	O	—	X
Freeson, R.	Brent E	O	O	O	O	O	O	—	X
Galpern, Sir M.	Glasgow S'leston	S	S	S	S	S	S	S	S
Garrett, J.	Norwich S	O	O	O	O	X	—	O	O
Garrett, E.	Wallsend	O	O	—	—	O	O	O	X
George, B.	Walsall N	O	O	—	—	O	X	X	—
Gilbert, J.	Dudley E	O	O	O	—	O	—	X	X
Ginsburg, D.	Dewsbury	O	O	—	—	X	X	X	X
Golding, J.	Newcastle-u-L'me	O	O	—	—	X	X	X	X
Gould, B.	Southampton T'st	O	O	—	O	O	O	O	O
Gourlay, H.	Kirkcaldy	O	O	—	—	O	X	X	—
Graham, E.	Edmonton	O	O	O	O	X	X	X	X
Grant, G.	Morpeth	O	O	—	—	X	—	O	X
Grant, J.	Islington C	O	O	—	O	X	X	X	X
Grocott, B.	Lichfield	O	O	X	—	—	—	O	O
Hamilton, J.	Bothwell	O	O	X	X	O	—	X	X
Hamilton, W.	Fife C	O	O	—	O	X	X	X	X
Hardy, P.	Rother Valley	O	O	X	—	O	—	—	X
Harper, J.	Pontefract	O	O	—	—	X	X	X	X
Harrison, W.	Wakefield	O	O	X	—	O	X	X	X
Hart, Mrs J.	Lanark	O	O	—	—	O	—	—	—
Hattersley, R.	B'ham S'brook	—	O	X	—	X	X	X	—
Hayman, Mrs H.	Welwyn	O	O	O	O	X	—	O	O
Healey, D.	Leeds E	—	O	—	—	X	X	X	X
Heffer, E.	Liverpool Walton	O	O	—	—	O	O	O	—
Hooley, F.	Sheffield Heeley	O	O	—	—	O	O	X	—
Horam, J.	Gateshead W	O	O	X	—	X	X	X	X
Howell, D.	B'ham S Heath	O	O	—	—	X	X	X	X
Hoyle, D.	Nelson	O	O	—	O	O	O	O	—

LAB MP	Constituency	D P1	D P2	A 1	A 2	EUROPE D R	P E	R	W
Huckfield, L.	Nuneaton	O	O	O	—	O	—	O	X
Hughes, C.	Anglesey	O	O	—	—	X	X	X	—
Hughes, M.	Durham	O	O	X	—	O	—	—	X
Hughes, R.	Aberdeen N	O	O	O	—	O	X	O	X
Hughes, R.	Newport	—	O	X	—	O	O	O	—
Hunter, A.	Dunfermline	O	O	X	X	O	O	O	X
Irvine, Sir A.	Liverpool E Hill	O	O	X	—	O	—	—	—
Irving, S.	Dartford	O	O	X	—	X	—	X	—
Jackson, C.	Brighouse	O	O	X	—	X	X	X	—
Jackson, Miss M.	Lincoln	O	O	O	O	O	—	O	—
Janner, G.	Leicester W	O	O	—	—	X	X	O	—
Jay, D.	Battersea N	O	O	O	O	O	O	O	X
Jeger, Mrs L.	Holborn	O	O	O	O	—	O	O	—
Jenkins, H.	Putney	O	O	O	O	O	O	O	O
John, B.	Pontypridd	O	O	—	—	O	X	X	X
Johnson, J.	Hull W	O	O	X	—	X	X	X	—
Johnson, W.	Derby S	O	O	—	—	X	X	X	—
Jones, A.	Rhondda	O	O	—	—	O	X	—	X
Jones, B.	Flint E	O	O	—	—	X	X	X	X
Jones, D.	Burnley	O	O	X	X	X	X	X	—
Judd, F.	Portsmouth N	O	O	—	—	O	X	X	—
Kaufman, G.	M'chester A'wick	O	O	—	—	O	X	X	X
Kelley, R.	Don Valley	O	O	—	O	O	O	—	—
Kerr, R.	Feltham	O	O	O	O	O	O	O	—
Kilroy-Silk, R.	Ormskirk	O	O	O	O	O	O	O	O
Kinnock, N.	Bedwellty	O	O	—	O	—	O	—	—
Lambie, D.	Ayrshire C	—	O	—	—	O	O	X	X
Lamborn, H.	Peckham	O	O	—	O	X	X	X	X
Lamond, J.	Oldham E	O	O	X	X	O	—	O	X
Latham, A.	Paddington	O	O	—	—	O	O	O	O
Leadbitter, E.	Hartlepool	O	O	X	O	O	O	—	X
Lee, J.	B'ham H'dsworth	O	—	—	—	—	O	O	O
Lestor, Miss J.	Eton	O	O	O	—	O	O	O	—
Lever, H.	Manchester C	O	O	—	—	X	X	X	X
Lewis, A.	Newham NW	X	X	—	—	O	O	O	—
Lewis, R.	Carlisle	O	O	—	—	O	—	O	X
Litterick, T.	B'ham Selly Oak	O	O	O	O	O	O	O	O
Lomas, K.	Huddersfield W	O	—	—	—	X	X	O	—
Loyden, E.	Liverpool G'ston	O	—	X	O	O	O	O	—
Luard, E.	Oxford	O	O	—	—	X	X	X	X
Lyon, A.	York	O	O	O	O	X	X	O	—
Lyons, E.	Bradford W	O	O	O	O	X	X	X	—
Mabon, Dr D.	Greenock	O	O	X	X	X	X	X	X
McCartney, H.	Dunbarton C	O	O	—	—	—	O	O	X
McDonald, Dr O.	Thurrock	N	N	N	O	N	—	O	—
McElhone, F.	Glasgow Q Park	O	O	X	X	O	—	X	X
MacFarquhar, R.	Belper	O	O	O	O	X	X	X	X

163

LAB MP	Constituency	D P1	D P2	A 1	A 2	EUROPE D R	E	P R	W
McGuire, M.	Ince	—	O	X	X	X	—	X	X
Mackenzie, G.	Rutherglen	O	O	X	X	X	X	X	X
Mackintosh, J.	Berwick & E Loth	O	O	—	—	X	—	—	—
Maclennan, R.	Caithness	O	O	—	—	X	X	X	X
McMillan, T.	Glasgow C	O	O	X	X	O	O	O	—
McNamara, K.	Hull C	O	O	X	X	O	—	—	—
Madden, M.	Sowerby	O	O	—	O	O	O	O	O
Magee, B.	Leyton	O	O	—	O	X	X	X	X
Mahon, S.	Bootle	O	O	X	—	X	X	—	—
Mallalieu, J.	Huddersfield E	O	O	—	—	X	X	X	—
Marks, K.	M'chester Gorton	O	O	X	—	X	X	X	X
Marshall, E.	Goole	O	O	—	—	O	X	X	X
Marshall, J.	Leicester S	O	O	—	—	—	—	O	X
Mason, R.	Barnsley	O	O	X	X	X	—	X	X
Maynard, Miss J.	Sheffield B'side	O	O	—	—	O	O	O	O
Meacher, M.	Oldham W	O	O	O	—	O	—	O	—
Mellish, R.	Bermondsey	O	O	X	X	X	X	—	—
Mikardo, I.	Bethnal Green	O	O	—	O	O	O	O	O
Millan, B.	Glasgow C'gton	O	O	X	X	X	O	—	X
Miller, Dr M.	E Kilbride	O	O	X	O	O	—	—	—
Mitchell, A.	Grimsby	N	N	N	N	N	O	—	—
Mitchell, R.	Southampton It'n	O	O	—	—	X	X	—	—
Molloy, W.	Ealing N	O	—	—	O	O	—	O	—
Moonman, E.	Basildon	O	O	—	—	X	—	—	O
Morris, A.	M'chester Wyth	O	O	—	—	—	—	O	X
Morris, C.	M'chester O'shaw	O	O	X	X	O	—	—	X
Morris, J.	Aberavon	O	O	—	—	X	X	X	—
Moyle, R.	Lewisham E	O	O	O	O	—	—	—	X
Mulley, F.	Sheffield Park	—	O	—	O	—	X	X	X
Murray, R. K.	Leith	O	O	—	—	—	—	X	—
Newens, S.	Harlow	O	O	O	O	O	O	O	X
Noble, M.	Rossendale	O	O	X	X	O	—	O	—
Oakes, G.	Widnes	O	O	X	X	X	X	X	X
Ogden, E.	L'pool W Derby	O	O	O	O	X	X	X	—
O'Halloran, M.	Islington N	O	O	X	X	O	X	O	X
Orbach, M.	Stockport S	O	O	—	—	O	—	O	—
Orme, S.	Salford W	O	O	—	O	—	O	—	X
Ovenden, J.	Gravesend	O	O	—	O	O	O	O	—
Owen, Dr D.	Plymouth D'port	O	O	—	—	X	—	X	—
Padley, W.	Ogmore	O	O	X	X	X	X	—	—
Palmer, A.	Bristol NE	O	O	—	—	X	—	X	X
Park, G.	Coventry NE	O	O	O	—	—	—	—	X
Parker, J.	Dagenham	O	O	—	O	O	X	X	X
Parry, R.	L'pool Scotland	O	O	X	X	—	—	—	O
Pavitt, L.	Brent S	O	O	O	O	O	O	O	O
Pendry, T.	Stalybridge	O	O	X	—	O	—	O	—
Perry, E.	Battersea S	O	O	—	—	X	—	X	X

| | | | | | | EUROPE | | | |
LAB MP	Constituency	D P1	D P2	A 1	A 2	D R	E	P R	W
Phipps, Dr C.	Dudley W	O	O	—	—	X	—	X	—
Prescott, J.	Hull E	O	O	—	O	O	—	O	—
Price, C.	Lewisham W	—	O	O	—	O	O	O	O
Price, W.	Rugby	O	O	X	—	X	X	X	X
Radice, G.	Chester-le-Street	O	O	O	O	X	X	X	X
Rees, M.	Leeds S	O	O	—	—	X	X	X	X
Richardson, Miss J.	Barking	O	O	O	O	O	O	O	O
Roberts, A.	Normanton	O	O	—	—	X	—	O	—
Roberts, G.	Cannock	O	O	—	—	O	O	O	—
Robinson, G.	Coventry NW	N	N	N	—	N	O	O	X
Roderick, C.	Brecon	—	O	—	O	—	O	—	
Rodgers, G.	Chorley	O	O	X	—	O	O	O	O
Rodgers, W.	Stockton	O	O	—	—	X	X	X	X
Rooker, J.	B'ham Perry Barr	O	O	—	O	O	O	O	—
Roper, J.	Farnworth	O	O	O	O	X	X	X	X
Rose, P.	M'chester B'ckley	O	O	X	—	X	X	X	—
Ross, W.	Kilmarnock	O	O	—	X	O	—	X	X
Rowlands, E.	Merthyr	O	O	X	—	X	X	—	X
Ryman, J.	Blyth	O	—	X	—	O	—	O	X
Sandelson, N.	Hayes	O	O	X	O	X	X	X	X
Sedgemore, B.	Luton W	O	O	—	O	O	—	O	X
Selby, H.	Glasgow Govan	O	O	—	—	—	O	—	—
Sever, J.	B'ham Ladywood	N	N	N	N	N	—	X	X
Shaw, A.	Ilford S	O	O	O	O	O	O	O	O
Sheldon, R.	Ashton-u-Lyne	O	O	—	O	X	X	X	X
Shore, P.	Stepney	O	O	O	O	O	—	O	X
Short, Mrs R.	Wol'hampton NE	O	O	O	O	O	—	O	—
Silkin, J.	Deptford	O	O	O	O	O	—	—	X
Silkin, S.	Dulwich	O	O	O	O	X	X	X	X
Silverman, J.	B'ham Erdington	O	O	—	—	O	O	X	X
Skinner, D.	Bolsover	O	O	O	O	O	O	O	O
Smith, J.	Lanark N	O	O	X	X	X	X	X	X
Snape, P.	W Bromwich E	O	O	—	O	O	—	X	X
Spearing, N.	Newham S	O	O	O	O	O	O	O	O
Spriggs, L.	St Helens	—	O	X	X	O	—	O	X
Stallard, J.	St Pancras N	O	O	—	—	O	—	X	—
Stewart, M.	Fulham	O	O	—	O	X	X	X	X
Stoddart, D.	Swindon	O	O	X	O	O	O	O	X
Stott, R.	Westhoughton	O	O	X	—	O	X	X	—
Strang, G.	Edinburgh E	O	O	O	O	X	—	X	X
Strauss, G.	Vauxhall	O	O	O	O	O	O	O	—
Summerskill, Dr S.	Halifax	O	O	O	—	X	X	X	X
Swain, T.	Derbyshire SE	O	O	—	—	O	—	—	—
Taylor, Mrs A.	Bolton W	O	O	O	O	—	—	—	—
Thomas, J.	Abertillery	O	O	—	—	X	X	X	—
Thomas, M.	Newcastle E	O	O	O	O	X	X	X	X
Thomas, R.	Bristol NW	O	O	O	O	O	O	O	O

LAB MP	Constituency	D P1	D P2	A 1	A 2	EUROPE D R	E R	R	W
Thorne, S.	Preston S	O	O	O	O	O	O	O	O
Tierney, S.	B'ham Yardley	O	O	—	—	O	—	O	—
Tilley, J	Lambeth C	N	N	N	N	N	N	N	O
Tinn, J	Redcar	O	O	X	X	X	X	—	X
Tomlinson, J.	Meriden	O	O	—	—	X	X	X	X
Tomney, F.	Hammersmith N	—	—	—	—	X	—	—	—
Torney, T.	Bradford S	O	O	—	—	O	O	O	O
Tuck, R.	Watford	O	O	—	—	—	—	—	—
Urwin, T.	Houghton-le-S'ng	O	O	X	—	O	O	O	—
Varley, E.	Chesterfield	O	O	—	—	—	X	—	—
Wainwright, E.	Dearne Valley	O	O	X	—	X	—	X	X
Walker, H.	Doncaster	O	—	—	—	O	—	X	—
Walker, T.	Kingswood	O	O	X	X	—	X	X	X
Ward, M.	Peterborough	O	O	O	O	X	X	X	—
Watkins, D.	Consett	O	O	X	O	X	X	X	X
Watkinson, J.	Glo'stershire W	O	O	—	—	O	—	X	—
Weetch, K.	Ipswich	O	O	O	O	O	—	X	—
Weitzman, D.	Hackney N	O	—	—	O	X	X	—	—
Wellbeloved, J.	Erith	O	O	—	—	X	—	X	X
White, F.	Bury & Radcliffe	O	O	X	—	X	X	X	X
White, J.	Glasgow Pollok	O	O	X	X	X	—	—	X
Whitehead, P.	Derby N	O	—	O	O	X	X	O	O
Whitlock, W.	Nottingham N	—	O	—	O	X	—	X	O
Willey, F.	Sunderland N	O	O	X	X	X	X	O	O
Williams, A.	Swansea W	O	O	—	—	X	X	X	—
Williams, A. Lee.	Hornchurch	O	O	—	X	X	X	X	X
Williams, Mrs S.	Hertford	O	O	—	—	X	X	X	—
Williams, Sir T.	Warrington	O	O	—	—	—	X	—	—
Wilson, Sir H.	Huyton	O	O	—	X	X	X	—	—
Wilson, W.	Coventry SE	O	O	O	O	O	O	X	X
Wise, Mrs A.	Coventry SW	O	O	—	O	O	O	O	O
Woodall, A.	Hemsworth	O	O	X	—	—	X	X	X
Woof, R.	Blaydon	O	O	X	—	O	O	O	—
Wrigglesworth, I.	Thornaby	O	O	X	—	X	X	X	X
Young, D.	Bolton E	O	O	X	—	—	—	X	—

CON MP	Constituency	D P1	D P2	A 1	A 2	EUROPE D R	E R	R	W
Adley, R.	Christchurch	X	X	—	O	X	—	O	—
Aitken, J.	Thanet E	X	X	X	—	X	O	—	—
Alison, M.	Barkston Ash	X	X	—	X	—	X	O	—
Amery, J.	Brighton Pavilion	O	O	—	X	X	X	O	—
Arnold, T.	Hazelgrove	X	X	—	—	X	X	O	X
Atkins, H.	Spelthorne	X	X	X	X	X	X	X	—
Atkinson, D.	Bournemouth E	N	N	N	N	N	N	O	—
Awdry, D.	Chippenham	X	X	—	O	X	X	X	—

CON MP	Constituency	D P1	D P2	A 1	A 2	EUROPE D R	D P E	R	W
Baker, K.	St Marylebone	—	O	—	O	X	X	X	—
Banks, R.	Harrogate	X	X	X	X	X	—	O	X
Bell, R.	Beaconsfield	X	X	—	X	O	O	O	—
Bennett, Sir F.	Torbay	X	X	—	X	X	X	—	—
Bennett, Dr R.	Fareham	X	X	—	—	X	X	O	—
Benyon, W.	Buckingham	O	O	X	X	X	X	X	X
Berry, A.	Southgate	O	X	—	X	X	X	O	X
Biffen, J.	Oswestry	X	X	—	—	O	O	O	O
Biggs-Davison, J.	Epping F	X	X	X	X	X	X	O	—
Blaker, P.	Blackpool S	X	X	—	X	X	X	O	—
Body, R.	Holland	O	O	—	—	O	O	O	O
Boscawen, R.	Wells	X	X	—	X	X	X	O	—
Bottomley, P.	Woolwich W	N	—	N	X	N	X	X	—
Bowden, A.	Brighton Kemp T	X	X	X	X	X	X	O	O
Boyson, R.	Brent N	X	X	X	—	X	X	O	—
Braine, Sir B.	Essex SE	X	X	X	X	—	X	O	—
Brittan, L.	Cleveland	X	X	X	—	X	X	O	—
Brocklebank-Fowler, C.	Norfolk NW	O	O	—	—	—	X	X	—
Brooke, P.	L'don & W'm'ster	N	N	N	N	N	X	X	X
Brotherton, M.	Louth	X	X	X	X	X	X	O	—
Brown, Sir E.	Bath	X	X	—	X	X	X	O	—
Bryan, Sir P.	Howden	X	X	—	—	X	X	O	—
Buchanan-Smith, A.	Angus N	X	X	—	—	X	X	X	—
Buck, A.	Colchester	O	O	X	O	X	X	O	—
Budgen, N.	Wolv'ampton SW	O	O	—	X	X	O	O	—
Bulmer, E.	Kidderminster	X	X	—	—	X	X	X	—
Burden, F.	Gillingham	X	X	X	X	X	X	O	—
Butler, A.	Bosworth	X	X	—	—	X	X	O	X
Carlisle, M.	Runcorn	X	X	—	—	X	X	X	X
Chalker, Mrs L.	Wallasey	X	X	X	—	X	X	X	X
Channon, P.	Southend W	O	O	X	X	X	X	O	—
Churchill, W.	Stretford	X	X	X	X	X	X	O	X
Clark, A.	Plymouth Sutton	X	X	—	X	O	O	O	X
Clark, W.	Croydon S	X	X	—	X	X	X	O	—
Clarke, K.	Rushcliffe	O	O	—	O	X	X	O	X
Clegg, W.	Fylde N	—	X	—	X	X	X	O	X
Cockcroft, J.	Nantwich	—	X	—	X	X	X	X	—
Cooke, R.	Bristol W	X	—	—	—	X	X	O	—
Cope, J.	Gloucestershire S	X	X	—	X	X	X	O	X
Cormack, P.	SW Staffs	X	X	X	X	X	O	O	—
Corrie, J.	Ayr N & Bute	X	X	—	X	X	—	O	—
Costain, A.	Folkestone	X	X	X	X	X	X	O	X
Critchley, J.	Aldershot	X	X	—	—	X	X	X	X
Crouch, D.	Canterbury	X	X	O	O	X	X	X	X
Crowder, P.	Ruislip	X	X	—	—	X	X	O	—
Davies, J.	Knutsford	X	X	—	—	X	X	—	—
Dean, P.	Somerset N	—	X	—	X	X	X	X	—

CON MP	Constituency	D P1	D P2	A 1	A 2	EUROPE			
						D R	E	P R	W
Dodsworth, G.	Herts SW	O	O	—	O	X	X	X	—
Douglas-Hamilton, Lord J.	Edinburgh W	O	O	X	—	O	X	X	X
Drayson, B.	Skipton	—	X	—	O	X	X	X	X
Du Cann, E.	Taunton	X	X	—	—	—	—	O	—
Durant, A.	Reading N	X	X	X	X	X	X	O	—
Dykes, H.	Harrow E	—	O	X	X	X	X	O	—
Eden, Sir J.	Bournemouth W	X	X	—	—	X	X	O	—
Edwards, N.	Pembroke	X	X	—	—	X	X	O	—
Elliott, Sir W.	Newcastle N	O	X	X	—	X	—	—	—
Emery, P.	Honiton	X	X	—	—	X	—	O	X
Eyre, R.	B'ham Hall Green	X	X	X	—	X	X	O	—
Fairbairn, N.	Kinross	X	X	—	—	X	X	X	—
Fairgrieve, R.	Aberdeenshire W	X	O	X	—	—	X	X	X
Farr, J.	Harborough	X	X	—	—	—	—	O	—
Fell, A.	Yarmouth	X	X	X	X	X	—	O	X
Finsberg, G.	Hampstead	X	X	—	—	X	X	O	—
Fisher, Sir N.	Surbiton	O	O	—	—	X	X	X	—
Fletcher, A.	Edinburgh N	X	X	—	—	X	X	X	—
Fletcher-Cooke, C.	Darwen	X	X	X	—	X	—	O	—
Fookes, Miss J.	Plymouth Drake	X	X	—	X	—	X	O	O
Forman, N.	Carshalton	N	N	N	—	N	X	O	O
Fowler, N.	Sutton Coldfield	X	X	X	—	X	X	O	—
Fox, M.	Shipley	X	X	—	—	X	X	O	—
Fraser, H.	Stafford	X	X	X	X	X	O	O	—
Fry, P.	Wellingborough	X	X	X	—	X	O	O	—
Galbraith, T.	Glasgow H'head	X	X	X	X	X	X	O	—
Gardiner, G.	Reigate	X	X	—	O	—	X	O	—
Gardner, E.	S Fylde	X	X	X	—	X	X	O	—
Gilmour, Sir I.	Amersham	O	O	—	—	X	X	X	—
Gilmour, Sir J.	Fife E	X	X	—	—	X	—	O	—
Glyn, Dr A.	Windsor	X	X	—	X	X	X	O	X
Godber, J.	Grantham	X	X	—	X	X	X	—	—
Goodhart, P.	Beckenham	X	X	—	—	X	X	O	X
Goodhew, V.	St Albans	X	X	X	X	X	X	O	—
Goodlad, A.	Northwich	O	O	—	—	X	X	X	—
Gorst, J.	Hendon N	O	X	X	X	X	X	O	—
Gow, I.	Eastbourne	X	X	—	X	X	O	O	O
Gower, Sir R.	Barry	X	X	—	—	X	X	X	—
Grant, J. A.	Harrow C	X	X	—	X	X	X	—	—
Gray, H.	Ross & Cromarty	X	X	X	—	X	X	O	X
Grieve, P.	Solihull	X	X	X	—	X	X	O	—
Griffiths, E.	Bury St E	X	X	—	X	X	X	O	—
Grist, I.	Cardiff N	O	O	—	O	X	X	O	O
Grylls, M.	Surrey NW	X	X	O	—	X	X	O	—
Hall-Davis, A.	Morecambe	O	O	—	—	X	X	O	—
Hamilton, M.	Salisbury	X	X	—	X	X	X	O	X
Hampson, K.	Ripon	X	X	—	—	X	X	X	—

CON MP	Constituency	D P1	D P2	A 1	A 2	EUROPE D R	P E R	W
Hannam, J.	Exeter	X	X	—	—	X	X	O	X
Harrison, Sir H.	Eye	X	X	—	—	X	X	—	—
Harvie Anderson, Miss B.	Renfrew E	X	X	X	X	X	—	O	—
Haselhurst, A.	Saffron Walden	N	N	N	N	N	X	X	—
Hastings, S.	Mid-Beds	X	—	—	—	X	X	O	—
Havers, Sir M	Wimbledon	X	X	—	X	X	X	O	—
Hawkins, P.	Norfolk SW	X	X	—	—	—	—	O	—
Hayhoe, B.	Brentford	O	O	X	X	X	X	X	X
Heath, E.	Bexley	O	O	—	—	X	X	X	—
Heseltine, M.	Henley	O	O	—	—	X	X	O	X
Hicks, R.	Bodmin	X	X	—	—	X	—	—	O
Higgins, T.	Worthing	O	O	—	—	X	X	O	X
Hodgson, R.	Walsall N	N	N	N	O	X	X	O	—
Holland, P.	Carlton	X	X	X	—	X	X	O	—
Hordern, P.	Horsham	X	X	—	X	X	X	O	—
Howe, Sir G.	Surrey E	O	O	—	—	X	X	O	—
Howell, D.	Guildford	X	X	—	—	X	X	O	X
Howell, R.	Norfolk N	—	X	—	—	X	X	O	X
Hunt, D.	Wirral	N	N	N	X	N	X	X	O
Hunt, J.	Ravensbourne	X	X	O	O	—	X	—	—
Hurd, D.	Mid Oxon	O	O	—	X	X	X	O	—
Hutchison, M. C.	Edinburgh S	O	O	—	—	O	O	O	—
Irvine, B. G.	Rye	X	X	—	S	X	S	S	S
Irving, C.	Cheltenham	O	—	—	—	X	X	O	O
James, D.	Dorset N	X	X	X	X	X	X	—	—
Jenkin, P.	Wanstead	X	X	—	—	X	X	O	X
Jessel, T.	Twickenham	X	X	X	X	—	X	O	—
Johnson Smith, G.	E Grinstead	X	X	X	X	X	—	X	X
Jones, A.	Daventry	X	X	—	X	X	X	O	X
Jopling, M.	Westmorland	—	X	—	—	X	X	O	X
Joseph, Sir K.	Leeds NE	X	X	—	X	X	X	O	—
Kaberry, Sir D.	Leeds NW	X	X	—	—	X	X	—	—
Kellett-Bowman, Mrs E.	Lancaster	X	X	—	X	X	X	O	X
Kershaw, A.	Stroud	X	X	X	—	X	X	X	X
Kimball, M.	Gainsborough	X	X	—	—	X	—	O	—
King, E. M.	Dorset S	O	O	—	—	X	X	X	—
King, T.	Bridgwater	X	X	—	X	X	X	O	X
Kitson, Sir T.	Richmond, Yorks	X	X	X	—	X	—	O	X
Knight, Mrs J.	B'ham E'gbaston	X	X	—	X	X	X	O	—
Knox, D.	Leek	O	O	—	—	X	X	X	X
Lamont, N.	Kingston-o-T'mes	O	O	—	—	X	X	O	—
Langford-Holt, Sir J.	Shrewsbury	X	X	—	—	X	X	O	O
Latham, M.	Melton M'bray	X	X	—	X	X	X	X	—
Lawrence, I.	Burton	X	X	X	X	X	X	O	—
Lawson, N.	Blaby	X	X	—	—	X	X	O	X
Le Marchant, S.	High Peak	X	X	X	X	X	X	O	X
Lester, J.	Beeston	X	X	X	X	X	X	X	X

CON MP	Constituency	D P1	D P2	A 1	A 2	D R	E	P R	W
Lewis, K.	Rutland	X	X	-	-	X	X	X	-
Lloyd, I.	Havant	O	O	X	-	X	-	X	-
Loveridge, J.	Upminster	-	X	-	X	X	X	O	-
Luce, R.	Shoreham	X	X	-	X	X	X	-	-
McAdden, Sir S.	Southend E	-	X	X	X	-	-	O	-
McCrindle, R.	Brentwood	X	X	-	-	X	X	O	X
MacFarlane, N.	Sutton	X	X	X	-	X	X	O	-
MacGregor, J.	Norfolk S	O	X	-	X	X	X	O	-
Mackay, A.	B'ham Stechford	N	N	N	N	N	X	O	-
Macmillan, M.	Farnham	O	O	-	-	X	-	O	-
McNair Wilson, M.	Newbury	O	O	X	X	X	-	O	-
McNair Wilson, P.	New Forest	X	X	-	-	X	X	O	-
Madel, D.	Beds S	O	O	-	-	X	X	-	-
Marshall, M.	Arundel	O	-	-	-	X	X	O	-
Marten, N.	Banbury	X	X	-	-	O	O	O	-
Mates, M.	Petersfield	X	X	-	O	X	X	O	-
Mather, C.	Esher	X	X	X	X	X	X	O	X
Maude, A.	Stratford	X	X	X	-	X	X	-	-
Maudling, R.	Barnet	X	X	-	-	X	X	X	-
Mawby, R.	Totnes	X	X	-	-	X	X	X	-
Maxwell-Hyslop, R.	Tiverton	X	X	-	O	X	O	O	X
Mayhew, P.	Tunbridge Wells	X	X	-	-	X	X	X	-
Meyer, Sir A.	Flint W	X	X	X	X	X	X	X	X
Miller, H.	Bromsgrove	X	-	X	-	X	X	O	X
Mills, P.	Devon W	X	-	-	-	X	X	O	O
Miscampbell, N.	Blackpool N	X	X	-	-	X	X	X	-
Mitchell, D.	Basingstoke	X	X	-	-	X	X	X	-
Moate, R.	Faversham	-	X	-	X	O	O	O	X
Monro, H.	Dumfries	X	X	X	-	X	X	O	X
Montgomery, F.	Altrincham	X	X	-	X	X	X	O	-
Moore, J.	Croydon C	X	X	-	-	X	X	O	-
More, J.	Ludlow	X	X	-	-	-	-	O	-
Morgan, G.	Denbigh	X	X	-	-	-	X	O	-
Morgan-Giles, Rear-Ad M.	Winchester	X	-	X	-	X	-	O	-
Morris, M.	Northampton S	X	X	-	-	X	X	-	O
Morrison, C.	Devizes	O	O	X	-	X	X	X	-
Morrison, P.	Chester	X	X	X	X	X	X	O	X
Mudd, D.	Falmouth	X	X	-	-	-	-	O	O
Murton, O.	Poole	S	S	S	S	S	S	S	S
Neave, A.	Abingdon	X	X	-	-	X	X	O	-
Nelson, A.	Chichester	O	O	O	-	X	-	O	-
Neubert, M.	Romford	X	X	X	X	X	X	O	X
Newton, A.	Braintree	O	O	-	X	X	X	X	O
Normanton, T.	Cheadle	-	X	X	-	X	X	O	X
Nott, J.	St Ives	X	X	-	-	X	X	O	-
Onslow, C.	Woking	X	X	X	X	X	X	-	-
Oppenheim, Mrs S.	Gloucester	X	X	-	X	X	X	O	-

CON MP	Constituency	D P1	D P2	A 1	A 2	EUROPE R	D E	P R	W
Osborn, J.	Sheffield Hallam	X	X	—	—	X	X	O	X
Page, J.	Harrow W	—	X	X	X	X	—	O	—
Page, R. G.	Crosby	X	X	X	X	X	X	O	X
Page, R.	Workintgon	N	N	N	—	N	X	O	X
Parkinson, C.	S Herts	X	X	X	—	X	X	O	—
Pattie, G.	Chertsey	X	X	X	X	X	X	O	X
Percival, I.	Southport	X	X	X	X	X	X	O	—
Peyton, J. ·	Yeovil	O	X	—	—	X	X	—	—
Pink, R. B.	Portsmouth S	X	X	—	—	X	X	—	—
Prentice, R.	Newham NE	O	O	—	—	X	X	—	—
Price, D.	Eastleigh	X	X	X	X	X	X	O	—
Prior, J.	Lowestoft	X	X	—	—	X	—	X	—
Pym, F.	Cambridgeshire	X	X	—	—	X	X	O	X
Raison, T.	Aylesbury	X	X	—	—	X	X	—	—
Rathbone, T.	Lewes	O	O	—	—	X	X	X	X
Rees, P.	Dover	X	X	—	X	X	X	O	—
Rees-Davies, W.	Thanet W	X	X	—	X	X	X	O	—
Renton, Sir D.	Huntingdon	X	X	X	—	X	X	O	—
Renton, T.	Mid-Sussex	X	X	—	—	X	X	O	—
Rhodes James, R.	Cambridge	N	N	N	O	N	X	X	O
Rhys Williams, Sir B.	Kensington	O	O	X	X	X	X	X	X
Ridley, N.	Cirencester	X	X	—	O	X	X	O	X
Ridsdale, J.	Harwich	X	X	X	—	X	X	O	—
Rifkind, M.	Ed'burgh P'tlands	O	X	X	—	X	X	X	—
Rippon, G.	Hexham	X	X	—	X	X	X	O	—
Roberts, M.	Cardiff NW	X	X	X	X	X	X	O	—
Roberts, W.	Conway	X	X	—	—	X	X	O	—
Rodgers, Sir J.	Sevenoaks	—	X	X	—	X	—	O	—
Rossi, H.	Hornsey	X	X	X	X	X	X	O	—
Rost, P.	Derbyshire SE	X	X	—	—	X	—	O	—
Royle, Sir A.	Richmond	—	O	—	—	X	X	O	—
Sainsbury, T.	Hove	O	O	—	—	X	X	—	—
St John-Stevas, N.	Chelmsford	O	O	X	X	X	X	—	—
Scott, N.	Paddington	O	O	—	O	X	X	X	—
Scott-Hopkins, J.	Derbyshire W	X	X	—	X	X	X	O	—
Shaw, G.	Pudsey	X	X	—	—	X	X	O	X
Shaw, M.	Scarborough	—	X	—	—	X	—	—	X
Shelton, W.	Streatham	X	X	X	X	X	X	O	—
Shepherd, C.	Hereford	O	X	—	—	X	X	O	X
Shersby, M.	Uxbridge	X	X	X	X	X	X	O	X
Silvester, F.	M'chester W'gton	X	—	X	X	X	X	O	—
Sims, R.	Chislehurst	X	X	X	X	X	X	O	X
Sinclair, Sir G.	Dorking	X	X	—	O	X	X	X	—
Skeet, T.	Bedford	—	X	—	X	X	—	O	X
Smith, D.	Warwick	X	X	X	—	X	X	O	O
Smith, T.	Ashfield	N	N	N	N	N	X	X	X
Speed, K.	Ashford	X	X	X	X	X	X	O	—

CON MP	Constituency	D P1	D P2	A 1	A 2	D R	P E	R	W
Spence, J.	Thirsk	X	X	—	—	—	X	O	—
Spicer, J.	Dorset W	X	X	—	X	X	X	O	X
Spicer, M.	Worcs S	X	X	—	—	X	X	O	X
Sproat, I.	Aberdeen S	X	X	—	—	X	X	O	—
Stainton, K.	Sudbury	X	X	X	X	X	X	O	—
Stanbrook, I.	Orpington	X	X	X	X	X	X	O	O
Stanley, J.	Tonbridge	X	X	X	—	X	X	O	—
Steen, A.	L'pool Wavertree	X	X	X	X	X	X	O	X
Stewart, I.	Hitchin	O	X	—	X	X	X	X	—
Stokes, J.	Halesowen	X	X	—	—	X	O	O	—
Stradling Thomas, J.	Monmouth	O	O	—	X	X	X	O	X
Tapsell, P.	Horncastle	X	X	—	—	X	X	O	—
Taylor, E.	Glasgow C'cart	X	X	X	X	O	X	O	X
Taylor, R.	Croydon NW	X	X	—	X	X	—	O	—
Tebbit, N.	Chingford	X	X	X	X	X	—	O	X
Temple-Morris, P.	Leominster	X	X	—	—	X	X	X	X
Thatcher, Mrs M.	Finchley	X	X	—	—	X	X	O	—
Thomas, P.	Hendon S	O	O	X	X	X	X	O	—
Townsend, C.	Bexleyheath	O	O	X	O	—	X	X	—
Trotter, N.	Tynemouth	X	X	—	—	—	X	O	—
Van Straubenzee, W.	Wokingham	X	X	—	X	X	X	O	—
Vaughan, Dr G.	Reading S	X	X	X	X	X	X	O	—
Viggers, P.	Gosport	X	X	—	O	X	—	X	X
Wakeham, J.	Maldon	X	X	—	X	X	X	O	—
Walder, D.	Clitheroe	X	X	X	X	X	X	O	—
Walker, P.	Worcester	O	O	—	—	X	X	X	—
Walker-Smith, Sir D.	Herts E	X	X	—	O	X	X	O	—
Wall, P.	Haltemprice	X	—	—	X	X	X	—	X
Walters, D.	Westbury	O	O	X	—	X	X	X	—
Warren, K.	Hastings	X	X	X	X	—	—	O	—
Weatherill, B.	Croydon NE	X	X	X	X	X	X	O	X
Wells, J.	Maidstone	X	X	—	X	X	X	O	X
Whitelaw, W.	Penrith	O	O	—	—	X	X	O	X
Wiggin, J.	Weston-s-Mare	X	X	—	X	X	X	O	—
Winterton, N.	Macclesfield	X	X	X	X	O	O	O	X
Wood, R.	Bridlington	X	X	—	X	X	X	X	—
Young, Sir G.	Acton	X	—	—	—	X	X	X	—
Younger, G.	Ayr	X	X	—	—	X	X	X	X

LIB MP	Constituency	D P1	D P2	A 1	A 2	D R	P E	R	W
Beith, A.	Berwick	O	O	X	X	X	X	X	O
Freud, C.	Isle of Ely	O	O	—	O	X	X	X	O
Grimond, J.	Orkney	O	—	—	—	X	X	X	—
Hooson, E.	Montgomery	O	O	—	—	X	—	X	O
Howells, G.	Cardigan	O	O	—	—	X	X	X	O
Johnston, R.	Inverness	O	—	—	—	X	X	X	O

173

ULSTER – OTHERS MP	Constituency	D P1	D P2	A 1	A 2	EUROPE D R E	P R	D R	W
Fitt, G. (*SDLP*)	Belfast W	O	O	—	X	—	X	—	—
Maguire, F. (*Ind*)	Fermanagh	O	O	X	X	—	—	—	—

Table 20·2: MAIN LABOUR REBELLIONS

These voting records show Labour MPs who voted against the government in 9 of the most significant backbench rebellions of the Parliament. (MPs no longer in the house are excluded.)
They are:

ER   Vote to prevent the government relaxing the earnings rule for pensioners, 29 January 1975. The Labour rebellion meant the government was defeated.

IP   Vote against the government's incomes policy, 22 July 1975

NI   Vote against the Prevention of Terrorism Bill, renewing and strengthening special powers in Northern Ireland, 29 November 1975

PE   Abstentions (not votes) which caused the government's defeat on the issue of public expenditure cuts, 10 March 1976 (Symbol O).

PB   Vote against government policy on pay beds, 12 October 1976

IMF   Vote against the cuts resulting from the government deal with the IMF, 21 December 1976

DEF   Vote against 'inadequate' extent of cuts in defence expenditure, 12 January 1977

SWG   Vote against the guillotine on the Scotland and Wales Bill, 22 February 1977, causing a government defeat

REF   Insertion of a 40% 'hurdle' in the Scottish referendum, 25 January 1977 – again causing a government defeat

Labour Rebellions

MP	Constituency	ER	IP	NI	PE	PB	IMF	DEF	SWG	REF
Abse, L.	Pontypool	—	—	—	—	—	—	—	X	X
Allaun, F.	Salford E	—	X	—	O	X	X	X	—	—
Anderson, D.	Monmouth	—	—	—	—	X	—	—	—	—
Ashton, J.	Bassetlaw	—	—	—	O	—	—	—	—	—
Atkins, R.	Preston N	—	X	—	O	—	X	X	—	—
Atkinson, N.	Tottenham	—	X	—	O	—	—	X	—	—
Bennett, A.	Stockport N	—	X	X	O	—	X	X	—	—
Bidwell, S.	Southall	—	X	X	O	—	—	X	—	X
Boothroyd, Miss B.	W Bromwich W	—	—	—	—	—	—	—	—	X
Brown, R.	Hackney S	—	—	—	—	—	—	—	X	—

MP	Constituency	ER	IP	NI	PE	PB	IMEF	DEF	SWG	REF
Buchan, N	Renfrew W	—	X	—	—	X	—	X	—	—
Butler, Mrs J.	Wood Green	—	—	—	—	—	—	X	—	—
Callaghan, J.	Middleton	—	X	—	O	X	—	X	—	—
Canavan, D.	Stirling W.	—	—	X	O	—	X	X	—	—
Carmichael, N.	Kelvingrove	—	—	—	—	—	X	X	—	—
Carter-Jones, L.	Eccles	—	—	—	—	—	—	X	—	—
Clemitson, I.	Luton E	—	—	—	—	X	—	X	—	—
Colquhoun, Ms M.	Northampton N	—	—	X	O	X	X	X	—	X
Cook, R. F.	Edinburgh C	—	—	—	O	X	X	X	—	X
Corbett, R.	H'mel Hempstead	—	—	X	—	X	—	X	—	—
Cowans, H.	Newcastle C	—	—	—	—	—	—	—	X	—
Crowther, S.	Rotherham	—	—	—	—	—	—	X	—	—
Cryer, R.	Keighley	—	X	—	O	—	—	—	—	—
Cunningham, G.	Islington S	X	—	—	—	—	—	—	X	X
Dalyell, T.	W Lothian	—	—	—	—	—	—	—	X	X
Davies, B.	Enfield	—	—	—	—	—	X	—	—	—
Dean, J.	Leeds W	—	—	—	—	—	—	—	X	X
Doig, P.	Dundee W	—	—	—	—	—	—	—	—	X
Douglas-Mann, B.	Mitcham	X	—	—	—	—	—	—	X	X
Dunwoody, Mrs G.	Crewe	—	—	—	—	—	—	—	X	—
Edge, G.	Aldridge	—	—	—	O	X	X	X	—	—
Edwards, R.	W'hampton SE	—	—	—	—	—	—	X	—	—
Ellis, J.	Brigg	—	—	—	—	—	—	X	—	—
Evans, A.	Caerphilly	—	—	—	—	—	—	—	X	—
Evans, I.	Aberdare	—	—	—	—	X	—	X	—	X
Fernyhough, E.	Jarrow	—	—	—	—	X	—	X	—	—
Flannery, M.	Hillsborough	—	X	X	O	X	X	X	—	X
Fletcher, E.	Darlington	—	—	—	O	—	—	X	—	X
Garrett, E.	Wallsend	—	—	—	—	—	—	—	X	X
Garrett, J.	Norwich S	—	—	—	—	—	—	X	—	—
George, B.	Walsall S	—	—	—	—	X	—	—	—	—
Grocott, B.	Lichfield	—	—	—	—	X	—	X	—	—
Hamilton, W.	Fife C	X	—	—	—	—	—	—	X	X
Hart, Mrs J.	Lanark	—	X	—	.	—	—	X	—	—
Hayman, Mrs H.	Welwyn	—	—	—	—	—	—	X	—	X
Heffer, E.	Walton	—	X	—	O	X	—	X	—	X
Hooley, F.	Heeley	X	—	—	—	—	—	X	—	—
Hoyle, D.	Nelson	—	X	—	O	X	X	X	—	—
Huckfield, L.	Nuneaton	X	—	—	—	—	—	—	—	—
Hughes, R.	Aberdeen N	—	X	—	—	X	—	X	—	—
Hughes, R.	Newport	—	X	—	—	X	—	X	—	—
Jay, D.	Battersea N	—	—	—	—	—	—	—	—	X
Jeger, Mrs L.	Holborn	—	—	—	—	—	—	X	—	—
Jenkins, H.	Putney	—	—	—	—	—	—	X	—	—
Kelley, R.	Don Valley	—	—	—	—	—	—	X	—	—
Kerr, R.	Feltham	—	X	—	O	—	X	X	—	—
Kilroy-Silk, R.	Ormskirk	—	—	—	—	X	—	X	—	—

MP	Constituency	ERR	IPl	NI	PE	PEB	IMF	DEF	SWG	REF
Kinnock, N.	Bedwellty	—	—	—	O	—	—	X	—	—
Lambie, D.	C Ayrshire	—	X	—	O	X	X	X	—	—
Lamond, J.	Oldham E	—	—	—	—	—	—	X	X	—
Latham, A.	Paddington	—	—	X	O	—	X	X	—	—
Leadbitter, E.	Hartlepool	—	—	—	—	—	—	—	X	—
Lee, J.	Handsworth	—	X	—	O	—	X	X	—	—
Lestor, Miss J.	Eton	—	—	—	O	X	—	X	—	—
Lewis, A.	Newham NW	—	X	—	—	—	—	—	X	—
Litterick, T.	Selly Oak	—	X	X	O	X	X	—	—	—
Lomas, K.	Huddersfield W	—	—	—	—	X	—	X	—	—
Loyden, E.	Garston	—	X	X	O	X	X	—	—	—
Lyon, A.	York	—	—	—	—	—	X	X	—	X
McDonald, Dr O.	Thurrock	—	—	—	—	X	X	X	—	—
McMillan, T.	Glasgow C	—	—	—	—	X	—	X	—	—
Madden, M.	Sowerby	—	X	—	—	—	X	—	—	—
Marshall, J.	Leicester S	—	—	—	—	—	—	X	—	—
Maynard, Miss J.	Brightside	—	X	X	O	X	X	X	—	X
Mikardo, I.	Bethnal Green	—	X	X	O	—	X	X	—	—
Miller, Dr M.	E. Kilbride	—	—	—	O	—	—	—	—	—
Moonman, E.	Basildon	—	—	—	—	—	—	—	X	X
Newens, S.	Harlow	—	X	—	O	—	X	X	—	X
Noble, M.	Rossendale	—	—	—	—	X	—	—	—	—
Ogden, E.	L'pool W Derby	—	—	—	—	—	—	—	—	X
Orbach, M.	Stockport S	—	—	—	—	—	—	—	—	X
Ovenden, J.	Gravesend	—	—	—	—	—	—	X	X	—
Palmer, A.	Bristol NE	—	—	—	—	—	—	—	—	X
Parker, J.	Dagenham	—	—	—	—	—	—	X	—	—
Parry, R.	L'pool Scotland	—	X	—	—	—	X	X	—	—
Pavitt, L.	Brent S	—	—	—	—	X	—	X	—	—
Phipps, C.	Dudley W	X	—	—	—	—	—	—	X	—
Prentice, R.	Newham NE*	—	—	—	—	—	—	X	—	—
Price, C.	Lewisham W	—	—	—	—	—	—	X	—	—
Richardson, Miss J.	Barking	—	X	X	O	X	X	X	—	X
Roberts, G.	Cannock	—	—	—	—	X	—	X	—	—
Robinson, G.	Coventry NW	—	—	—	—	—	—	—	—	X
Roderick, C.	Brecon	—	—	—	—	—	X	—	—	—
Rodgers, G.	Chorley	—	X	—	O	—	X	X	—	X
Rooker, J.	Perry Bar	—	—	—	—	X	—	X	—	—
Rose, P.	Blackley	—	—	X	—	X	—	—	—	—
Ryman, J.	Blyth	—	—	—	—	—	—	X	—	—
Sedgemore, B.	Luton W	—	X	—	O	—	X	—	—	—
Selby, H.	Govan	—	X	X	O	—	X	X	—	—
Short, Mrs R.	W'hampton NE	—	—	—	O	X	—	—	—	X
Silverman, J.	Erdington	—	—	—	—	X	—	X	—	—
Skinner, D.	Bolsover	—	X	—	O	X	X	X	—	X
Spearing, N.	Newham S	—	—	—	—	—	X	—	—	—
Spriggs, L.	St Helens	X	—	—	—	—	—	—	—	X

176

MP	Constituency	E R	I P	N I	P E	P B	I M F	D E F	S W G	R E F
Swain, T.	Derbyshire SE	—	X	—	—	—	—	X	—	—
Taylor, Mrs A.	Bolton W	—	—	—	—	X	—	—	—	—
Thomas, R.	Bristol NW	—	X	X	O	X	X	X	—	X
Thorne, S.	Preston S	—	X	X	O	X	X	X	—	—
Tinn, J.	Cleveland	X	—	—	—	—	—	—	—	—
Torney, T.	Bradford S	—	—	—	—	—	—	X	—	X
Urwin, T.	Houghton	—	—	—	—	—	—	—	X	—
Wilson, W.	Coventry SE	—	—	—	—	—	—	X	—	—
Wise, Mrs A.	Coventry SW	—	X	—	O	X	X	X	—	X
Woof, R.	Blaydon	—	—	—	—	X	—	—	—	—

* Subsequently Conservative.

Table 20-3: LIBERAL AND NATIONALIST VOTING ON 12 MAJOR BILLS
Tables show how MPs voted on second reading of each Bill: X is vote for government, O is vote against, N means the MP was not yet elected when the vote was taken

Liberals	1 Trade Union and Lab Rel. 7 May 1974	2 Trade U. and L.R. Amendment 3 December 1974	3 Industry 18 February 1975	4 Sex Discrimination 26 March 1975	5 Employment Protection 28 April 1975	6 Community Land 29 April 1975	7 Petroleum and Pipelines 30 April 1975	8 Aircraft and Shipbuilding 2 December 1975	9 Education 4 February 1976	10 Dock Work Regulation 10 February 1976	11 Race Relations 4 March 1976	12 Rent (Agriculture) 4 May 1976
Beith, A.	X	O	O	–	–	O	O	O	X	–	X	X
Freud, C.	X	O	O	X	O	O	O	O	X	O	X	X
Grimond, J.	X	O	O	–	O	O	O	O	–	O	–	–
Hooson, H.	X	O	O	–	–	O	O	O	X	O	X	X
Howells, G.	X	O	O	–	O	O	O	O	X	O	–	X
Johnston, D.	X	O	O	X	–	–	–	O	X	O	–	–
Pardoe, J.	X	O	O	–	–	O	O	O	X	O	–	X
Penhaligon, D.	N	O	O	X	O	O	O	O	–	O	X	X
Ross, S.	X	O	O	–	O	O	O	O	X	O	X	X

	1	2	3	4	5	6	7	8	9	10	11	12
Smith, C.	X	O	O	—	O	O	O	O	O	O	—	X
Steel, D.	X	—	O	X	O	O	O	—	X	O	X	—
Thorpe, J.	X	O	O	X	O	O	—	O	X	O	O	—
Wainwright, R.	X	O	O	—	—	O	O	O	—	O	—	—

Scottish Nationalist

	1	2	3	4	5	6	7	8	9	10	11	12
Bain, Mrs M.	N	X	O	—	X	O	—	O	—	O	—	—
Crawford, G.	N	X	O	—	X	—	X	O	—	O	—	—
Ewing, Mrs W.	—	X	O	—	X	—	—	—	—	O	—	—
Henderson, D.	X	X	O	—	X	—	X	O	—	O	—	—
MacCormick, I.	X	X	—	—	X	—	—	O	—	O	X	—
Reid, G.	X	X	O	—	X	—	X	O	—	O	X	—
Stewart, D.	X	X	O	—	X	—	X	O	—	O	—	—
Thompson, G.	N	X	O	X	X	—	X	O	—	O	X	—
Watt, I.	X	—	O	—	X	—	—	O	—	O	—	—
Welsh, A.	N	X	O	X	X	—	X	O	—	O	—	—
Wilson, R.	X	X	O	—	X	—	X	O	—	O	X	—

Welsh Nationalist

	1	2	3	4	5	6	7	8	9	10	11	12
Evans, G.	N	X	X	—	—	X	X	O	X	O	—	—
Thomas, D.	X	—	X	—	—	X	—	O	—	—	—	X
Wigley, D.	X	X	X	—	X	X	—	O	X	—	—	—

See also direct election voting on pp. 172-4 and voting on devolution (by Scottish and Welsh MPs) on pp. 136-9

Part III
The Voting Analysed

Part III
The Voting Analysed

1 Background to the October 1974 Election

Introduction

The Dissolution of Parliament announced on 20 September 1974 ended the shortest Parliament of the present century. It had lasted only 184 days and during that time only one by-election had taken place. This was at Newham South, a seat made vacant by the appointment of Sir Elwyn Jones as Lord Chancellor. In an ultra-safe Labour stronghold, which the party easily retained, turnout fell to a miserable 25·9% and the Conservative candidate was beaten into fourth place by the National Front who collected 11·5% of the vote.

On 20 September the state of the parties was:

Table 1: THE STATE OF THE PARTIES, SEPTEMBER 1974

The Speaker	1
Lab	298
Con	296
Lib	15
UUUC	11
SNP	7
PC	2
Social Dem and Lab	1
Dem Lab	1
Ind Lab	1
Vacant (Newcastle upon Tyne E and Swansea E, both formerly held by Lab)	2
Total	635

The Nominations

A record number of candidates (2252, compared to 2135 in February) was nominated for the 10 October election.

The candidates brought forward by the parties (with the February figures in parentheses) are set out below:

Table 2: CANDIDATES IN OCTOBER 1974

	Oct	Feb
Lab (inc N Ireland Labour)	623	627
Con (exc all Ulster Unionists)	622	622
Lib	619	517
SNP	71	70
PC	36	36
NF	90	54
Com	29	44
The Speaker	1	1
Others*	160	164
	2252	2135

* Including 12 United Ulster Unionist Coalition, 10 Workers' Revolutionary Party, 9 Social Democratic and Labour Party and 5 Alliance Party.

The Outcome

Despite widespread predictions that Labour would win with a fairly massive majority, the result proved to be yet another cliff-hanger. In the event, Labour won 319 seats, the Conservatives 277, Liberals 13, the Scottish Nationalists 11 and Plaid Cymru three. The full results are set out below:

Table 3: GENERAL ELECTION RESULT, OCTOBER 1974

Party	Total votes	% share of total votes	Candidates	MPs
Con*	10,464,317	35·8	623	277
Lab†	11,457,079	39·2	623	319
Lib	5,346,754	18·3	619	13
SNP	839,617	2·9	71	11
PC	166,321	0·6	36	3
NF	133,843	0·4	90	0
Com	17,426	0·1	29	0
Others‡	783,321	2·7	161	12
Total	29,189,178	100·0	2252	635

* Excluding all types of Unionist candidates in Northern Ireland but including the Speaker of the House of Commons (Rt Hon J. S. B. Lloyd).

† Including the three candidates of the Northern Ireland Labour Party.

‡ Including all candidates contesting seats in Northern Ireland.

Labour's majority, though even smaller than that of 1964, was, in fact, in terms of practical politics, considerably more comfortable than it appeared. The following table sets out Labour's majority over its chief rivals:

Table 4: LABOUR'S MAJORITY

Lab majority over Con	43
Lab majority over Con and Lib combined	30
Lab (plus Fitt and Maguire) majority over Con, Lib and UUUC	22

Labour's great danger was to come when, after by-election reverses had revealed growing electoral unpopularity, the Conservatives, Liberals and Nationalists all combined.

The Seats Which Changed Hands

In all, Labour gained 19 seats, losing only one constituency (Carmarthen) to Plaid Cymru. The Conservatives suffered 22 losses with only two gains – Hazel Grove and Bodmin, both taken from the Liberals. The Scottish Nationalists gained 4 seats (all from the Conservatives) to take their total to 11. The full list of seats to change hands is set out below:

Table 5: SEATS WHICH CHANGED HANDS

Lab from Con (17)

Berwick and East Lothian	Lichfield and Tamworth
Birmingham, Selly Oak	Nelson and Colne
Bolton W	Oxford
Bristol NW	Peterborough
Bury and Radcliffe	Rochester and Chatham
Hemel Hempstead	Rossendale
Ilford N	Southampton Test
Ipswich	Welwyn and Hatfield
Leicester S	

Lab from Ind Lab (1)
Lincoln

Con from Lib (2)

Bodmin	Hazel Grove

Lib from Con (1)
Truro

PC from Lab (1)
Carmarthen

SNP from Con (4)

Angus S	Galloway
Dunbartonshire E	Perth and East Perthshire

Ind from UUUC (1)
Fermanagh and South Tyrone

2 How the Marginals Behaved

Over the whole country, Labour achieved a swing of 2·2% from Conservative. But in the key Conservative-held marginals that they needed to win they only achieved a small swing of 1·2%. Table 6 sets out the facts and figures of these marginals:

Table 6: THE MARGINALS

	Swing needed (%)	Swing achieved (%)	Result
Peterborough	0·02	1·8	Lab Gain
Hemel Hempstead	0·2	0·4	Lab Gain
Ipswich	0·2	1·4	Lab Gain
Nelson and Colne	0·3	1·1	Lab Gain
Northampton S	0·3	0·0	Con Hold
Ilford N	0·3	1·0	Lab Gain
Bury and Radcliffe	0·3	0·6	Lab Gain
Berwick and E Lothian	0·6	3·4	Lab Gain
Bristol NW	0·6	1·2	Lab Gain
Norfolk NW	0·6	−0·5	Con Hold
Rochester	0·7	2·7	Lab Gain
Brentford	0·7	0·4	Con Hold
Oxford	0·7	1·6	Lab Gain
Bolton W	0·8	1·9	Lab Gain
Rossendale	1·0	1·2	Lab Gain
Upminster	1·0	0·2	Con Hold
Southampton Test	1·2	1·7	Lab Gain
Lichfield	1·2	1·4	Lab Gain
Bosworth	1·2	1·0	Con Hold
Croydon C	1·3	1·0	Con Hold
Pembroke	1·3	0·5	Con Hold
Welwyn	1·3	1·7	Lab Gain
Wellingborough	1·6	0·3	Con Hold
Leicester S	1·6	2·7	Lab Gain
Acton	1·7	0·6	Con Hold
Braintree	1·9	0·7	Con Hold
Beeston	2·1	1·9	Con Hold

As the above table shows, Labour failed to win 11 of those marginals that needed a swing of under 2·2% and only one constituency, the Selly Oak division of Birmingham which fell to a 3·5% swing was won on a higher swing than 2·2%.

Labour's worst results were Northampton South, where Labour candidate John Dilks achieved no swing at all, and

Norfolk North-West which (in true East Anglian fashion) actually swung 0·5% to the Conservatives. Outer London proved a particularly bad area for Labour. The party failed to capture such ultra-marginals as Upminster, Brentford, Acton and Croydon Central from the Conservatives.

What, then, was the explanation behind this Labour failure to capture these vital seats? The Conservatives claimed that their organisation in the marginals had been brought to a peak of efficiency. While it is clear that a major allocation of their resources was put into their 'critical seats' campaign, this does not explain why the Labour-held marginals (in which the Tories had made equally determined efforts) swung by an average 2% to Labour (compared to a mere 1·2% swing in Tory-held marginals).

Two factors seem partly to account for Labour's poor showing in Tory-held marginals. The first was the decline in the Liberal vote. The fall in Liberal support was greater in the Conservative-held marginals than elsewhere and in these key seats Liberals lost on average nearly 6% of the vote. Indeed, there were 5 Conservative marginals where the Liberal vote fell by an average of nearly 10%. In these seats the swing to Labour was less than 1%. In Conservative marginals where there was a really big drop in Liberal support it looks as though this was because the Tories persuaded an unusually large number of Liberals to come back to them. Because of this the Conservatives held on to a few seats which they might have expected to lose, in particular Bosworth, Braintree, Wellingborough and several London suburban seats.

Partly, no doubt, this late swing from Liberal to Tory in the last days of the campaign was prompted by the predictions in the opinion polls of a vast Labour majority. There seems, however, to have been a regional and indeed rural factor also at work. Several key marginals – especially in the East Midlands and Outer London – were in areas which swung by relatively small amounts to Labour regardless of whether the seat was marginal or not. Thus in the rural East Midlands neither safe Blaby nor marginal Bosworth or Beeston swung to Labour very much, but urban South Leicester produced a Labour gain on a 2·7% swing. Similarly, Norwich South showed a 4% swing to Labour, but rural Norfolk North-West swung 0·5% to the Tories.

3 Regional Patterns in the Voting

Apart from the small swing occurring in Conservative-held marginal seats, distinct regional variations occurred within Britain. Thus Scotland swung 3·9% to Labour whereas within England itself the swing was markedly lower, especially in East Anglia and the South West:

Table 7: REGIONAL VARIATIONS IN SWING TO LABOUR

	% swing
Northern England	2·2
Midlands	1·8
London	1·8
South-West	1·4
East Anglia	1·1

The large swings in the North – in Cumbria, Durham and Northumberland – were partly explained by the appearance of Liberal candidates who hurt the Conservatives more than Labour. Even allowing for this however, seats such as Newcastle North showed very heavy pro-Labour swings. In this respect, Newcastle was representative of a general trend of heavy swings to Labour in the largest cities:

Table 8: HOW THE MAJOR CITIES VOTED

City	% swing	City	% swing
Newcastle	5·3	Inner London	3·5
Cardiff	4·7	Stoke	5·7
Liverpool	4·0	Hull	5·7

The cities showing the least swing to Labour were Bradford, Bristol and Coventry. Not only did Labour do well in the cities, but it polled best in virtually all of its safe seats. The safer the seat, the better Labour fared, as the table below sets out:

Table 9: HOW THE SWING TO LABOUR VARIED

	Safe seats	Medium-safe seats	Marginal seats
% swing to Lab:			
In Con-held seats	2·6	2·1	1·6
In Lab-held seats	3·5	2·9	1·9

To this extent, Labour tended to pile up its vote in exactly those constituencies where it mattered least, in areas such as central Leeds, Lambeth and Liverpool (see table 10). In the mining seats, Labour also did well, achieving an average 2·7% swing. In addition to piling up votes in seats already solidly safe, Labour ironically recovered much lost ground in the Tory heartland of Southern England, taking back votes from the Liberals in such true-blue seats as Thanet West and Hove. Labour's success in hopeless seats and its failure in many key marginals was a strange feature of the October election.

Table 10: LARGEST SWINGS TO LABOUR IN ENGLAND AND WALES (4·5%+)

Leeds W	6·4
Liverpool Kirkdale	6·0
(Hove)	(5·6)
Birmingham, Small Heath	5·3
Sunderland N	5·2
Leeds S	5·2
Peckham	5·1
Sunderland S	4·9
Lambeth, Vauxhall	4·9
(Weston-super-mare)	(4·9)
Cardiff W	4·8
Cardiff SE	4·7
Lambeth Central	4·7
Sheffield Park	4·7
Holborn and St Pancras S	4·6
(West Thanet)	(4·6)

The October election also reinforced the division of England into two nations: the Tory shires and the Labour cities. The Conservatives have rarely returned fewer MPs for the big cities while Labour are further than ever from making inroads into the counties. In the 50 most agricultural seats, Labour could achieve a swing of only 1·6%. Labour's sole loss at the election (Carmarthen) was its most agricultural seat, whilst the only Tory marginal seat actually to swing Conservative was Norfolk North-West, one of the most agricultural seats in the country. Rural Norfolk was not alone in going against the Labour swing. It was joined by a handful of seats which defied the national trend and swung Conservative. The most notable of these was Falmouth and Camborne, where a 1·7% swing to Conservative confirmed a steady drift to the right in what had been a Labour seat from 1945 to 1966. Other swings to the right occurred in Gloucestershire West (1·0%), Rugby (0·6%),

Gosport (0·1%), Brent North (0·1%) and Norfolk North-West (0·5%) – this latter marginal constituency continuing East Anglia's traditional defiance of any national trend. A very few seats with a very high proportion of owner-occupiers (who might presumably have found favour with Tory mortgage plans) also swung fractionally Conservative – most notably South-East Essex and Southend East. No swing at all occurred in two vital marginal seats which Labour had hoped to win – Buckingham and Northampton South, fought for Labour respectively by Robert Maxwell and John Dilks.

Features of the Labour Victory

In addition to the markedly different behaviour of these key marginal seats and variations in regional voting, there were a variety of other unusual features in Labour's victory. In England, for example, Labour won more seats than the Conservatives and it was only the third occasion in history that this has happened (the previous elections were 1945 and 1966). No less than 18 of the 19 seats gained by Labour were in England. Thus England now had 251 Labour MPs compared to 248 Conservatives – unlike 1964, when Labour could muster only 246 to the Conservatives' 261. Labour won a variety of seats in October 1974 that it had failed to win in 1964 – including Oxford, Middleton and Prestwich and Preston North. Indeed, Labour came near to winning such seats as Hornsey, Lowestoft and Wallasey which it had failed to win even in the triumph of 1966. But perhaps the single most noticeable result of the Labour victory (and the inroads caused by third parties) has been the massive increase in the number of seats now held on a minority vote and the change in the areas of Labour and Tory predominance. These two changes deserve closer analysis.

Seats Won on a Minority Vote

One result of the impact of Liberal and Nationalist candidates has been the large number of seats now won on a minority vote. The change has been particularly marked for the Conservatives – 224 of their 276 seats are now held with under half the votes cast.

	Total seats	Won on minority vote	%
Lab	319	131	41·1
Con	276	224	81·2
Lib	13	11	84·6
SNP	11	9	81·8
PC	3	3	100·0
Others	13	2	15·4
	635	380	59·8

Labour, with only 131 of its 319 seats won on a minority vote, has escaped relatively unscathed, except in Scotland. No less than 56 of Scotland's 71 seats were won by a candidate polling under 50% of the votes cast – the most extreme case was in East Dunbartonshire, won by Margaret Bain for the SNP with 31·2% of votes cast.

The Safest Conservative and Labour Seats

A remarkable transformation has occurred as a result of the 1974 elections in terms of the safe seats held by each of the major parties. The Liberal upsurge, the SNP breakthrough in rural Scotland, and the split with the Ulster Unionists, has left the Conservatives with only 52 seats in which they polled a majority of votes cast. The 25 safest seats (where Conservatives obtained over 52·5% of all votes cast) are set out below:

Table 12: THE SAFEST CONSERVATIVE SEATS

Chelsea	61·1%	Rushcliffe	54·7%
Worthing	58·2%	Eastbourne	54·7%
Penrith and the Border	58·1%	Epsom and Ewell	54·0%
Croydon S	57·9%	Southgate	53·9%
Christchurch and Lymington	57·4%	Surrey NW	53·8%
Sutton Coldfield	57·1%	Harrogate	53·8%
Richmond (Yorks)	56·9%	Honiton	53·8%
Rye	56·9%	Hove	53·6%
South Fylde	56·8%	Thirsk and Malton	53·2%
Arundel	56·2%	Wanstead and Woodford	53·2%
Esher	55·8%	East Grinstead	53·2%
North Fylde	55·5%	Solihull	52·7%
St Marylebone	54·9%		

As the above table demonstrates, in only one constituency (Chelsea) have Conservatives more than 60% of the total vote. In very marked contrast Labour have no less than 76 seats with over 60% of the total vote, and 15 seats with over 70% of all votes cast. In the safest Labour seat of all (Liverpool, Scotland Exchange) more than 4 out of every five votes cast were for Labour (see table below). At Rhondda, the Labour *majority* was a massive 34,481. In England, the Yorkshire mining seat of Hemsworth produced a 31,572 majority.

Table 13: THE SAFEST LABOUR STRONGHOLDS

Liverpool Scotland Exchange	80·2%	Newcastle Central	71·8%
Stepney and Poplar	77·6%	Peckham	71·6%
Rhondda	77·1%	Sheffield Park	71·4%
Hemsworth	76·5%	Bedwellty	70·9%
Abertillery	75·9%	Merthyr	70·6%
Ebbw Vale	74·1%	Bolsover	70·5%
Dearne Valley	74·1%	Pontefract and Castleford	70·4%
Bermondsey	73·4%		

This striking difference between the rock-solid Labour seats and the relatively few safe seats held by other parties is set out below:

Table 14: NUMBER OF SAFE SEATS BY PARTY

	Lab	Con	Lib	SNP	UUUC
Above 80%	1	—	—	—	—
Above 75%	5	—	—	—	—
Above 70%	15	—	—	—	3
Above 65%	35	—	—	—	—
Above 60%	76	1	—	1	5
	76	1	0	1	5

Apart from the Labour strongholds, three Ulster Unionist constituencies (Antrim North, 72·6%, Down North, 71·9% and Antrim South, 71·5%) have been won by candidates obtaining over 70% of votes cast. Indeed, the largest majority of all in the election was at Antrim South, where James Molyneaux obtained a 38,432 majority. The safest Liberal seat remains Orkney and Shetland (Jo Grimond's seat, where he took 56·2% of votes cast). The SNP's safest seat is the Western Isles (61·4% of votes cast).

4 The Performance of the Minor Parties

Introduction

In the February General Election, the outcome of the third-party challenge, at least in terms of votes polled, had been outstanding. Almost 25% of the electorate, compared to only 10·6% in June 1970, had voted for candidates of the Liberal and Nationalist parties. Thus, in the October election, the third parties were optimistic, particularly the Liberals with their massive field of 619 candidates. But it was the SNP which achieved the most substantial advance. Their representation increased from 7 to 11 (and Plaid Cymru went up from two to three), and the Liberals fell from 15 (if Christopher Mayhew is included) to 13. Even so, Liberal and Nationalist representation combined is higher than on any previous occasion since the 1930s.

Table 15: COMBINED LIB AND NAT REPRESENTATION AT WESTMINSTER

Election	Lib	Nat	Total
1955	6	0	6
1959	6	0	6
1964	9	0	9
1966	12	0	12
1970	6	1	7
(Feb) 1974	14	9	23
(Oct) 1974	13	14	27

The extent to which the two-party system has been eroded can be seen even more clearly in the votes cast for minor parties (set out in table below).

Table 16: VOTES CAST FOR MINOR PARTIES, 1951–74

Election	% share of vote for Con and Lab	% share of vote for minor parties
1951	96·8	3·2
1955	96·1	3·9
1959	93·2	6·8
1964	87·5	12·5
1966	90·0	10·0
1970	89·4	10·6
(Feb) 1974	75·4	24·6
(Oct) 1974	75·1	24·9

While, throughout the United Kingdom, some 75·1% of all voters supported Conservative or Labour candidates (compared to a massive 96·8% in 1951), the break-up of the two-party stranglehold was most noticeable outside England. In Scotland, Wales and Ulster, 43·6% of all votes cast were for minor parties. (In Scotland, 39% voted for minor party candidates, in Wales 26·6%.)

A The Liberal Party

The Liberals entered the October election with their largest-ever field of candidates and with high hopes that the 6 million votes secured in February would prove a spring-board for parliamentary success. They came out of the battle with fewer votes, a reduction in seats and with morale having suffered a severe setback.

The Liberals managed only a solitary gain in October 1974, at Truro, where David Penhaligon, an able Liberal who had been widely tipped to secure the seat, was in by 464 votes. Meanwhile two seats were lost to the Conservatives, Hazel Grove and Bodmin, lost by Michael Winstanley and Paul Tyler. Not one of the many hoped-for Liberal gains materialised. Bath defied Christopher Mayhew's assault, whilst Leominster, Newbury, Skipton and Hereford all survived a strong Liberal attack.

The total Liberal vote fell from 6,063,470 (19·3%) cast in February to 5,346,800 (18·3%) in October. This decrease tended to disguise the fact that, with 102 more candidates than in February, their vote in most constituencies had fallen quite considerably. In 93% of constituencies contested by Liberals on both occasions, the Liberal share of the vote declined. Nor did the Liberal leaders fare as well as they had in February. With the exception of Richard Wainwright in Colne Valley and Jo Grimond in Orkney and Shetland, all the sitting Liberals had their majority cut – by 6% in the case of Jeremy Thorpe and 11·5% for Cyril Smith at Rochdale. As a result only four Liberals possessed majorities over their nearest rivals of more than 10%.

As a result of the October election, the areas of relative Liberal strength and weakness also saw some changes. The South-West (and most particularly Devon and Cornwall) remained the best area for the Liberals, followed by the suburban metropolitan areas, while East Anglia lost much of the February upsurge.

The change in areas of traditional Liberal strength can perhaps best be seen in comparison with the 1970 results.

	% 1970	% Oct 1974
Devon and Cornwall	20·6	31·5
Rural Wales	15·0	20·5
Rural Scotland	13·1	13·7
South-East (Outer)	12·7	23·3
Outer Metropolitan Area	11·0	23·2
South-West (excl Devon and Cornwall)	11·0	25·3

In 1970, Liberals were strongest in Devon and Cornwall; their two next best areas were both their traditional Celtic fringe strongholds, rural Wales and rural Scotland. By 1974, while Liberal strength in the South-West had firmed greatly, and Liberal strength in the Home Counties had doubled or even more than doubled, rural Scotland had hardly changed in percentage terms. To this extent, the SNP upsurge had achieved what may well be the end of Liberalism as the party of the Celtic fringe.

Meanwhile, the areas of greatest Liberal weakness had seen less change. Industrial Scotland remained barren Liberal territory (and rural Scotland was now nearly as bad), while the West Midland conurbation and South Yorkshire remained equally desolate. Merseyside, once the great hope of the 'New Liberalism', slipped back in October 1974 to become one of the Party's weakest areas.

One of the greatest single disappointments for the Liberals in October 1974 was the almost complete absence of 'tactical voting', whereby supporters of a party in a hopeless position would vote Liberal to unseat the sitting Conservative or Labour Member. In such seats as Bath, Chippenham, Hereford, Newbury, South Bedfordshire and Leominster, Liberals had entertained high hopes that the Labour vote would go over to their camp. In one or two seats (such as Truro) a very limited amount of tactical voting occurred (and in Colne Valley and Cardiganshire Tories seem to have voted Liberal to keep Labour out) but such examples were rare in the extreme. The number of Labour lost deposits dropped from 28 in February to only 13 in October, thus reflecting the rise in the Labour vote even in the most hopeless of constituencies. Indeed, far from losing votes to the Liberals in strong Liberal areas, Labour appeared to have recaptured votes lost in February.

The election of October 1974 had thus seemed to set the seal on the high hopes of the 1973 revival. The party, despite its ability to poll a very large number of votes, had seemed to have come full circle to the situation of 1966.

Since October 1974 (as page 216ff of this Guide shows), Liberals have fared disastrously in by-elections. If this tide continues against the Liberals in the next election, they face possible serious losses. As the table below shows, nine of the Liberal seats are held with less than a 10% majority over the nearest challenger.

Table 18: LIBERAL SEATS IN ORDER OF MARGINALITY

Constituency	Maj	% maj	Challenger
Berwick	73	0·2	Con
Truro	464	0·8	Con
Inverness	1134	2·8	SNP
Isle of Wight	2040	3·1	Con
Colne Valley	1666	3·3	Lab
Isle of Ely	2685	5·1	Con
Rochdale	2753	5·8	Lab
Cardiganshire	2410	6·9	Lab
Cornwall N	3856	9·2	Con
Devon N	6721	11·5	Con
Montgomery	3859	14·7	Con
Roxburgh, Selkirk and Peebles	7433	16·2	Con
Orkney and Shetland	6852	39·0	SNP

It must be emphasised, however, that despite their by-election record, Liberals have often retained their strongholds even when the national tide is against them. Moreover, even in the most adverse conditions, Liberals might still pick up an isolated seat where local factors or a strong candidate defy the predictions of the pollsters. In October 1974 the Liberals still remained in second place in some 102 constituencies, 92 of these held by Conservatives and 10 by Labour.

The table below sets out the 17 Tory-held seats vulnerable to a 5% swing to the Liberals.

Table 19: TORY-HELD SEATS VULNERABLE TO THE LIBERALS

Constituency	Maj	% maj
Skipton	590	1·4
Bodmin	665	1·4
Leominster	579	1·7
Newbury	1022	1·8
Hereford	1110	2·5
Chippenham	1949	3·3
Bath	2122	4·3
Hazel Grove	2831	5·1
Louth	2880	5·6
Aberdeenshire W	2468	5·8
Chelmsford	4002	6·3
Gainsborough	3968	8·6
Salisbury	4180	8·9
Pudsey	4581	9·0
Denbigh	4551	9·4
Orpington	5010	9·6
Tiverton	5254	9·9

The number of Liberal gains if they *can* secure success in Tory-held seats at the next election is set out below:

% swing	No. of gains	Seats in Parliament
1	4	17
2	6	19
3	10	23
4	11	24
5	17	30
7·5	34	47
10	52	65

If the Liberals do secure any Labour votes in Tory-held seats as a result of the Lib-Lab pact, it is the above seats which are the ones to watch for Liberal surprises.

B Scottish National Party

After the six million votes polled in February 1974 by the Liberal Party, the greatest success in the election for the smaller parties was undoubtedly that won by the Nationalists in Scotland. The party entered the election defending two seats (Western Isles and Glasgow Govan). Although Govan was lost to Labour, the party returned seven-strong to Westminster. The seats to return SNP members are set out below:

Table 20: THE SCOTTISH NATIONALIST STRONGHOLDS:
         FEBRUARY 1974

(Seats arranged in % maj)

Constituency	% maj over
Western Isles	47·9 Lab
Aberdeenshire E	15·8 Con
Banffshire	11·6 Con
Argyll	10·3 Con
Stirlingshire E and Clackmannan	7·0 Lab
Moray and Nairn	5·9 Con
Dundee E	5·8 Lab

These successes were mainly at the expense of the Tories. Four of their 6 gains were from the Tories – at Argyll, Moray and Nairn, Banff, and Aberdeenshire East. Labour victims of the SNP were Richard Douglas at Stirlingshire East and Clackmannan and George Machin at Dundee East.

Less happily for the SNP, they failed to win back Hamilton or to make any advance in West Lothian. Nor did their candidates make any real impression in Glasgow or Edinburgh. Apart from these relative setbacks, however, the SNP had every reason for satisfaction. Compared to 11·4% of the Scottish vote in 1970, they obtained 21·9% on this occasion. Only 6 deposits were lost (compared with 43 in 1970).

In many respects, the 1974 election provided the SNP with an ideal springboard for a further major Parliamentary advance. In October 1974 the SNP went on to achieve precisely this – its total of seats increased from 7 to 11, all four gains coming in Conservative-held rural territory. The seats captured were Galloway, Perth and East Perthshire, East Dunbartonshire and Angus South. The 11 seats now held by the SNP are set out below in order of marginality:

Table 21: SEATS HELD BY SNP IN ORDER OF MARGINALITY

Constituency	Maj	% maj	Challenger
Dunbartonshire E	22	0·0	Con
Galloway	30	0·1	Con
Moray and Nairn	367	1·2	Con
Perth and E Perthshire	793	1·9	Con
Angus S	1824	4·7	Con
Banffshire	1851	8·0	Con
Aberdeenshire E	4371	13·0	Con
Argyll	3931	13·0	Con
Stirlingshire E and Clackmannan	7341	14·3	Lab
Dundee E	6983	15·1	Lab
Western Isles	5232	36·7	Lab

These SNP victories have now changed the face of Scottish politics. The table below sets out how the political representation of Scotland has changed since 1945:

Table 22: *PARLIAMENTARY REPRESENTATION IN SCOTLAND 1945–74*

Election	Con	Lab	Lib	SNP	Others	Total
1945	27	37	—	—	7	71
1950	31	37	2	—	1	71
1951	35	35	1	—	—	71
1955	36	34	1	—	—	71
1959	31	38	1	—	1	71
1964	24	43	4	—	—	71
1966	20	46	5	—	—	71
1970	23	44	3	1	—	71
(Feb) 1974	21	40	3	7	—	71
(Oct) 1974	16	41	3	11	—	71

In terms of votes cast the change has been even more dramatic over the last 10 years:

Table 23: *VOTES CAST FOR SNP, 1964–74*

Election	Vote	% in Scotland
1964	64,044	2·4
1966	128,474	5·0
1970	306,802	11·4
(Feb) 1974	632,032	21·9
(Oct) 1974	839,617	30·0

With over 800,000 votes – some 30% of all votes cast in Scotland – the SNP had replaced the Conservatives as the second largest party and the natural alternative to Labour in Scotland. Indeed, in parts of rural Scotland the SNP had emerged as the largest single party. The table below sets out the regional growth of the SNP:

Table 24: *SNP STRENGTH BY REGION, 1970–74*

	1970	Feb 1974	Oct 1974	+ Feb–Oct 1974
Strathclyde	9·0%	18·4%	27·7%	+9·3%
East Central Scotland	12·1%	22·8%	31·0%	+8·2%
Rural Scotland	13·2%	26·7%	34·6%	+7·9%

Only a slightly heavier push would have given the SNP an even greater parliamentary representation. For example, Kinross and West Perthshire, formerly the rock-solid seat of Sir Alec Douglas-Home, was only retained by Nicholas Fairbairn by a majority of 53 after two recounts. The SNP failed by a whisker to make the vital breakthrough they had hoped for in the industrial seats of West Central Scotland – although they came second in 36 of Labour's 41 seats. Indeed, Labour only narrowly retained Lanark (Judith Hart's seat) by 698 votes over Tom McAlpine, SNP spokesman on industrial affairs. Labour suffered a similar close shave at East Kilbride and at Midlothian.

Even more significant than the success achieved by the SNP in October was the foundation which was laid for future advances. If the SNP momentum continued, the Labour Party could face disaster at the next General Election. In October 1974, the SNP achieved 42 second-places, compared to 17 in February. No fewer than 35 of these were in Labour-held seats, 5 in Conservative and two in Liberal. Even on a 10% swing to SNP from Labour, 23 seats would fall. Despite the implications of the poor SNP performance at the Hamilton by-election and in the 1978 local elections, Labour will have to poll its full vote to keep the SNP out of these seats.

Table 25: LAB-HELD SEATS VULNERABLE ON A 10% SWING TO SNP

Constituency	% maj
Stirlingshire W	0·8
Lanark	1·7
Stirling, Falkirk and Grangemouth	3·4
West Lothian	4·4
Dunbartonshire W	4·5
East Kilbride	5·2
Dundee W	5·9
Midlothian	5·9
Hamilton	8·2*
Glasgow Govan	8·5
Renfrewshire W	9·9
Dunbartonshire Central	11·1
Caithness and Sutherland	11·4
Dunfermline	11·5
Paisley	11·7
Motherwell and Wishaw	12·8
Kirkcaldy	13·4
Kilmarnock	15·5
Fife Central	18·5
Rutherglen	19·1
Edinburgh E	19·3
Lanarkshire N	19·4
Glasgow Garscadden	19·7*

* by-election has since taken place

The Conservatives – if only because they have been battered to the sidelines of Scottish politics – have far less to lose from a further SNP advance. Their 6 most vulnerable seats are listed below:

Table 26: CON-HELD SEATS VULNERABLE TO SNP ADVANCES

Constituency	% maj
Kinross and West Perthshire	0·2
Ross and Cromarty	3·2
East Fife	7·0
Angus N and Mearns	9·4
Renfrewshire E	18·1

However, the SNP vote could go down, as it did in the wake of the Hamilton by-election victory of 1968. In this event, the Conservatives have most to gain. A 5% swing from SNP to Conservative would produce 6 Conservative victories. A similar 5% swing from SNP to Labour would not give Labour a single victory.

C Plaid Cymru

Unlike the Nationalists in Scotland, Plaid Cymru had a very mixed result in Wales. Although the party captured Carmarthenshire – which it had missed by only three votes in February, thereby increasing its parliamentary representation to three, it came nowhere near to victory in any other seat. Its total share of the Welsh vote was 10·8%, virtually unchanged from the 10·7% achieved in February and still below the 11·5% secured in June 1970. Meanwhile, Labour, with 49·5% of the total vote, still dominates Welsh politics, while the Liberal revival in Wales in October has acted as another check on progress by the Plaid (Liberals polled relatively well in Wales in October 1974, their total vote declining by only 0·2% compared to February). However, no amount of disappointment in the total vote achieved by the Plaid could disguise the tonic achieved by the triumphant return of Gwynfor Evans – for 28 years the President of the party – for Carmarthenshire. The Plaid's three seats are:

Constituency	Maj	% maj	Sitting MP
Merioneth	2592	11·5	Dafydd Thomas
Caernarvon	2894	8·4	Dafydd Wigley
Carmarthenshire	3640	7·0	Gwynfor Evans

All three are rural Welsh-speaking constituencies where the cultural and linguistic nationalism of the party has strong appeal.

Apart from these three seats, the Plaid finished nowhere else within sight of victory. In rural Anglesey, which some had seen as a potential Plaid gain, the party finished in third place with only 19·1% of the vote. In the South Wales valleys, as the table below shows, even in the 6 seats where the Plaid came second to Labour, their chances of future victory seem remote. In each seat, Labour's percentage majority had increased since the February election.

Table 27: *LAB-HELD SEATS IN WHICH PC CAME SECOND*

Constituency	Lab maj	Lab % maj	(Feb)
Caerphilly	13,709	32·1	(29·7)
Aberdare	16,064	42·0	(29·6)
Neath	17,723	43·5	(40·7)
Merthyr	16,805	55·8	(41·4)
Abertillery	18,355	66·8	(59·4)
Rhondda	34,481	68·8	(57·8)

Thus the Plaid seems unlikely to break out of its rural strongholds in Welsh-speaking North Wales. All this, however, provides only relative comfort for Labour, whose loss of Carmarthenshire has reduced their representation in Wales to 23, a new 'low' for the post-war period.

Table 28: *PARLIAMENTARY REPRESENTATION IN WALES 1945–74*

Election	Lab	Con	Lib	Others	Total
1945	25	4	6	—	35
1950	27	4	5	—	36
1951	27	6	3	—	36
1955	27	6	3	—	36
1959	27	7	2	—	36
1964	28	6	2	—	36
1966	32	3	1	—	36
1970	27	7	1	1*	36
(Feb) 1974	24	8	2	2†	36
(Oct) 1974	23	8	2	3‡	36

* Ind Lab (S. O. Davies) in Merthyr
† Plaid Cymru in Caernarvonshire and Merioneth
‡ Plaid Cymru in Caernarvonshire, Merioneth and Carmarthenshire

D National Front

The National Front, with 90 candidates in the field compared to 54 in February, launched their widest yet challenge for the October election. All 90 candidates lost their deposits – indeed, none secured over 10% of the votes cast – thereby contributing

£13,500 to the Exchequer. The Front later claimed that the prime purpose of the election had been to launch a 'giant advertising drive'. Undoubtedly the party's 90 candidates (and television and radio time) attracted considerable publicity. Nor did the Front poll nearly as badly as the fringe candidates of the left. Twelve National Front candidates secured over 5% of votes cast (only Jimmy Reid for the Communists achieved this degree of success, and no Workers' Revolutionary Party candidate managed even 2%).

The Front's best result was in Hackney South and Shoreditch, where, at the first attempt, Robin May secured 2544 votes (9·4% of the votes cast).

Table 29: SEATS IN WHICH NF POLLED OVER 4% OF VOTE, OCTOBER 1974

Constituency	%	Constituency	%
Hackney S and Shoreditch	9·4	Barking	4·9
Tottenham	8·3	Bermondsey	4·8
Wood Green	8·0	Deptford	4·8
Bethnal Green and Bow	7·6	Edmonton	4·6
Newham NE	7·0	Wolverhampton SE	4·6
Leicester E	6·4	Battersea N	4·5
Walthamstow	5·5	Blackburn	4·4
West Bromwich W	5·4	West Bromwich E	4·3
Leyton	5·4	Wolverhampton	4·2
Islington Central	5·3	Leicester S	4·1
Leicester W	5·0	Rochdale	4·1

Of these 23 seats in which the National Front captured over 4% of the poll, the best results were obtained in London, especially in the East End and in the Tottenham and Wood Green areas. Indeed, a curious feature of the results was that the National Front tended to slip back where they had been strong in February (as in parts of Leicester and West Bromwich) and do well in parts of London. Apart from the Front's few good results, as the table below shows, the great majority of candidates polled less than 2·5%:

Table 30: % OBTAINED BY NF

10 and above	nil
7·5 – 10	5
5 – 7·5	7
2·5 – 5	34
0 – 2·5	44

E The Communist Party

The Communists, fielding only 29 candidates compared to

40 in February, suffered yet another disastrous and humiliating contest. Having done badly in February, October proved even worse. Only in Dunbartonshire Central (where Jimmy Reid was the standard-bearer) could the party poll even moderately respectably – with 8·7% of the vote, down from 14·4% in February. Not a single Communist candidate saved his deposit, and none except Jimmy Reid even managed 3% of the vote. The 6 best results for the party are set out below:

Table 31: WHERE COMM POLLED BEST

Constituency	%	(% in Feb 1974)
Dunbartonshire Central	8·7	(14·4)
Liverpool, Scotland Exchange	2·9	(2·5)
Aberdare	2·7	(2·1)
Motherwell and Wishaw	2·4	(2·7)
Fife Central	2·4	(4·4)
Stepney and Poplar	2·0	(3·6)

Even in constituencies with some Communist tradition, such as Fife Central and Motherwell, their vote was badly down – from 2019 to 1040 in Fife Central and from nearly 2000 in 1970 to only 946 in Motherwell. On average, Communist candidates saw a third of their meagre February vote evaporate still further, while in seats such as Stepney and Dagenham their vote halved.

The steady decline in Communist support since the heady days of 1945 when the party secured 102,000 votes and returned two MPs is set out below:

Table 32: THE COMM VOTE: 1945–74

Election	Candidates	MPs elected	Forfeited deposits	Total votes	% of UK total
1945	21	2	12	102,780	0·4
1950	100	—	97	91,765	0·3
1951	10	—	10	21,640	0·1
1955	17	—	15	33,144	0·1
1959	18	—	17	30,896	0·1
1964	36	—	36	46,442	0·2
1966	57	—	57	62,092	0·2
1970	58	—	58	37,970	0·1
(Feb) 1974	44	—	43	32,741	0·1
(Oct) 1974	29	—	29	17,426	0·1

It was, perhaps, some small comfort for the Communist Party that the other left-wing candidates suffered equally severely.

F Workers' Revolutionary Party

With 10 candidates in the field, the WRP fared disastrously. No candidate obtained more than the 572 votes (1·5%) of the vote polled by Vanessa Redgrave in Newham NE. As the table below shows, WRP votes were invariably below the February level, in several cases more than halved.

*Table 33: CONSTITUENCIES CONTESTED BY WRP CANDI-
DATES*

Constituency	Votes	% vote	Vote Feb.
Newham NE	572	1·5	(760)
Lambeth Central	233	0·9	(337)
Hayes and Harlington	198	0·5	—
Hackney N and Stoke Newington	159	0·6	—
Aberavon	427	0·9	—
Wallsend	435	0·7	(1108)
Liverpool, Toxteth	365	1·3	(263)
Pontefract and Castleford	457	1·1	(991)
Coventry NE	352	0·8	—
Swindon	206	0·4	(240)
	3404	0·8	

Average vote for WRP candidates: 340
Average % vote for WRP candidates: 0·8%

If the WRP performance was abysmal, the five candidates fielded by the Marxist Leninists fared even worse. Only one candidate secured more than 1% of the vote and the other four fell back from their vote in February.

G The Labour Independents

Just as the Communist and the 'New Left' candidates went down to defeat, so the Labour rebels in the shape of Eddie Milne, Dick Taverne and Eddie Griffiths were all beaten. Taverne, who had held Lincoln in February by 1293 votes after winning his by-election triumph with a 13,000 majority, was ousted in October by Margaret Jackson who won the seat with a 984 majority on a 6·4% swing to Labour. Meanwhile, at Blyth, Eddie Milne lost by a mere 78 votes after a determined Labour assault on the seat. In the Sheffield Brightside constituency, where Eddie Griffiths had been ousted by his local party, Joan Maynard retained the seat comfortably for Labour, although Griffiths polled 10,182 votes (27·9% of the vote).

205

Along the Fringe

These left-wing and Independent Labour candidates were joined in their attempts to woo the voters by a variety of independents, fringe groups and downright cranks. The 7 candidates fielded by the Irish Civil Rights Association all forfeited their deposits, as did the 11 candidates of the United Democratic Party. The Campaign for a More Prosperous Britain, led by a 61-year-old Oldham millionaire, forfeited all its 25 deposits (presumably contributing in this way at least to a more prosperous Exchequer). Of the other candidates, the Gay Liberation Front polled 223 votes in Lambeth Norwood, a Women's Rights candidate in Sutton and Cheam polled 298 votes, and the Cornish Nationalists (Mebyon Kernow) polled 384 votes in Truro.

Lost Deposits

Some 442 candidates in the election duly lost their deposits. The totals (by party) were:

Table 34: LOST DEPOSITS

Party	Candidates	Money forfeited
Con	28	£4,200
Lab	13	£1,950
Lib	125	£18,750
NF	90	£13,500
Com	29	£4,350
PC	26	£3,900
Others	131	£19,650
	442	£66,300

5 Turnout

In the February election, turnout rose for the first time since the 1959 election – from 72% to 79%. In October, turnout slipped back to 72·8%.

Table 35: TURNOUT AT BRITISH GENERAL ELECTIONS 1945–74

Election	%	Total electorate
1945	72·7	33,240,391
1950	83·9	34,412,255
1951	82·6	34,919,331
1955	76·8	34,852,179
1959	78·7	35,397,304
1964	77·1	35,894,054
1966	75·8	35,957,245
1970	72·0	39,342,013
(Feb) 1974	78·7	39,798,899
(Oct) 1974	72·8	40,072,971

Some particularly heavy falls in turnout occurred in the major cities:

Table 36: FALL IN TURNOUT

	% voting	Feb–Oct 1974 (%)
Greater London	66·6	8·1
Glasgow	68·7	4·4
Leeds	64·7	9·4
Sheffield	67·7	8·5
Bradford	70·6	9·1
Nottingham	66·7	9·5

The following tables show the 10 seats with the highest turnout, the lowest turnout and the seats with the lowest turnout decrease in October 1974.

Table 37: TURNOUT, OCTOBER 1974

Seats with highest turnout Oct 1974 %	Seats with lowest turnout Oct 1974 %
88·7 Fermanagh & S Tyrone	50·0 Chelsea
85·6 Carmarthen	51·5 Stepney & Poplar
84·1 Kingswood	51·6 Newham NE
84·0 Merionethshire	52·6 Lambeth C
83·1 Berwick & E Lothian	52·8 Lambeth Vauxhall
83·0 Keighley	52·8 Hackney N & Stoke Newington
82·4 Hazel Grove	52·8 Hackney C
82·3 Bodmin	53·1 Bethnal Green & Bow
82·2 Lanark	53·2 City of London & Westminster S
82·1 Skipton	53·4 Manchester C

Seats with lowest turnout decrease
Oct 1974
%

+6·6 Down S
+2·2 Carmarthen
+1·8 Greenock & PG
+1·3 Fermanagh & S Tyrone
+1·3 Londonderry
+0·7 Bury & Radcliffe
+0·2 Armagh
−0·3 Whitehaven
−0·5 Neath
−0·6 Workington

6 Constituencies with Special Characteristics

(1) The following chart shows the 20 constituencies where the proportion of student voters exceeds 5%.

8·7 Bristol W	6·2 Cardiff N
7·6 Cambridge	6·1 Hampstead
7·3 Oxford	5·9 Sheffield, Hallam
6·9 Edinburgh S	5·9 Edinburgh N
6·9 Chelsea	5·8 Glasgow, Kelvingrove
6·7 Manchester, Withington	5·8 Cardigan
6·4 Aberdeen S	5·8 Glasgow, Hillhead
6·4 Leeds NW	5·7 Edinburgh C
6·4 Hendon S	5·5 Hornsey
6·4 Newcastle N	5·5 Kensington

(2) Constituencies where the numbers employed in agriculture exceed 20%.

30·8 Montgomery	24·2 Banff
29·4 Orkney & Shetland	24·1 Leominster
29·2 Cardigan	23·5 Penrith & the Border
28·2 Carmarthen	21·5 Howden
25·9 Aberdeenshire E	21·3 Aberdeenshire W
25·5 Holland with Boston	20·8 Angus N & Mearns
25·0 Galloway	20·6 Norfolk SW
24·8 Devon W	20·2 Ludlow

(3) Constituencies where the numbers employed in mining exceed 10%.

32·9 Bolsover	16·1 Newark
32·4 Hemsworth	16·1 Bedwellty
28·4 Houghton-le-Spring	15·9 Rother Valley
23·8 Dearne Valley	14·8 Caperhilly
23·8 Morpeth	14·3 Blyth
23·4 Easington	14·3 Cannock
22·4 Mansfield	14·0 Normanton
21·2 Ashfield	13·1 Ogmore
20·5 Don Valley	12·3 Bassetlaw
20·2 Pontefract & Castleford	12·0 Derbyshire NE
19·4 Abertillery	10·3 Ebbw Vale
17·2 Barnsley	10·1 Goole
17·0 Ayrshire S	10·0 Durham
16·3 Aberdare	

(4) Constituencies where the percentage of persons either born in the New Commonwealth, or with at least one parent born in the New Commonwealth, exceeds 15%.

29·6 Birmingham, Ladywood	18·9 Birmingham, Sparkbrook
27·1 Birmingham, Handsworth	18·7 Islington N
25·4 Southall	18·0 Hornsey
25·3 Tottenham	17·6 Hackney C
24·6 Brent S	17·2 Birmingham, Small Heath
19·4 Lambeth C	16·4 Battersea S
19·3 Brent E	15·7 Lambeth, Norwood
19·2 Bradford W	15·4 Islington, C
19·0 Hackney N & Stoke Newington	15·3 Newham, NW

(5) Constituencies where the percentage of persons born in Ireland exceeds 5%.

12·0 Brent E	6·1 Hampstead
9·2 Hammersmith N	5·9 Birmingham, Small Heath
8·6 Islington N	5·5 Kensington
8·3 Birmingham, Sparkbrook	5·5 Islington C
7·7 Brent S	5·5 Glasgow, Queen's Park
7·5 Manchester, Ardwick	5·3 Birmingham, Handsworth
7·2 Paddington	5·2 Fulham
6·9 Manchester, Moss Side	5·1 Luton E
6·8 St Pancras N	5·1 Holborn & St Pancras S
6·5 Coventry SE	5·1 Birmingham, Erdington
6·5 Acton	5·0 Birmingham, Ladywood

SOURCES: These figures are derived from the official census returns and as such are some years old. They are conveniently set out in the indispensable Nuffield election studies, edited by David Butler.

7 The New Marginals

This chart shows the seats in which each party has the best chance of ousting its rivals in the coming election. Figures indicate the percentage majority of the successful party in October 1974.

Conservative Held:

% maj over Lab		% maj over Lib		% maj over SNP	
Hertfordshire SW	9·9	Tiverton	9·9		
		Orpington	9·6		
Chislehurst	9·5				
Hexham	9·4				
Harrow E	9·4			Angus N and Mearns	9·4
Leeds NW	9·3	Denbigh	9·3		
Basingstoke	9·3				
Worcester	9·1				
		Salisbury	9·0		
Glasgow Hillhead	8·9	Pudsey	8·9		
Colchester	8·9				
Chester	8·8				
Bedfordshire S	8·8				
		Gainsborough	8·6		
Gillingham	8·5				

% maj over Lab		% maj over Lib		% maj over SNP	
Carlton	8·2				
Streatham	7·9				
Ayr	7·8				
Edinburgh S	7·7				
Carshalton	7·5				
Bedford	7·2				
Gloucester	7·2				
Nantwich	7·2				
Shipley	7·2				
Conway	7·1			Fife E	7·1
Gloucestershire S	6·8				
Romford	6·7				
Liverpool Wavertree	6·6				
Leek	6·5				
		Chelmsford	6·4		
Harrow	6·3				
Cardiff N	6·2				
		Aberdeenshire W	5·8		
Kensington	5·6	Louth	5·6		
Brighton, Kemptown	5·6				
Birmingham, Edgbaston	5·5				
Birmingham, Hall Green	5·5				
Hitchin	5·5				
Barry	5·4				
Tynemouth	5·4				
Cambridge	5·2				
Croydon NE	5·2				
Horsham-Crawley	5·2				
Bexleyheath	5·1	Hazel Grove	5·1		
Faversham	5·0				
Manchester, Withington	5·0				
Uxbridge	4·8				
Hendon N	4·7				
Buckingham	4·6				
Glasgow Cathcart	4·6				
Hertfordshire S	4·5				
Yarmouth	4·3	Bath	4·3		
High Peak	4·3				
Exeter	4·3				
Hampstead	4·3				
Dover and Deal	4·0				
Burton	3·9				
Croydon NW	3·9				

% maj over Lab		% maj over Lib		% maj over SNP	
Monmouth	3·9				
Lancaster	3·6	Chippenham	3·6		
Wallasey	3·6				
Lowestoft	3·4				
Cleveland-Whitby	3·3				
				Ross and Cromarty	3·2
Bromsgrove and Redditch	3·0				
Edinburgh, Pentlands	3·0				
Wellingborough	2·5	Hereford	2·5		
Derbyshire SE	2·3				
Stretford	2·3				
Norfolk NW	2·2				
Acton	2·1				
Braintree	2·1				
Hornsey	2·0				
Newcastle N	1·8	Newbury	1·8		
		Leominster	1·7		
		Bodmin	1·5		
Pembroke	1·4	Skipton	1·4		
Upminster	1·4				
Halesowen and Stourbridge	1·4				
Reading N	1·1				
Aberdeen S	0·7				
Brentford and Isleworth	0·5				
Northampton S	0·5				
Bosworth	0·4				
Croydon C	0·4				
Beeston	0·2			Kinross and W Perthshire	0·2
Plymouth Drake	0·1				
Totals	79		17		4

N.B. The following Conservative-held marginals have resulted from the large by-election swings against Labour. It would appear likely that some at least of these seats will return to their Labour allegiance.

Marginal Conservative By-election Gains:

Constituency	% maj	% swing to Con at by-election
Ashfield	0·6	20·8
Workington	2·6	13·2
Birmingham Stechford	5·4	17·6
Woolwich W	6·7	7·6
Ilford N	12·4	6·9
Thurrock	9·9	10·6
Walsall N	11·8	22·6

Labour Held:

% maj over Con		% maj over Lib	% maj over other parties	
			Renfrewshire W (SNP)	9·9
Swansea W	9·8			
Birmingham Yardley	9·7			
Belper	9·7			
Preston S	9·6			
Norwich S	9·6			
Bebington and Ellesmere Port	9·5			
Battersea S	9·4			
Luton E	9·3			
Watford	9·1			
Bolton E	8·9			
Halifax	8·8			
Woolwich W	8·5		Glasgow Govan (SNP)	8·5
Leicester E	8·3			
Birmingham Perry Barr	8·3			
Darlington	8·0			
Keighley	7·2			
Derby N	6·9			
Brecon and Radnor	6·8			
Paddington	6·5			
Middleton and Prestwich	6·4			
York	6·3			
Plymouth, Devonport	6·2			

% maj over Con		% maj over Lib	% maj over other parties	
Putney	5·9		Dundee W (SNP)	5·9
Berwick and E Lothian	5·9		Midlothian (SNP)	5·9
Liverpool Garston	5·7			
Kingswood	5·5			
Ealing N	5·3			
			E Kilbride (SNP)	5·2
Aldridge-Brownhills	5·1			
Preston N	4·5			
Chorley	4·4		Dunbartonshire W (SNP)	4·4
Ilford S	4·4		W Lothian (SNP)	4·4
Stockport N	4·4			
Loughborough	4·3			
Brighouse and Spenborough	4·3			
Northampton N	4·1			
Rochester and Chatham	4·1			
Coventry SW	3·9			
Peterborough	3·7			
Huddersfield W	3·4		Stirling, Falkirk and Grange-mouth (SNP)	3·4
Gravesend	3·4			
Portsmouth N	2·6			
Ipswich	2·5		Lincoln (DLP)	2·5
Bolton W	2·4			
Leicester S	2·2			
Oxford	1·9			
Nelson and Colne	1·8		Lanark (SNP)	1·8
Sowerby	1·7			
Ilford N	1·6			
Bristol NW	1·2			
Welwyn and Hatfield	1·0			
Southampton W	1·0			
Birmingham Selly Oak	0·8		Stirlingshire W (SNP)	0·8
Bury and Radcliffe	0·8			
Gloucestershire W	0·8			
Hemel Hempstead	0·7			
Rossendale	0·5			
Lichfield and Tamworth	0·5			
			Blyth (Ind Lab)	0·1

Projected effects of a given swing between the two main parties (allowing for the consequences of this swing for gains and losses among other parties).

Swing to Conservatives (based on October 1974 voting):

Size of swing (%)	Lab to Con	Lib/SNP to Con	Lab to SNP/Ind	Over-all maj
1	13	4	2	none
2	21	6	3	none
3	35	6	4	1
4	43	7	5	19
5	57	8	7	49
10	122	9	11	181

Swing to Labour:

Size of swing (%)	Con to Lab	Lib/Nat to Lab	Con to Lib/SNP	Over-all maj
1	13	1	1	30
2	29	1	5	63
3	51	1	6	107
4	66	2	8	139
5	82	2	8	171

SOURCE: Michael Steed *The British General Election of October 1974*
(Macmillan)

By-Elections since October 1974

        Where the result has been substantially affected by the increase or decrease in the vote polled by a third party, swing calculations tend to be misleading. They have therefore been omitted in these cases.

As a check on the swing figures, or a substitute where none are given, the chart gives figures of vote retained. These show the percentage of its October 1974 vote which each party obtained in the subsequent by-election. Thus a figure of more than 100 shows that the vote was actually increased compared with the general election: a figure of 50 means that it was halved.

26 June 1975   Woolwich West

Votes cast	P. J. Bottomley (Con)	17,280
	J. Stayner (Lab)	14.898
	Mrs S. M. Hobday (Lib)	1884
	Mrs R. M. Robinson (NF)	856
	R. S. Mallone (FP)	218
	Dr F. H. Hansford-Miller (ENP)	140
	R. E. G. Simmerson (Ind Con)	104
	P. H. H. Bishop (Ind)	41
Result	**Con majority 2382 Con gain from Lab**	
Turnout	62·3 (73·9) Swing 7·6 to Con	
Party %	Con 48·8; Lab 42·1; Lib 5·3; NF 2·4; FP 0·6; ENP 0·4; Ind Con 0·3; Ind 0·1	
	Lib, NF, FP, ENP, Ind Con and Ind lost deposit	
Votes retained	Con 107·5 Lab 76·0 Lib 31·6	

4 March 1976   Coventry North-West

Votes cast	G. Robinson (Lab)	17,118
	J. B. Guinness (Con)	13,424
	A. Leighton (Lib)	4062
	A. Fountaine (NF)	986
	J. K. Read (NP)	208
	T. L. Keen (CFMPB)	40
	W. S. Dunmore (Ind)	33
Result	**Lab majority 3694 no change**	
Turnout	72·9 (75·2) Swing 5·0 to Con	
Party %	Lab 47·7; Con 37·4; Lib 11·3; NF 2·8; NP 0·6; CFMPB 0·1; Ind 0·1	
	Lib, NF, NP, CFMPB and Ind lost deposit	
Votes retained	Lab 89·1 Con 114·6 Lib 70·0	

11 March 1976 Carshalton

Votes cast	F. N. Forman (Con)	20,753
	C. J. Blau (Lab)	11,021
	J. Hatherley (Lib)	6028
	T. Denville-Faulkner (NF)	1851
	R. E. G. Simmerson (Ind Con)	251
	W. S. Dunmore (Ind)	133
	W. G. Boaks (Ind)	115
Result	**Con majority 9732 no change**	
Turnout	60·5 (74·3) Swing 8·4 to Con	
Party %	Con 51·7; Lab 27·5; Lib 15·0; NF 4·6;	
	Ind Con 0·6; Ind 0·3; Ind 0·3	
	NF, Ind Con, Ind and Ind lost deposit	
Votes retained	Con 92·0 Lab 58·5 Lib 72·9	

11 March 1976 The Wirral

Votes cast	D. J. F. Hunt (Con)	34,675
	A. E. Bailey (Lab)	10,563
	M. R. D. Gayford (Lib)	5914
	Dr F. H. Hansford-Miller (ENP)	466
	D. H. Jones (Ind Con)	307
Result	**Con majority 24,112 no change**	
Turnout	55·5 (75·5) Swing 13·6 to Con	
Party %	Con 66·8; Lab 20·3; Lib 11·4; ENP 0·9;	
	Ind Con 0·6	
	Lib, ENP and Ind Con lost deposit	
Votes retained	Con 97·1 Lab 47·5 Lib 47·9	

24 June 1976 Rotherham

Votes cast	J. S. Crowther (Lab)	14,351
	D. N. Hinckley (Con)	9824
	Miss E. M. Graham (Lib)	2214
	G. K. Wright (NF)	1696
	P. H. H. Bishop (Ind)	129
	R. L. Atkinson (Ind)	99
Result	**Lab majority 4527 no change**	
Turnout	46·8 (65·5) Swing 13·3 to Con	
Party %	Lab 50·7; Con 34·7; Lib 7·8; NF 6·0; Ind 0·5;	
	Ind 0·3	
Votes retained	Lab 55·5 Con 111·1 Lib 41·4	

15 July 1976   **Thurrock**

Votes cast	Dr O. A. McDonald (Lab)	22,191
	P. W. C. Lomax (Con)	17,352
	R. A. Charlton (Lib)	5977
	J. Roberts (NF)	3255
	Dr F. H. Hansford-Miller (ENP)	187
	P. H. H. Bishop (Ind)	72
Result	**Lab majority 4839 no change**	
Turnout	54·1 (68·6) Swing 10·6 to Con	
Party %	Lab 45·3; Con 35·4; Lib 12·2; NF 6·6; ENP 0·4; Ind 0·1	
	Lib, NF, ENP and Ind lost deposit	
Votes retained	Lab 65·1 Con 115·8 Lib 48·8	

4 November 1976   **Newcastle Central**

Votes cast	H. L. Cowans (Lab)	4692
	A. S. Ellis (Lib)	2854
	T. R. H. Sowler (Con)	1945
	D. W. Hayes (SWP)	184
	B. C. Anderson-Lynes (NF)	181
Result	**Lab majority over Lib 1838 no change**	
Turnout	41·0 (58·4)	
Party %	Lab 47·6; Lib 29·0; Con 19·7; SWP 1·9; NF 1·8	
	SWP and NF lost deposit	
Votes retained	Lab 44·5 Lib 166·3 Con 80·0	

4 November 1976   **Walsall North**

Votes cast	R. G. Hodgson (Con)	16,212
	D. J. Winnick (Lab)	11,833
	S. Wright (Ind)	4374
	J. C. Parker (NF)	2724
	Mrs F. M. Oborski (Lib)	1212
	J. McCallum (SWP)	574
	Mrs M. Powell (Ind NP)	258
	J. R. Tyler (EP)	181
	W. G. Boaks (Ind)	30
Result	**Con majority 4379 Con gain from ENP**	
Turnout	51·5 (66·6) Swing 22·6 to Con	
Party %	Con 43·4; Lab 31·6; Ind 11·7; NF 7·3; Lib 3·2; SWP 1·5; Ind NP 0·7; EP 0·5; Ind 0·1	
	Ind, NF, Lib, SWP, Ind NP, EP and Ind lost deposit	
Votes retained	Con 130·2 Lab 41·8 Lib 19·0	

4 November 1976 **Workington**

Votes cast	R. L. Page (Con)	19,396
	D. N. Campbell-Savours (Lab)	18,331
	B. N. Wates (Lib)	2480
Result	**Con majority 1065 Con gain from Lab**	
Turnout	74·2 (75·8) Swing 13·2 to Con	
Party %	Con 48·2; Lab 45·6; Lib 6·2	
	Lib lost deposit	
Votes retained	Con 149·3 Lab 81·3 Lib 52·4	

2 December 1976 **Cambridge**

Votes cast	R. V. R. James (Con)	19,620
	M. H. Smith (Lab)	9995
	M. W. B. O'Loughlin (Lib)	3051
	G. J. N. Sharpe (Ind)	711
	J. E. Wotherspoon (NF)	700
	P. M. Sargent (Ind)	374
Result	**Con majority 9625 no change**	
Turnout	49·2 (69·6) Swing 9·9 to Con	
Party %	Con 51·0; Lab 26·0; Lib 18·3; Ind 1·9; NF 1·8;	
	Ind 1·0	
	Lib, Ind, NF and Ind lost deposit	
Votes retained	Con 90·0 Lab 52·6 Lib 63·4	

24 February 1977 **City of London and Westminster South**

Votes cast	Hon P. L. Brooke (Con)	11,962
	M. M. Noble (Lab)	3997
	A. M. E. Scrimgeour (Lib)	1981
	P. T. Kavanagh (NF)	1051
	P. C. B. Mitchell (Ind)	449
	M. Lobb (NP)	364
	D. W. Delderfield (Ind)	306
	W. G. Boaks (Ind)	61
	W. F. Thompson (Ind)	43
	R. O. Herbert (Ind)	37
Result	**Con majority 7965 no change**	
Turnout	39·6 (53·2) Swing 9·3 to Con	
Party %	Con 59·1; Lab 19·7; Lib 9·8; NF 5·2; Ind 2·2;	
	NP 1·8; Ind 1·5; Ind 0·3; Ind 0·2; Ind 0·2	
	Lib, NF, Ind, NP, Ind, Ind, Ind and Ind lost deposit	
Votes retained	Con 83·3 Lab 46·5 Lib 48·1 NF 153·2	

31 March 1977 **Birmingham Stechford**

Votes cast	A. J. Mackay (Con)	15,731
	T. A. G. Davis (Lab)	13,782
	A. H. W. Brons (NF)	2955
	G. A. Gopsill (Lib)	2901
	B. Heron (IMG)	494
	P. M. Foot (SWP)	377
Result	**Con majority 1949 Con gain from Lab**	
Turnout	58·8 (64·1) Swing 17·6 to Con	
Party %	Con 43·4; Lab 38·0; NF 8·2; Lib 8·0; IMG 1·4; SWP 1·0	
	NF, Lib, IMG and SWP lost deposit	
Votes retained	Con 141·1 Lab 59·7 Lib 49·5	

28 April 1977 **Ashfield**

Votes cast	T. J. Smith (Con)	19,616
	M. R. L. Cowan (Lab)	19,352
	H. C. Flint (Lib)	4380
	G. A. Herrod (NF)	1734
	Mrs J. Hall (SWP)	453
Result	**Con majority 264 Con gain from Lab**	
Turnout	59·7 (74·7) Swing 20·8 to Con	
Party %	Con 43·1; Lab 42·5; Lib 9·6; NF 3·8; SWP 1·0	
	Lib, NF and SWP lost deposit	
Votes retained	Con 157·5 Lab 54·7 Lib 55·0	

28 April 1977 **Grimsby**

Votes cast	A. V. Mitchell (Lab)	21,890
	R. Blair (Con)	21,370
	A. De Freitas (Lib)	3128
	M. Stanton (SWP)	215
	P. H. H. Bishop (Ind)	64
	M. L. Nottingham (Ind)	30
Result	**Lab majority 520 no change**	
Turnout	70·2 (69·4) Swing 7·0 to Con	
Party %	Lab 46·9; Con 45·7; Lib 6·7; SWP 0·5; Ind 0·1; Ind 0·1	
	Lib, SWP, Ind and Ind lost deposit	
Votes retained	Lab 101·1 Con 145·6 Lib 33·0	

7 July 1977 **Saffron Walden**

Votes cast	A. G. B. Haselhurst (Con)	22,692
	A. W. Phillips (Lib)	10,255
	B. R. M. Stoneham (Lab)	5948
	W. O. Smedley (Ind)	1818
Result	**Con majority 12,437 no change**	
Turnout	64·8 (78·1)	
Party %	Con 55·7; Lib 25·2; Lab 14·6; Ind 4·5	
	Ind lost deposit	
Votes retained	Con 106·6 Lib 69·4 Lab 47·0	

18 August 1977 Birmingham Ladywood

Votes cast	E. J. Sever (Lab)	8227
	J. Q. Davies (Con)	4402
	P. A. F. Reed-Herbert (NF)	888
	K. G. Hardeman (Lib)	765
	R. Ahsan (Ind Soc)	534
	J. Hunte (Ind)	336
	K. Gordon (SWP)	152
	G. P. Matthews (Ind Con)	71
	P. B. Courtney (Ind)	63
	W. G. Boaks (Ind)	46
Result	**Lab majority 3825 no change**	
Turnout	42·6 (56·9) Swing 8·8 to Con	
Party %	Lab 53·1; Con 28·4; NF 5·7; Lib 4·9; Ind Soc 3·5;	
	Ind 2·2; SWP 1·0; Ind Con 0·5; Ind 0·4; Ind 0·3	
	NF, Lib, Ind Soc, Ind, SWP, Ind Con, Ind and	
	Ind lost deposit	
Votes retained	Lab 55·5 Con 86·7 Lib 24·8	

24 November 1977 Bournemouth East

Votes cast	D. A. Atkinson (Con)	15,235
	J. B. N. Goodwin (Lab)	3684
	D. Matthew (Lib)	3212
	J. P. Pratt (NB)	1127
	K. McWilliam (NF)	725
	W. G. Boaks (Ind)	42
Result	**Con majority 11,551 no change**	
Turnout	42·6 (70·4) Swing 8·7 to Con	
Party %	Con 63·4; Lab 15·3; Lib 13·4; NB 4·7; NF 3·0;	
	Ind 0·2	
	NB, NF and Ind lost deposit	
Votes retained	Con 73·2 Lab 43·7 Lib 31·7	

2 March 1978 Ilford North

Votes cast	V. Bendall (Con)	22,548
	T. Jowell (Lab)	17,051
	J. Freeman (Lib)	2248
	J. Hughes (NF)	2126
	T. Iremonger (Ind Con)	671
	C. Rowe (ELPF)	89
	A. Burr (NB)	48
	W. G. Boaks (Ind)	38
Result	**Con majority 5497 Con gain from Lab**	
Turnout	68·2 (74·4) Swing 6·9 to Con	
Party %	Con 50·4; Lab 38·0; Lib 5·0; NF 4·7; Ind Con 1·5;	
	ELPF 0·2; NB 0·1; PS 0·1	
	Lib, NF, Ind Con, ELPF, NB and PS lost deposit	
Votes retained	Con 113·6 Lab 82·7 Lib 27·8	

13 April 1978   Glasgow Garscadden

Votes cast	D. Dewar (Lab)	16,507
	K. Bovey (SNP)	11,955
	I. Lawson (Con)	6746
	Mrs S. Farrell (SLP)	583
	S. Barr (Comm)	407
	P. Porteous (SWP)	166
Result	**Lab majority 4552 no change**	
Turnout	69·0 (70·9) Swing (3·6 from Lab to SNP)	
Party %	Lab 45·4; SNP 32·9; Con 18·6; SLP 1·6;	
	Comm 1·1; SWP 0·6	
	SLP, Comm and SWP lost deposit	
Votes retained	Lab 83·6 SNP 98·7 Con 134·8	

20 April 1978   Lambeth Central

Votes cast	J. Tilley (Lab)	10,311
	J. Hanley (Con)	7170
	Mrs H. Stevens (NF)	1291
	D. Blunt (Lib)	1104
	J. Chase (Soc Un)	287
	C. Redgrave (WRP)	271
	A. Bogues (SWP)	201
	B. McNeeney (SPGB)	91
	A. Whereat (Ind)	55
	S. Munro (SLPF)	38
	W. G. Boaks (Ind)	27
Result	**Lab majority 3141 no change**	
Turnout	44·5 (52·3) Swing 9·3 to Con	
Party %	Lab 49·5; Con 34·4; NF 6·2; Lib 5·3; Soc Un 1·4;	
	WRP 1·3; SWP 1·0; SPGB 0·4; Ind 0·3; SLPF 0·2;	
	Ind 0·1	
	NF, Lib, Soc Un, WRP, SWP, SPGB, Ind,	
	SLPF and Ind lost deposit	
Votes retained	Lab 67·0 Con 106·9 Lib 34·4	

27 April 1978   Epsom and Ewell

Votes cast	A. Hamilton (Con)	28,242
	T. Mooney (Lab)	7314
	M. Anderson (Lib)	5673
	J. King (Roy)	2350
	J. Sawyer (NF)	823
Result	**Con majority 20,928 no change**	
Turnout	54·8 (73·7) Swing 6·2 to Con	
Party %	Con 63·6; Lab 16·4; Lib 12·8; Roy 5·3; NF 1·9	
Votes retained	Con 88·0 Lab 63·8 Lib 35·9	

27 April 1978 Wycombe

Votes cast	R. Whitney (Con)	29,677
	T. Fowler (Lab)	14,109
	H. Warschauer (Lib)	3665
	Mrs S. Jones (NF)	2040
Result	**Con majority 15,568 no change**	
Turnout	59·0 (74·3) Swing 7·9 to Con	
Party %	Con 60; Lab 28·5; Lib 7·4; NF 4·1	
Votes retained	Con 91·4 Lab 78·2 Lib 32·3	

31 May 1978 Hamilton

Votes cast	G. Robertson (Lab)	18,880
	Mrs M. MacDonald (SNP)	12,388
	Lord Scrymgeour (Con)	4818
	F. McDermid (Lib)	949
Result	**Lab majority 6492 no change**	
Turnout	72·0 (77·2)	
Party %	Lab 51·0; SNP 33·4; Con 13·0; Lib 2·6	
Votes retained	Lab 102·1 SNP 81·4 Con 130·7 Lib 60·9	

13 July 1978 Manchester Moss Side

Votes cast	G. Morton (Lab)	12,556
	T. Murphy (Con)	10,998
	P. Thornson (Lib)	2502
	H. Andrew (NF)	623
	V. Redgrave (WRP)	394
Result	**Lab majority 1558 no change**	
Turnout	51·6 (62·9) Swing 3·6 to Con	
Party %	Lab 46·3; Con 40·6; Lib 9·2; NF 2·3; WRP 1·5	
Votes retained	Lab 82·5 Con 99·1 Lib 44·0	

13 July 1978 Penistone

Votes cast	A. McKay (Lab)	19,424
	I. Dobkin (Con)	14,053
	D. Chadwick (Lib)	9241
Result	**Lab majority 5371 no change**	
Turnout	59·8 (74·6) Swing 8·8 to Con	
Party %	Lab 45·5; Con 32·9; Lib 21·6	
Votes retained	Lab 71·6 Con 117·0 Lib 84·8	

Miscellaneous By-Election Statistics

Largest swing to Con	Walsall N	22·6%
Lowest swing to Con	Coventry NW	5·0%
Best Lab result (vote retained)	Grimsby	101·1%
Worst Lab result (vote retained)	Walsall N	41·8%
Best Con result (vote retained)	Ashfield	157·5%
Best Lib result (vote retained)	Newcastle C	166·3%
Worst Lib result (vote retained)	Walsall N	19·0%
Highest turnout	Workington	74·2%
Lowest turnout	City of London & Westminster S	39·6%
Best NF result	Birmingham Stechford	8·2%
Lowest vote polled by anyone	W. G. Boaks (Lambeth Central)	27